GARLAND STU

Entrepreneurship

STUART BRUCHEY
University of Maine

GENERAL EDITOR

A Garland Series

Edgar B. Davis and Sequences in Business Capitalism

From Shoes to Rubber to Oil

Riley Froh

Garland Publishing, Inc.
New York & London
1993

Library of Congress Cataloging-in-Publication Data

Froh, Riley, 1938–
Edgar B. Davis and sequences in business capitalism : from shoes to rubber to oil / Riley Froh.
p. cm. — (Garland studies in entrepreneurship)
ISBN 0-8153-0993-7 (alk. paper)
1. Davis, Edgar B. (Byrum), b. 1873. 2. Businessmen—United States—Biography. 3. Entrepreneurship—United States. I. Title. II. Series.
HC102.5.D38F76 1993
338'.04'092—dc20 92-33550
[B] CIP

Printed on acid-free, 250-year-life paper

Manufactured in the United States of America

This book is dedicated to
Mary Binz Froh
and to the memory of
David M. Figart

Mary and David

Two Kindred Spirits
Across the miles
And across the years

CONTENTS

ILLUSTRATIONS

PREFACE

Edgar B. Davis is mainly remembered today in folklore and myth as an eccentric wildcatter who was extremely generous with his money. Certainly he was a legend in his own time, for long before he ever sent a drill bit spinning down into unproved territory in search of elusive black gold, he had made two separate fortunes in the shoe business and the international rubber industry.

Already well known in the business world, he entered the petroleum game at age forty-two. In the next thirty-two years he discovered three oil fields, concluded the biggest oil deal in Texas as of 1926, pioneered profit sharing in the Southwest, established two major charitable foundations, underwrote several literary and artistic projects, financed much civic philanthropy, and backed the biggest flop on Broadway. He was known world-wide for his financial extravagances, but beneath this peculiar exterior dwelt a solid businessman.

This biography tells the story of the man behind the legend, the entrepreneur who brought his country into the plantation rubber industry in the first decade of this century and who built an enterprise that stands as a model to this unique figure in the annals of American capitalism. Few people who met him after he started his quest for oil ever realized that the driving force behind his desire for the wealth oil could bring him was his grand ambition to return to the plantation rubber industry though a giant scheme of international cooperation. Even fewer knew of his political aspirations.

As a study in business history, Davis emerges as a major figure in the development of the American free enterprise system, a capitalist who really understood what Calvin Coolidge meant when he noted that the business of America is business. A modern Calvinist, Davis proved time and again that the Puritan work ethic of his ancestry embodied a successful philosophy for his era. That he never followed Franklin's adage of a penny saved was more evidence of the faith Davis placed on his own abilities which he believed to be guided by Providence.

Though Davis' major dreams never materialized, he set examples of eternal optimism in his quest. What he did accomplish over seven decades makes quite a story and provides insight into the role of the entrepreneur in the development of the national economy.

ACKNOWLEDGEMENTS

I have tried on the dedication page to show my debt to my wife Mary Froh for her many and varied and valuable contributions to this book. From the start she has helped not only research the Davis story but also edit, proofread, and revise the entire manuscript. Mary conducted interviews and selected the photographs included in this publication. Mary is a rare individual in the realm of the spiritual that is easier sensed than seen.

My mother Inez Griffin was Edgar B. Davis' private secretary the last seven years of his life. During these twilight years, he reminisced endlessly about his long and extraordinary life. As a result, Inez knew Davis and his story as well as anyone. Her fascination for him influenced me to write his biography, and she was delighted with the project and helped in many ways with the research and writing. Inez had an amazing sense of humor, a real talent for writing songs and poetry, and a winning personality that made her many friends and no enemies. She did so want to see this finished, and she cheerfully encouraged Mary and me to go on with it. Inez died May 1, 1992. She told me in April that she had lived a long life and a good life and was ready to go.

David M. Figart was one of the brightest and kindest men I ever knew. He knew Edgar B. Davis better than anyone else. Although I only visited David once, he and I were pen pals for over twenty years, and we became very close. David enriched the lives of everyone who had the good fortune to know him and he provided documents and encouragement, and acted as a willing sounding board to me in the writing of this biography. I have tried to say goodbye to my old friend in a way that means something to me in this dedication.

The Caylor family enriched this study over a lifetime in personal and professional ways too numerous to mention here. Tommy and Ethel are gone now, but my old friends Patsy Caylor Krauskopf and T. Caylor still share with me the valuable Davis records that Tommy preserved in addition to a thousand treasured memories. They provided most of the photographs for this book.

Working with Claudia Hirsch, Assistant Editor of Garland Press, has been a pleasure. Her expertise is made even more helpful by a sincere courtesy, and her suggestions and assistance are truly appreciated.

Finally I would like to thank Dr. Stuart Bruchey, Professor Emeritus of American Economic History at Columbia University, for his interest in including this biography of Edgar B. Davis in this series on entrepreneurs under his editorship. I am very pleased to have the story appear here.

Edgar B. Davis and Sequences in Business Capitalism

Chapter I
THE YANKEE AND HIS MISSION

Obey the voice at eve obeyed at prime.

Ralph Waldo Emerson

Puritan New England ran deep in the Davis heritage, for Edgar B. Davis descended from those great, grim, earnest men of whom Ralph Waldo Emerson spoke so admiringly, and a strain of Calvinism cropped up in thought, word, and deed to the day he died. Tracing the family back to the *Mayflower* through genealogical records was a source of family pride, and Davis sprang from the solid, hard-working stock typical of the Massachusetts of his time. It was into this environment that Davis was born.

When Stephen Davis married Julia Anna Copeland on New Year's Day 1859, he undoubtedly planned to support his bride and prospective family in his small, independent shoe-cutting business located in North Bridgewater, Massachusetts.[1] Stephen was twenty-five; Julia Anna, one year younger. Both were in the eighth generation from John and Priscilla Alden[2] and had descended from a long line of New England residents who were equipped mentally, physically, and spiritually for endurance; both were from immediate farm backgrounds.[3]

Born in Falmouth, Massachusetts, on December 24, 1834, Stephen Davis was the son of William Davis whose father Stephen Davis descended from Dolar Davis, who emigrated from Chester, England in 1634.[4] William Davis was married to a Falmouth girl, Deborah Dimmock, whose grandfather, General Joseph Dimmock, had commanded the American troops who foiled the British landing from the Frigate *Nimrod* during the War of 1812.[5]

Julia Anna Copeland had been born in North Bridgewater to Marcus Morton and Rebecca Copeland on August 9, 1835; her father was a direct descendant of Sir Lawrence Copeland of Scotland, whereas her mother descended from Colonel Cyrus Porter, a veteran of the Revolutionary War.[6] The house into which Julia Copeland was born had been built in 1830, four years before her arrival. Still in good condition and occupied to this day,[7] it is a tribute to the Scotch strain of hardihood in the Copeland family--a quality which led the family physician to observe that, "The Copelands would get a living on a hill where a sheep would starve."[8]

Julia and Stephen Davis had their home and business life interrupted while Stephen served for a time in the Massachusetts Heavy Artillery during the Civil War. His unit saw no action, and he was soon back at the shoe-cutting trade.[9]

The craftsman at his bench was faced with new problems during the northern post-Civil War boom, however, because of the machinery developed to mass produce boots and shoes during the recent conflict. Moreover, the factory-built shoe was cheaper and more comfortable than the old hand-made product, and by 1867 one Massachusetts factory could outproduce thirty thousand individual shoemakers.[10] Still, Stephen Davis' single proprietorship remained intact, for he knew leather and excelled at his trade.[11] The unprecedented boom in industry was of eight years' duration.

The family began to grow; but at a time when a single proprietor's wealth was in his sons, Stephen Davis may have worried as Mable, Evelyn, and Amy Davis arrived at intervals during the 1860s. On July 25, 1870, however, Oscar Copeland arrived in the Davis household,[12] and on February 2, 1873, Edgar Byram Davis, the last child of Stephen and Julia, was born.[13]

In this same year two major events occurred which directly or indirectly influenced the Davises, especially young Edgar Byram, always fascinated by coincidental dates and mystical incidents.[14] The year 1873 stretched an inflated prosperity to the breaking point; and throughout the summer over-building of railroads, inflation of credit, heavy investment in new farm lands, fluctuation of currency, and general overexpansion in many areas resulted in the Panic of 1873,[15] a depression which broke wide open with the failure of Jay Cooke, the railroad financier whom the nation considered indissoluble.[16] The small businessman was hit hard, and the employee suffered at all levels. In Davis' home state, wages, which in 1872 were thirty-six percent higher than comparable salaries in 1860, dropped ten percent and fifteen percent respectively by 1875 and 1878.[17] Consequently, the Davis shoe-cutting business became one of the 5,830 business failures in the first year of the depression and was sold to George E. Keith. The following year, Keith founded his own company and Stephen Davis went to work for him.[18] Keith somehow survived the five or six years of hard times and rode successfully into the better days which followed.

Farther from New England, other events were taking shape to pattern Edgar Davis' destiny. In May, 1873, a man known only as Farris landed in England with two thousand Hevea seeds which he had smuggled from Brazil. Hevea trees produce excellent sap to make rubber, and Brazil forbade exportation of seeds or plants. A movement, headed by Sir Clements Markham, who had recently stolen quinine plants from South America, was underway in England to receive these ill-gotten seeds, but only six grew and thrived at the Royal Botanical Gardens at Kew. Although most of the seeds died, the idea germinated, and Sir William Jackson Hooker, director of Kew Gardens, began corresponding with Henry A. Wickham, an Englishman experienced in extracting Hevea milk in the Amazon. It took time and some extraordinary luck on Wickham's part, but by 1876 he was able to peer through the glass at Kew greenhouses and see nearly 3,000 young rubber plants growing from the seeds he had illegally slipped out of Brazil.[19] Davis was destined to benefit from these plants in the future.

While the Hevea plants were thriving in beautiful Kew Gardens, the Davises of New England were having a difficult time financially. Fortunately, the Scotch strain on the maternal side had prepared Julia Anna Copeland for the meager years in the Davis family. Always exhibiting a strong faith in God, she dealt with straitened circumstances gracefully by keeping her household neat and the children's clothes mended.[20] A deeply religious person, Julia Copeland Davis met each crisis in life with the Calvinism in Job 13:15, "Though he slay me, yet will I trust Him."[21] This stoic approach to life's problems passed on to the children, the patience of Job and his quotation remaining a life-long habit of the youngest Davis.

Out of his mother's belief in the Bible, young Edgar Davis began to form his own idea of faith. Faith became such a definite part of his religion that he eventually capitalized it in his writing style.[22] Davis took the word *faith* from Second Timothy 1:5,[23] "When I call to remembrance the unfeigned faith that is in thee, which dwelt first in thy grandmother Lois, and thy mother Eunice; and I am persuaded that in thee also." The fact that the faith in this quotation in inherited from the mother is undoubtedly significant to the verse choice. That the mother's spirit made a permanent impression on her youngest son is obvious in Edgar B. Davis's poem "Mother," written in the 1920s.[24]

Tis not thy face, thy hair, thine eyes,
Though Beauty owns thee near of kin,
That mark thee, loved one!
Thy face so gentle and serene,
Scarce tells the tale of battles won,
But augurs of a world unseen,
And a lofty Spirit in work begun,
So not of Beauty would I sing,
Nor strength, nor grace, nor anything
But the glory of thy useful life
The triumph of thy soul.

Stephen Davis also ingrained strength of character into his sons. "My father taught us the rugged principle," wrote Davis,

> that if we wanted anything in this world we must do it ourselves, and held up at all times that stern virtue; but the one word which covered his life was obedience for he took his medicine without squealing, and that covered a period of invalidism for twenty-four years, following unsuccess in business.[25]

In the Davis home, "it was an honor to work but it was a dishonor to loaf;"[26] and John Calvin's philosophy lived on as the Davises survived.

Both Davis boys entered the Huntington Grammar School in nearby Brockton, the city of which North Bridgewater is now a part. Although they honored their father and mother, the two boys were bitter rivals as youths. They fought constantly between themselves and among other companions, for each had his own group of followers. Oscar, three years older than his brother, usually emerged victorious in their struggles; consequently, their battles once reached such a stage that the younger of the two actually hid with a club to ambush the other, who, unexpectedly and fortunately, took a different route home. Always large for his age, Edgar Davis eventually outgrew his brother and won their last fight by throwing Oscar Davis over a fence. Apparently seeing the futility of future struggles, the older brother changed tactics and invited his family opponent to a dance that night. Afterwards, they fought no more, and an entirely different relationship resulted.[27]

Oscar Davis had the reputation of being a clever wit with a generous nature. Soon friendly relations between the Davis brothers grew into a bond of devotion and loyalty.[28] The friendly truce is of added importance "because Edgar respected him and his judgment--although sometimes did not follow his, or anyone's, suggestions--and because at least two of Edgar's business opportunities came through his brother."[29] Politically, the brothers reserved some differences; Oscar Davis was always a staunch Republican, whereas his younger brother voted the Democratic ticket.[30]

One mutual friend recalls seeing the brothers together frequently; they were often trying to help others and just as often trying to have fun with their companions. One of Oscar Davis' favorite jokes was to slip his personal belongings into a visiting friend's suitcase, and, upon the friend's departure, to open the case, thereby exposing the "stolen" articles to the guest's chagrin.[31]

After graduating from Brockton High School, Oscar Davis took a one-year course in the Dwight L. Moody School for Boys in Northfield, Massachusetts, completing the study in June, 1885. This particular emphasis on Bible study at this institution greatly influenced Oscar toward much independent reflection on religion and worship.[32] These thoughts indirectly influenced his younger brother in his independent study of the Bible. In September Oscar Davis joined his father in George Keith's employ as an operator of one of the machines in the small factory[33] that had grown from what was once his father's shoe shop.

Edgar B. Davis graduated from Brockton High School in June, 1889, concluding all his formal education with the ten grades which the public schools contained at that time. He presented a dramatic recitation and sang with a vocal octet at the graduation exercises.[34] His family remembered him at graduation as a boy

> of rugged build and an iron determination that came out in his business career. An excellent athlete, he wanted nothing more than to go to Harvard and play left guard on the Harvard team. But money was scarce in the Davis family.[35]

With the scholarships available to athletes today, Edgar B. Davis would have had his college "education" had he been of this generation. He stood six feet in height and weighed over two hundred and fifty pounds in his prime and was fearsome on the high school gridiron.

With no college prospects, Davis sought a steady means of

livelihood. Edgar Davis had already delivered papers, sold soft drinks, and worked in a local fish market, and one of these part-time jobs became a motivating force in his life. Once his mother had made some lemonade which he was to deliver for a party for some children whom he knew but to whose party he had not been asked. He was told to take the delivery to the back door. It seems a simple incident that no doubt occurs often in the lives of children, but as Edgar B. Davis walked away from where he was not invited, he vowed secretly to himself that things would be different in the future.[36] They were.

After working a short time in the Montello shoe factory of Isaac H. Emerson, Davis tried reporting for the local Brockton *Gazette*; however, past environment proved too strong for him to break from family tradition, and as he explained, "I remember that I had started out in life--like all boys born in Brockton--to the smell of leather, and naturally gravitated into the shoe business."[37] His next job was in the office of Eaton and Terry, shoe manufacturers; from here, the eighteen-year-old began his climb in the business world. Two years later, in 1893, Charles A. Eaton established his own business, making Davis the bookkeeper with a five percent interest in the venture.[38] Meanwhile, in a rival firm, Oscar Davis advanced to personal assistant to the owner, George Keith.

Undoubtedly, Edgar, as well as Oscar Davis, was following the precepts of his parents by striving zealously in his position, for his rise certainly suggests a willingness on his part to work and a notice of the value by his employer. Edgar Davis himself was profoundly impressed by his achievements in the company and wrote:

> I remember two things in the shoe business: one when I had a triple promotion from ten dollars a week to fifteen dollars. I walked on air because they usually promoted you from $10.00 to $12.50 to $13.50 to $15.00. I give you my word that I got more of a thrill on that occasion, and again when I was made a member of the firm with a 5% interest in the business, than I did in later years when things had come in by the millions. So things are relative.[39]

At this time, the philosophy he later practiced of sharing the profits of capital with labor began to take root as Davis experienced the joy of profiting from a job well done.

Edgar Davis continued his successful climb; after the incorporation of the Charles A. Eaton Company, he was promoted to treasurer and later to sales manager with a twenty-five percent interest in the concern.[40] It was as treasurer of the prospering Eaton Shoe Company that Edgar B. Davis made his first trip abroad in 1901, which was "...intended for a little pleasure and business."[41] He found Europeans wearing what he termed an "ugly and grotesque shoe," and since his product did not sell in Europe at this time, he reasoned that it was because his shoes were too stylish for Europeans. He credited George Keith's European stores with finally promoting fashionable shoes in Europe and regarded Keith as an artist for the triumph over crude footwear. Purely nationalistic at the time, Davis was shocked, like many Americans who travel, to find that the British and the Europeans took little notice of America; therefore, he maintained, Theodore Roosevelt acted wisely in sending the sixteen battleships on their effective and imposing cruise around the world as an example of American power.[42] This nationalism decreased with the growing cosmopolitanism of Davis' later years.

Actually, Davis had little time for pleasure while he was engaged in the shoe business. Yet, it was during this time that he developed a proficiency in bridge and golf.[43] Edgar B. and Oscar Davis were excellent bridge players, and in order to execute the kind of bridge in which they indulged, they played often during the days in Brockton. Indeed, the lasting bond with many of Edgar Davis' close friends was the game of bridge.[44]

Davis also excelled in tennis and billiards.[45] The driving personality did not stop at mastering the technicalities of the game; in addition, he always played to win.

An interesting paradox of Davis' rather complex personality can be shown at this point by contrasting his adroitness in athletics and cards with his inability to grasp certain things mechanical. Although most people thought the chauffeur he later maintained merely a symbol of affluence, close associates knew a different story. Davis had no mechanical sense at all. In one respect he did listen to others and did not drive a car.[46] Davis must have made a lasting impression on his trial runs. He fared little better on his bicycle, for an 1895 Brockton *Enterprise* clipping reads that "in collision with another bicyclist, Edgar Davis was thrown at Grand and Nilsson Streets and suffered a bad cut over the right eye."[47] Close friends commented that "he rode a bicycle the way he used to drive an automobile."[48]

Skillful at games and expert at bridge, Edgar B. Davis also cultivated the aesthetic side of life. He loved music, formally studied singing, and gave recitals in Brockton.[49] He played the piano naturally by ear and also wrote music. Though he never played professionally, he was able to accompany well known opera stars at social functions.[50] How much he enjoyed music is indicated by the number of musicals he attended while on periodic visits to New York. In April and May of 1915, Davis took a friend to seven Broadway musicals, operas, and concerts.[51]

His varied interests in social circles naturally brought him into contact with many women of whom he was very fond, but Edgar B. Davis never married. Close friends knew that he had lost the girl whom he loved in his youth. There was one singular incident when Davis showed a particular interest in a woman. On this occasion Edgar B. Davis saw a beautiful woman walking through the lobby of the Belmont Hotel where he was living in New York. He traced her to Washington, D.C., but finding her engaged to be married, he dropped the matter at once. Though rumors that Davis had been in love persisted, there was never another romantic association with any woman in his long life.[52]

Edgar B. Davis did entertain some serious thoughts of matrimony at one time, although the girl was an imaginary composite of several girls whom he admired. Yet this suggests that he knew at least three different girls well enough to ascertain their best qualities. He described this perfect girl to his sister Amy Davis as one who could sing like Lyda, cook like Lillian, and be a gracious hostess like Alice. At that point, his sister, whom he considered the greatest influence in his life, deflated his ego with, "And what have you got to offer her?"[53] Whether he never found a girl who met his standards of perfection, took his sister's advice and assumed he had nothing to offer, or really somehow lost the girl whom he had loved, the fact remains that he never married. But he did cultivate and enjoy the company of women, especially bridge players and singers.

One anecdote remembered and repeated often by Davis may have seriously affected him. Edgar B. Davis once had a date with one of the socialites who had been at the party to which he had delivered the lemonade as a youth. The destination was an affair at an opulent home in front of which was a circular drive. Making a grand entrance around the oval track in a hired, expensive buggy, Davis suddenly ran the two wheels on his side up an incline, causing him to lean his huge frame to the opposite way. Gravity, his date, and a weak spring did the rest, resulting in Davis' landing heavily on his companion under the overturned buggy. The arrival was not as grand as planned, but it did get attention. "I wonder why she would never go with me again?" Davis would chuckle innocently when he repeated the story.[54]

Edgar Davis' brother's wife, it seems, appealed to Davis on a spiritual level. No doubt he had tremendous respect for her, for in his poetry file, next to the poem to his mother, is a poem addressed to his sister-in-law, Harriet Davis. This is the only other Davis poem addressed to a woman and probably shows a characteristic he admired in addition to the respect he felt for this particular woman. Harriet had died in childbirth with her fourth baby and on November 16, 1923, the sixteenth anniversary of her death, Davis wrote:[55]

To Harriet

When last I saw thee,
Radiant in thy coming motherhood,
How beautiful thou wert.
        With what expectant joy
Thou visualized the babe in arms.
        With what fine courage
Dids't thou face the test.

        But, --as tho' unwilling longer to loan
Such grace as thine, --God called thee
        Noble Sacrifice!
Happy and proud to be the mother of men!

Davis' poetry suggests a serious interest in literature. Emerson's essays appealed to him greatly, and he frequently quoted passages from "The Over-Soul."[56] He read widely and seriously in his formative years in Massachusetts.

To create leisure time for reading, Davis labored intently in the keen competition of the Brockton shoe business, and his diligence had earned this enterprising young man an interest in the Charles A. Eaton Shoe Company. Sound business principles seemed to be natural with him, and he enjoyed the strong spirit of rivalry between him and the local Jewish businessmen in the shoe trade: "A Yankee, with a natural trading instinct, he would have gotten the best of any bargaining. He had his 'eyeteeth cut when selling shoes to Jewish merchants.' Yet he merited the reputation for being more than fair and square in his dealings."[57] Remembering lessons learned in business, Davis often said, "I cut my eye teeth on the Jews and Oscar."[58] Although Oscar Davis was a sharp trader and Edgar Davis developed into one, both had the reputation of being scrupulously honest; nor would either take unfair advantage of anyone. In ball games, however, Oscar would carefully touch each bag, whereas Edgar admitted that he might "miss" one. A long time secretary saw Davis as "a man of many contradictions--I thought he epitomized to me at times a real Yankee--'praise the Lord and hang on--or rather, make a dollar.'"[59]

Davis became known for his toleration towards all religions and nationalities and for an almost absolute lack of anything savoring of anti-Semitism or religious discrimination. Still, he imagined that good business instincts were a natural endowment of his chief Jewish rival, Nayors, and Davis even mimicked Nayors' brother's speech patterns in recounting his favorite anecdote. Davis had devised some clever plan to corner the market in one of the many new shoe deals being promoted. Somehow, the Jewish concern beat Davis to the wire and reaped the first and most fruitful profits. While contemplating a new strategy in his office, Davis was startled by the grinning brother of the victorious competitor who, thrusting his head through the slightly opened door, mocked, "Edgus! Edgus! Nes vus too smardt for you, vusen't he, Edgus?" Davis told this story good-humoredly and never failed to be amused himself, no matter how often he repeated it.[60]

Beneath the exterior joking mood dwelled the satisfaction that he had benefited from his experiences, that he ultimately profited. "Always remember," he advised, "there are people walking the streets of London tonight, wishing they had drawn trumps."[61] One of his mannerisms with intimates expressed the same pride that he had learned his lessons well. While pulling down his lower eyelid, he would ask, "Do you see any green here?"[62]

Not always outdone in his immediate endeavors, Davis is credited with bringing the concept of national advertising into the shoe industry. He even added to diverse advertising techniques by once placing the face of the proprietor on the sole of the shoe.[63] Thus, by 1903, he had risen in the business world, had become a world traveler, and had prospered financially--but he was working too hard.

He was an active member of the Congregational Church in Brockton and a devout Christian, who "tried to do everything according to the narrowest rules of the narrowest church--no smoking, etc."[64] Murdock Pemberton--author, publicity man, and one-time employee of Davis--was familiar with Davis' early religious life:

> As a kid, he had been a Y.M.C.A.'er, an insufferable little prig, he told me. When he came to later, the disdain for the old Puritan strain of running other people's morals and lives gave him a swell understanding viewpoint of the wider philosophy of life.[65]

If Davis took his work too seriously and took his religion too much to heart, this seriousness of purpose in all his affairs had brought a young man of little means to a financial vantage point in Brockton. He had not gone to Harvard but, as Davis himself put it, "I was educated in the University of Hard Knocks, whose colors were Black and Blue."[66]

About this time (1903), several of the "hardest knocks" were rapping at his door in the form of a series of events which always in Davis' mind were interrelated. Davis, in his own autobiographical sketch of 1949, gives the most definite date of these occurrences between 1903 and 1907.

> Something Happened in my life on December 1, 1904, which Led me to Believe that I had a Mission in Life, and I want to record the great Results which have come through my life of Faith in God which I have lived--very weakly at times I fear--ever since.[67]

The inability to express a mystical experience in words is commonplace in the literature of mysticism: consequently, Davis is not unique in vaguely stating that "Something Happened" in his notes. To those in whom he confided, though, Davis insisted that his mystical experience consisted of a "Voice" which detailed his "Mission" in these ten words: "Called of God to be President of the United States."[68] After the experience he would never utter this summons aloud but would reveal the message to intimate friends on a paper which he would immediately burn. He went through this ritual with a number of people and even kept a list of his enlightened friends in his safety deposit box.[69]

From the time of the "Voice" until his death, Davis' every action would be motivated by the "Mission" which he believed controlled his life,[70] and he endured stoically misfortunes which he believed a test of his "Faith." Calvinist Davis, noting the turning point in his heretofore rising tide, explained that,

> Immediately after this Event of December 1, 1904, I had a series of breakdowns and hospitalizations and suffered greatly thereby, but which I now see was for my own good (For whom the Lord loveth He chasteneth and scourgeth every Soul whom He receiveth). These hospitalizations left me with melancholia which I had great difficulty in overcoming for a number of years.[71]

Obviously, Edgar Davis, like other ambitious young men before and after him, had overburdened himself and suffered the penalty of a complete nervous breakdown and a halt to his soaring business career. There had been other problems. Some time before the mental depression, Davis had been in a New Haven railroad accident in which many persons were killed. Davis, the only person who did not file a claim against the railroad company, later suffered from a bump which he had received on his head, which may have been a factor in the nervous breakdown. To make matters worse, Charles A. Eaton gave his son a position in the company which Davis saw as rightfully his.[72] Deeply hurt by the loss of the promotion, Davis made a resolution while he was recovering from his illness: "I made up my mind to two things: I would not make a god of money and I would do something for the workingman."[73] Although difficult for Davis, this unfortunate experience was certainly a lucky "break" for his future employees.

After the sale of his business interests, which netted Davis his first million, Davis did not seriously enter any other undertaking until his venture with The United States Rubber Company in 1908. During the Christmas rush, he sold jewelry for his friends and bridge partners, Sanford and Mabell Gurney, who, besides owning a shop in Brockton, were his close neighbors.[74]Part-time work was of little help to Davis, however, whose fortune and health were decreasing simultaneously. Three years (1904-1907) of hospitalizations and doctor's fees, not to mention ordinary living expenses, exhausted Davis' first fortune built during the previous decade. The seriousness of the nervous disorder can be illustrated by one of Davis' irrational actions at the time. He was found by Oscar Davis and George Leach, a close friend, on the streets of Brockton preaching that he was Christ reincarnated.[75] His condition required some time in a sanitarium.[76]

Davis' convalescence was slow, but by the end of 1906, he had mended enough to take the advice of a Boston specialist who prescribed a long ocean voyage; consequently, on January 29, 1907, the *Moltke*, a German steamer bound for a Mediterranean cruise, carried Edgar B. Davis, accompanied by a group of friends, to his rendezvous with fortune.[77] Davis, undoubtedly on the lookout for any direction from Providence, considered himself a man with a mission; therefore, he was prepared to grasp any opportunity in spite of his poor health. Although many men never fully recover from a nervous breakdown, Davis considered his affliction a divine lesson; moreover, since he felt he was being guided, certain events took on added significance for him. For these reasons, when the doctor sent a very sick man on an ocean voyage purely for his health, the trip ironically became a success in more ways than one. Edgar B. Davis improved to the point that when opportunity whispered he heard the call loud and clear.

Chapter II
THE VOYAGE AND THE IDEA

The beginnings and endings of all human undertakings are untidy, the building of a house, the writing of a novel, the demolition of a bridge, and eminently, the finish of a voyage.

John Galsworthy

For three decades following the 1876 smuggling of rubber seeds out of Brazil by Henry Wickham, slow, steady progress was made in cultivation of the Hevea rubber tree in the East. From Kew Gardens, seedlings had been transported to Ceylon, the Dutch island of Java, and various sections of the Federated Malay States.[1] By the turn of the century, a practical method of tapping the trees without permanently damaging them had been developed, but in 1900 the Eastern plantations exported only four tons of rubber, for it was difficult to compete at a profit with the 35,000 tons of good, Brazilian wild rubber that easily met the manufacturing needs of the world.[2]

The law of supply and demand in a progressive, interrelated world is a fluctuating mark, and several changes were in the making which would reverse the balance, causing the quantity of plantation rubber to supplant that of wild rubber in only a few years. Already leading the world in rubber exportation, Brazil produced such an abundance of coffee for the world market in 1902 that the price of coffee fell proportionately with the over-supply. Falling coffee prices prompted Eastern planters to seek a more lucrative crop to replace the unprofitable coffee bean. As a result, planters in Ceylon, Malaya, and Sumatra gradually began to set out more rubber trees.[3] Meanwhile, the horseless carriage was gradually developing into a practical means of transportation, and the pneumatic tires for 1900 racing sulkies proved to be just the device to cushion the intricate internal combustion engine from damaging bumps.

At this time, Brazil, by monopolizing the market, ironically endangered its own interest in raw rubber production. Realizing that it produced most of the rubber supply to meet the demand, Brazil drastically raised the price of its crude rubber in 1905; consequently, the 174 tons exported from Ceylon and Malaya that year were also sold for fantastic profits. The next year, British and Dutch capital poured into Malaya, Ceylon, Java, and Sumatra in the rush to plant Hevea in place of such former crops as tea, tapioca, pineapple, and tobacco.[4] In 1905 there was a total of fifty thousand acres of rubber trees grown on Eastern plantations; during this same year, planters set out one hundred thousand additional acres of Hevea tress. This increase in planting continued, and by 1908 Eastern rubber planters had brought their holdings to 750,000 acres, but Brazil continued to lead the world in production of crude rubber. Since supply did not keep pace with demands, by 1910 Brazil was able to double the 1908 crude rubber price of $1.50 per pound. This top price of $3.00 per pound provided a wide margin of profit for the producers of crude rubber.[5]

Paradoxically, the greatest consumer of crude rubber, the United States, had no rubber-producing interests under its control; and as the first Model T Fords rolled from the assembly lines in mass production in 1907, demand for crude rubber supplies rose. At this same time, however, one of America's citizens, Edgar B. Davis, on a voyage for his health, was sailing into the early rubber boom of 1907.

Adventitious events were at work to complete a rare success story which was in the making as Davis began his cruise. As the ship steamed out of New York harbor, Davis ran into an acquaintance whom he had met at Lake Mohonk Mountain House, a fashionable resort in New York state. This friend, Walter B. Mahony, had begun a world cruise, whereas Davis was bound on a Mediterranean voyage. Mahony, like Davis, was a successful businessman. The son of a prominent real estate man in Columbus, Ohio, he was a descendent, on his mother's side, of the Morgan who had developed the famous Morgan horse in Vermont. After an outstanding record in college, he was extremely successful in the business of selling bonds. Subsequently, he studied law and later opened an office in New York City, although he did not practice law extensively.[6]

The chance meeting with Mahony prompted Davis to make a momentous change of plans which took place in the following way as Davis remembered it:

> I left my friends at Nice and journeyed down Italy to Rome and Naples; from there I took passage for Egypt with no intention of going further. However, Mahony became ill in Cairo and his Mother expressed the hope that I would accompany him on the voyage around the world which, as I already was a quarter of the way around, I finally decided to do.[7]

Davis was equipped socially to pass the leisure hours of a ship passenger, for, in addition to his ability at bridge, he had developed into an engrossing conversationalist. As one skilled in the art of conversation, he was naturally a good listener. He began to hear what he considered valuable information.

> We had not gone through the Suez Canal before the men we met in the smoking room told us about the rubber trees which were beginning largely to be planted in Ceylon, South India, Federated Malay States, Straits Settlements, and Java from which good dry rubber could be produced at a "shilling a pound." As rubber was selling at something like $1.25 a pound, I pricked up my ears at a possible profit like that.[8]

Obviously, the shrewd Yankee intellect was benefiting from the combination of rest, salt air, and sheer opportunity, for it had mended enough to grasp the significance of a favorable business situation. "Although neither Mahony nor I visualized streets filled with motor cars in connection with the things we heard," Davis later stated, "we both sensed that something of great importance economically was happening."[9] Davis would never lose this fascination for the rubber industry which enveloped him in the East, and there is a sort of nostalgic reverence in his description of his first glimpse of the foundation of the plantation rubber industry: "On Easter Sunday in April, 1907, Mahony and I saw our first Hevea Braziliensis rubber trees in the beautiful Peradeniya Gardens near Kandy, Ceylon."[10]

Mahony and Davis were becoming more and more absorbed in their findings in proportion to the distance they sailed eastward; consequently, they began investigations in a semi-professional manner. Arriving in the Straits Settlements, the men had an opportunity to tour the Federated Malay States; but Davis, still not fully recuperated, did not feel well enough to go. Mahony, however, visited some plantations and witnessed firsthand the system of cultivating rubber.[11] These facts fascinated Davis and thus was the American plantation rubber industry conceived in the mind of a determined Yankee who, not content to dream of vast possibilities and potentialities, set a course and followed it. In his own words, his desire was to make good "as I have set my teeth to do."[12] Indeed, as he left the East, the only thing which prevented him from launching his plan immediately was the distance left to travel home, for "upon our return to this country I made inquiries as to what was the largest rubber company in the country."[13]

That he sought out grand commercial exploitation is typical of Davis who thought on a large scale and seemed able to imagine vast undertakings much easier than small experimental ventures. For this reason, many associates could never understand him. "If you can make a little on a little, you can make a lot on a lot," was much of his business creed.[14]

Davis could not have approached a more receptive firm than the United States Rubber Company, at that time the largest rubber company in the world. It was the only American industry that had even remotely considered the possibilities of maintaining its own property for a source of its crude rubber supply. Founded in 1892, the company had early aimed at eventual control of its own raw materials, although little had been done to achieve this goal. Samuel P. Colt, who replaced Charles Ranlett Flint as president in 1901, succeeded in establishing purchasing agents to buy directly for the company instead of through other importers. The General Rubber Company, a $1,000,000 subsidiary of United States Rubber, was formed as a purchasing agency, with headquarters in Manaos and Para in South America. Colt's theory of acquiring actual production areas of crude rubber was not to develop plantations but to lease property for a wild rubber supply.[15] Edgar B. Davis changed that policy by persuading United States Rubber officials to accept his idea and to hire him along with it to develop the scheme.

Health is wealth, but the expenses for convalescence had depleted Davis' money, and although physically ready for a new enterprise, he had to call on the kindness of his brother to finance an entrance into a new shoe business.[16] Shoes had become a last resort, however, for Davis was intrigued with the rubber industry. Unfortunately, he was restricted in his plans by a lack of funds and time. Having made his first success through hard work and a steady climb up the ladder of preferment, Davis was forced by circumstances to change his tactics and become one of the most colorful characters in business circles, a promoter. Davis revealed a characteristic of the real salesman in his ability to recoup his resources after two initial failures to market his plan. A Brockton friend of his days in the shoe business arranged an interview for Davis with the general manager of United States Rubber, who, through a courteous talk, gave Davis the impression that the man knew almost nothing of plantation rubber.[17] He did, however, send Davis to the head of the General Rubber Company, the subsidiary which acquired the raw materials. Although this man had some understanding of the plantations of the East Indies, Davis records no further conversations in his autobiographical sketch,[18] but he made other unsuccessful attempts to present his plan. According to Bruce Barton, who wrote Davis' story without revealing his identity (letters to personal friends confirm that the story was based on the life of Davis), Davis was "literally thrown out of the office day after day."[19] This is probably exaggerated, but it reflects the Davis persistence. That he might fail probably did not enter Davis' mind, for unwavering determination had become a definite part of his personality. Of even greater influence was his belief that he was being divinely guided as a result of his mystical experience. After making a decision, he was able to stick to it with a grim determination no matter what the cost. Thus, the complex result was the hard-headed, mystic Yankee, following what he ambiguously called "Faith" but what was labeled by those who knew him well as eccentricity, madness, religious fanaticism, or other epithets.

Davis was hardly equipped with the background necessary to establish himself as knowledgeable on the subject of rubber. One trip through plantation areas by a man who had had business experience in leather and shoes could gain, it seems, only a bare understanding of a completely alien business. For all practical purposes, Davis was a novice, but, besides being cast in a determined mold, he had other qualities. As noted previously, he could compete at bridge with the best of them, converse easily and interestingly in social circles, and generally present an image of a polished gentleman. In addition to his own qualities, his brother Oscar, whose ability to mix with people exceeded that of his younger brother, acted as a lead to business associations. Davis had not spent over ten years in a highly competitive industry without picking up a few techniques of doing business. If one could not approach someone in one way, perhaps there was another method, and Davis was not a man to leave a stone unturned. He played the game of life as he played at cards--to win. He had another trump card, and he would use it, for he often compared his skill at bridge with his life.

The story of how Davis got in touch with John J. Watson, treasurer of the rubber company and the man who arranged for Davis to present his case to the executive board, has two versions. Davis formally told of his opportunity to approach United States Rubber officials in the following way:

> Meanwhile, in the summer of 1908, my brother who was Vice President of the George E. Keith Company, maker of the Walkover Shoes, had had a tough time making prices because of the fluctuation in leather. He was very tired and, as his wife was about to be confined and was unable to accompany him, he wanted me to go to Lake Mohonk Mountain House for a holiday. I demurred because I had been to such very heavy expenses with my hospitalizations, doctors' fees, and two trips abroad, but when I remembered how fine my brother Oscar had been in paying the household expenses of my Mother and Father during my illness and had given me a good sized check to go into a new shoe business--I was leaving the business I had been in since I was 20--I decided to go.
>
> Lake Mohonk was run by Quakers who had morning Prayers, did not sell liquor nor cigaretts nor allow card playing, but it appealed to the wealthy people of New York and Philadelphia because of the beauty of the place and a first class table. Card playing and other amusements were done behind closed doors. My brother made acquaintances and friends easily--he was a really great wit--and we immediately were in the select crowd behind the closed door entertainments. Here we met among others Mr. and Mrs. John J. Watson, Jr. of New York. (I am mentioning this as I feel that this trip to

> Lake Mohonk and this meeting with the Watsons was Providential.) As stated, everybody seemed to like Oscar, but Mr. Watson and I became good friends, although I never mentioned business with him. When the Watsons left he asked me to lunch with him when I came through New York on my return to Massachusetts, and gave me his card as Treasurer of United States Rubber Company. I afterward found that Mr. Watson was acting President of the Company during the illness of Colonel Samuel P. Colt. Then I immediately told him about what we had seen and learned in the East and, to make a long story short, he gave me an Opportunity to meet the leaders of the Rubber Company.[20]

The "providential" coincidence stressed by Davis in the above narrative was given another point of view in the revealing account he gave to several close associates. Davis said that he knew very well that John J. Watson was treasurer of the rubber company. Also, Oscar wanted to assist his brother in meeting someone prominent in the rubber business. Of no little significance is the statement made by Edgar Davis that "My brother made acquaintances and friends easily . . . and we immediately were in the select crowd behind closed door entertainments."[21] In telling the true side of the venture at Lake Mohonk years later, Davis, who took some pride in this successful promotion scheme, enjoyed depicting the image he and Oscar made in their immaculate linen suits: "We went at 'em in white!" he would say.[22]

That Davis finally approached the United States Rubber Company indirectly was only rarely hinted by him, however, for Davis would characteristically imply that initial connections were "Providential," and, indeed, the whole story suggests an extraordinary piece of luck. On the whole, it was a combination of many things, mostly culminating in Davis' rare ability, or as he put it, "Then an opportunity came to me--I pushed it a little!-- to interest the directors of the United States Rubber Company."[23]

Convincing John J. Watson that he had a plan worth investigating was not tantamount to success, but it was a concrete beginning. Watson sent Davis back to the East to collect more data for a report on the industry,[24] and Davis kept doggedly on, explaining in his own words, "I had made one trip. I made another trip around the world to make sure that rubber could be produced for less than a shilling per pound."[25]

Leaving shortly before Christmas, 1908, Davis embarked on a business voyage, even taking time to look into the Eastern shoe industry. As his home town paper recorded:

> Edgar B. Davis of 1330 Main Street returned June 4, 1909, from a six-month trip in which he circumnavigated the globe. Mr. Davis went to Ceylon in the interests of a New York company and spent a month on the island. While in Manila he visited a shoe factory run by an American named McGrath and the foreman of which was W. R. Joyce, a former Brocktonian. The basis of the force at that factory was a set of men who had been cobblers under the old regime and the results were excellent. The shoes turned out were almost as classy as the Brockton product and were by far the best he saw while abroad.[26]

Returning home, Davis found Colonel Samuel P. Colt back at the head of the United States Rubber Company. At a formal meeting, Davis presented his findings and recommendations to the board of directors of the United States Rubber Company. He approached the meeting confidently, but when it came his turn to talk, he was speechless for one of the few times in his life. "By that time I had had considerable experience," he remembered,

> and knew some important business men in different large cities in the country, but when I went in and saw those gentlemen, I was somewhat overawed that I had to sell them something that they knew practically nothing about, and none of them had ever been on the other end of the world.[27]

It seems that he was more worried about the directors' ignorance than his lack of information; yet, he continued:

> I started, but the words wouldn't come. I hemmed and I hawed,--and I hawed and I hemmed, and finally

> blurted out my story. Then when I left the room for the directors to discuss the question, I kicked myself all the way down the hall. I had made such a rotten showing. One of the Vice Presidents told me that he heard one of those capitalists say: "You know, I rather believed that Davis. He wasn't slick enough not to be telling the truth."[28]

It appears that the directors were shrewd enough to comprehend that unprecedented possibilities existed in Davis' scheme to create company properties, for negotiations to finance a plantation venture were begun in earnest. Davis recorded that Colt lent his influence to the scheme, which was obviously a vote with some weight.[29] Davis was not yet in the company, but the door was open. The main barrier between the directors and their new prospective member of the firm was a disagreement over the size of the initial investment. Davis proposed his usual maximum, whereas the company recommended a cautious minimum. The unusual terms agreed upon suggest that United States Rubber considered Davis either a valuable asset or a good risk. In complete charge of the plantations, he was to be a vice president with a salary of $12,000 a year plus expenses. In addition, Davis asked for a percentage of the profits he intended to make. This resulted in the agreement that when the plantations were in full production, Davis was to be paid 8 2/3 percent of the value at the time (above the original investment by United States Rubber) as indicated by an independent commission.[30]

The directors of the company appropriated $1,500,000, which was only ten percent of what Davis considered an adequate investment.[31] Even this figure had been reduced from an original executive committee recommendation of $3,000,000 by two influential company directors who had experienced financial problems with a tin company in Sumatra.[32] Nevertheless, Davis signed the contract on December 21, 1909.[33]

A natural business instinct is very much in evidence through an examination of Davis' handling of his contract. Considering the original appropriation too small, Davis, arranged to get a percentage of the value which he would eventually create so by the time he got the plantations in full production, his share would be based on an "adequate investment." "You will remember that I signed the contract on what I felt it was inevitable for the United States Rubber Company to invest, and not what they agreed to invest," he reminded confidants.[34] He was thinking much farther ahead of the firm he joined, for "later, this gave rise to a much larger sum than they had anticipated."[35] At settlement time, Davis had to retain Louis Brandeis who managed to collect out of court.[36]

The big payoff, however, was ten years in the future. Although greatly simplified, Davis' accomplishments at the close of 1909, as described by two rubber chroniclers, were as follows:

> In Malaya and Sumatra, the tourist saw some of the early rubber plantations and then and there the United States Rubber Company's Mid-East estates were born. Bursting with his subject, the super-salesman checked in with Colt's corporation, sold Samuel on the idea and went bouncing back to Malaya with the necessary financing behind him.[37]

Perhaps Davis did "bounce" a little in jubilation of having got the "rubber ball rolling" toward his plantation goal, for all in all, it seems he had overcome many handicaps. For instance, he did not have a background in the rubber industry. But in 1909 Davis convinced the largest rubber company in the world that he was worth over a million dollars to them because Davis was an impressive fellow with unusual capabilities.

In the first place Davis was physically impressive: "spectacled, benevolently round-faced, bald in front, over six feet in height and tipping the scales at more than 250 pounds-- that is the picture of the physical man in his prime."[38] Secondly, because he believed that he was being divinely guided, Davis radiated his driving force by his own confident demeanor. Another picture of Davis will bring to light his rare personality. Davis is discussed in the absorbing *Rubber, A Story of Glory and Greed*, which is the history of rubber from primitive man to the date of publication in 1936, because "his fathering of the factory-owned plantation idea constitutes his chief claim to a place in the rubber records . . ."[39] The following description is helpful to an understanding of Davis' image:

> not to its Flints, its Colts or any of its practical rubber men does United States owe this development, however, but to a singular character who breezed into

> and through its councils on the way from shoes to oil. Reader, we give you Edgar B. Davis, the most likable, the most unexpected and withal one of the ablest gentlemen in the whole centuries-long history of caoutchouc [India rubber] from Hernando Cortez to the brothers duPont.[40]

Impressive, able, and determined, he had made the most of rare opportunity. No longer in financial straits and obviously in improved health, early 1910 found him steaming once again out of New York Harbor, this time on a voyage "for his wealth."

Chapter III
THE DEVELOPMENT

It was a hundred miles from anything that could be described as civilization and the life had been lonely; but he had made money; during the rubber boom he had done very well...

W. Somerset Maugham

Edgar B. Davis, as a representative of the United States Rubber Company, was bound for a rich area of the globe, but it proved to be a locality which would only reluctantly give up its wealth. This graphic description pictures his exotic destination:

> On one side is the Bay of Bengal, on the other the Gulf of Siam and the South China Sea. This is southermost Asia thrusting down towards the equator in a goose-neck peninsula. The neck itself is a part of Siam, the head and the beak are that jumble of colonies and federated and unfederated protectorates loosely known as British Malaya. West of it across Malacca Strait lies the long length of the island of Sumatra, which runs on to the south and east and breaks off in a tail of subsidiary Dutch islands the closest and largest of which is Java. East of Malaya, east of Sumatra and north of Java is the squarish bulk of the Island of Borneo, mostly Dutch, but including also another jumble of British protectorates. This is the new world of rubber, and its capital, its Para, Manaos and Iquitas rolled into one, is stinking Singapore, a yellowman's city on a dot of an island at the southern extremity of the Malay Peninsula, halfway between India and China.[1]

Davis' immediate home was to be Sumatra, "a large, wild, green, hot

> island, and a grand spine of mountains runs from end to end of it, and in the mountains live savage tribes not pleasant to meet. So far as he--and U.S. Rubber--is concerned, Sumatra is a sixty-mile wide coastwise welter of lowland jungle, threaded together by a single railway and by good dirt and macadam roads."[2]

Davis wasted no time in organizing. By March 1, 1910, he was bound from Singapore to Sumatra to inspect tobacco property recommended for purchase.[3] Davis exhibited his nationalism, explaining that "a sense of patriotism to some extent" prompted him to push rubber plantation interests, when he heard other nationalities gloating over America's absence from the business made profitable by American purchases.[4] Possibly, Davis and Watson had discussed applying for a higher title for Davis in the Company, but Davis had decided to play his hand as it stood, reasoning,

> I have no doubt that a Vice-Presidency, without a Directorship, will meet every requirement altho I feel somewhat like a "four-flusher" every time the title is used. No, while I appreciate your willingness to submit the matter to the Directors, it is unnecessary. I feel confident that they are with me heartily in this work and would not fail to do me full justice if I make good, as I have set my teeth to do so.[5]

Davis surveyed matters bearing on the profitable operation of a rubber plantation such as adequate rainfall, drainage, soil richness, labor prospects, and transportation.[6] Men experienced in plantation development never withheld any information from Davis when he was new to the East, and having had to rely on the British and Dutch may have taught the nationalistic Yankee a lesson in international relations. Davis remembered the kindness shown to him:

> ... when the big money comes, I want to go abroad to pay my obligations to the Dutch planters who were with us in the East and will of course want Warren's advice and assistance. I also want to pay my

> obligations to the British--those who remain--for their services to me in teaching as green a forester as ever hit the pike but which Led to my first Fortune.[7]

In addition to receiving sound advice, Davis also continued to get his share of timely (or, as he put it, Providential) good fortune, for after arriving in Sumatra he recommended the purchase of the Nieuw Asahan Tobacco Co. So United States Rubber bought for 1,750,000 guilders (then $700,000) a fifty-two-year lease on some 88,000 acres of partially cleared and cultivated land, roads, buildings, and coolies thrown in. And Davis became Managing Director of Plantations.[8]

Davis took over during a good season of high tobacco prices; the crop in the ground was an excellent one,[9] and "that year's tobacco crop was sold for $300,000 so it cost United States Rubber only $400,000 to get into the rubber-plantation business."[10]

While Davis was building an organization and employing efficient personnel, Colonel Colt sent John Warren Bicknell east to make an independent report for the rubber company. Colt's own May, 1910, report to stockholders reveals his company's growing belief in its newest venture:

> ...special attention has been given to the initiation of plans for ourselves producing both in the"Far-East" and in Brazil the supply of crude rubber needed by the Company, which we confidently expect will result in our obtaining in the not distant future from our own rubber properties a substantial portion of our requirements.[11]

The report obviously omits that leading this "initiation of plans" was a novice not only new to the company but also a stranger to the plantation business.

However, "that was the first the stockholders heard of the 'Far-East' and the last they heard of Brazil,"[12] for Davis was carrying on in his typical enthusiastic fashion. To gain needed experience, he employed an Englishman, W. J. Gallagher, former Director of Agriculture for the Federated Malay States. He also engaged an able Dutch planter, Huibreght Ketner, a huge man weighing even more than Davis. Davis himself planted the first rubber seedling ever set out by an American in Sumatra and five million more were set under his leadership.[13] Actually, "the first purchase was made in May, 1910, the first planting done in June, 1910, which gives you some idea of how Edgar works."[14]

Edgar worked quickly, getting ahead of everyone right away. As he remembered, "although up to that time I never had heard of any company planting a thousand acres of rubber trees a year, Mr. Ketner planted *three thousand* the first year and *seventeen thousand* acres the second year."[15] Ketner strove to stay up with his boss's demands. Davis once even doubled the original planting outlines for an area. In answer to one of Davis' early queries from Ceylon, "How much will you plant next year?" Ketner answered by return wire: "Ten thousand acres." Davis' next wire read, "It must be twenty."[16]

The outcome of this large-scale gambling was spectacular. As a result,

> right along with the great plantation boom rode the United States, making its first actual estate investments in the East in 1910, bringing its plantation acreage to 32,500 (more than double the area of Manhattan Island) in 1912. By 1913 it had ten thousand coolies toiling for it in Sumatra; twenty thousand acres planted of eight thousand owned; 2,500,000 Hevea trees. One factor making for rapid progress was that much of the eighty thousand acres had been planted in tobacco and the task of conquering jungle before setting out the Heveas was avoided. Already in 1913 this development was the world's largest rubber plantation and it has continued expanding and retains that distinction to this day.[17]

Davis represented the successful entrepreneur. His primary goal was profits and his functional role was four-fold: establishing business objectives, creating the organization to fulfill stated aims, establishing company policy, and continuing and improving management techniques.

The determined character and domineering personality of Edgar B. Davis was in total charge. In the shoe business, Davis, as general sales manager, naturally had many employees under his direction, but this time he was in complete control. Any superiors he had were half way around the world. Giving orders came naturally to him. As his nephew remembers,

> my father was older by three years, but told me "Edgar orders me around as if I were a little boy." Don't we have here the "Faith" that would bowl over anything that got in the way, and command anything that would serve it?[18]

Of course Edgar B. Davis believed in power,[19] and "he was determined to have his own way and do things in his own good time."[20] He also found it difficult to admit that he was wrong.[21] The fact that he was right about the potentialities of rubber plantations and had overcome certain handicaps to make his dream a reality only strengthened his belief in his mission in life. To get his own way at times, he would rationalize his position by bringing up the "Voice" to his own mind in the plantation days and afterwards to those to whom he had revealed his secret.[22] In other words,

> on the spiritual side he would attribute his stand to Faith.... When he had an urge to do something, it was God's will; when anyone approached him for help, it was God bringing them together. Therefore he had the courage to do things which others would not do, for he was sure it would all work out for their benefit in the end.[23]

So the complex mixture emerges in Davis' character: a determined personality blended with a sincere desire to do the right thing through Divine guidance; but the domineering personality was a salient feature in spite of the excellent manners. Yet he was not obnoxious in his methods, many times going about quietly getting his own way. Those who knew him best over an association of many decades have left impressions of the Davis personality and character: "If I understand E.B.D.'s philosophy correctly, he is literally trying to submit to Divine Guidance for every action."[24] There are many written comments on Davis' chief goal always to have his own way: "And even in his Mission God was to perform a miracle, but only in the way that E.B.D. predetermined...."[25] Along the same line of thought Davis' nephew says, "He told me that he wanted 'the Holy Spirit of God' (He did not add that it was in order to carry out *his own* wishes–my personal opinion)."[26]

Perhaps Davis did not appear as overbearing as he was because of his ability to wait his opposition out: "He will not force his views, however. If others cannot work with him, he is willing to wait, confident that it is the best thing to do, and that God will work out things in His own way and time."[27] It appears that although Davis could be hard on his employees, he never threatened anyone's job as a means to achieve his desires. Yet, many employees and friends, fearing his dominating mentality, would often approach him through others instead of risking Davis' retorts directly.[28] It was extremely important, however, that men remain a part of his group:

> the fact that a man is in his organization means that God put him there, and E.B.D. will not remove him; he may, however, remove himself, but generally he is given every opportunity to reconsider.[29]

Nothing could stand in the way of what Davis considered divine guidance. Consequently, "if he has a view of how something should be done; if he has a responsibility for carrying out certain plans--no one may 'shove him off the driver's seat.'"[30]

There is some evidence to suggest that Davis suppressed this innate drive to achieve his ends as much as possible. There is only one occasion when Davis used his great physical power to subjugate anyone. This incident is unique in itself, for the opposition was minor:

> I remember a curious incident which happened in a hotel room in a mountain resort in Java--I think it was Garoot. Warren Bicknell and I were with him. Warren had just put on a freshly laundered white suit preparatory to going into the dining room. The walls of the bedroom were painted some light color--possibly blue--which rubs off--you will remember this from your trip to the East. Mr. Davis in an affectionate gesture put his hands on Warren's shoulders and, as Warren thought, was pushing him back against the wall, which would involve another change of clothes. Warren instinctively resisted, and in a flash Mr. Davis' anger got the best of him and he jammed Warren hard against the wall. It all passed almost instantly; but not many years before Warren

> died I recalled this to his mind and he had a vivid remembrance of it.[31]

Undoubtedly the childhood inclinations to fight were subdued with difficulty.

To balance an unusually strong force of will, Edgar Davis' nature was generous to the extreme, kindly, and free from false pretense, the soul of generosity, both material (when he had it) and spiritual; no friend in need of consolation was neglected--he always found time for that, but it was always done quietly and few knew about it."[32] On the other hand, his financial generosity was both concealed and obvious, depending on the mood and situation, for "he did a great deal for a great many people--much of which was faintly resented, much deeply appreciated."[33]

This assistance was not always welcome, possibly for the reason that Davis had to dominate in much of his giving. One of Davis' life-time associates, George Seybold, who once managed the plantations in Sumatra, told a revealing story about the Davis brand of hospitality:

> Mr. Davis in Singapore, gave a dinner party every night, with from anywhere from four to sixteen guests. It was always his party and he would never allow anyone to take the check. There was a man named Fitzgerland there who invited Mr. Davis to dinner one night. Mr. Davis said that he would accept provided he could pay for the dinner. Fitzgerland burst out, "You are the most selfish man I ever saw. I will never eat dinner with you again." And he never did. Davis was very much taken back and Fitzgerland said, "Don't you realize that other people have their own self respect and they don't want to be patronized by you all the time?"[34]

Although startled by this lecture, Davis never changed his habit of always picking up the check. Moreover,

> he never did social bookkeeping and never kept account of the things he did for other people. That was so automatic with him that there was no account outside of the fact that he wanted to do it.[35]

George Seybold considered this trait one of the most outstanding of Davis' character.[36]

Another characteristic of Davis was that he rarely found fault with his associates. George Seybold was forever impressed that he "never heard him condemn anyone for anything they ever did."[37] Thomas L. Caylor, who was closely associated with Davis for the last twelve years of his life, remembered more than anything else "his love for his fellow man. He recognized evil but refused to condemn those who were evil. That's pretty hard to do, especially when the evil acts are against one."[38] In later life, Davis often remarked of anyone who came under condemnation by others that, "There but for the grace of God, go I."[39]

Davis also avoided snobbery in many ways. "E.B.D. had no use for stuffy respectability," states his nephew;

> he decried pomposity and would look it straight in the eye. He liked good living but was no hedonist. Languishing in pleasure spots never appealed to him; if he visited them he had a purpose, maybe a vacation, but not a long one.[40]

One of the first things George Seybold noticed about Davis was that he had no use for any social hierarchy. No distinction in rank was made at any of his dinner parties. Seybold, when first associated with him in a minor position with United States Rubber, was asked to dinner parties for the dignitaries of Singapore or for high-ranking company officials.[41] Davis gradually withdrew from several exclusive clubs which he had joined while in the shoe business, and he refused invitations to join any private clubs after he had permanently returned from the rubber plantations.

His treatment of others was part of what he termed his life of "Faith"; and faith in his mission had become his religion as well as his life. He disassociated himself with any denomination after 1904, although he would sometimes attend a church service and even spoke periodically at churches.[42] Individual prayer and meditation took the place of formal, organized worship for Davis. But the influence of his Puritanism remained strong and pervasive when it came to any business deal. One of the legends grew out of Davis' break with his church. The story that Davis became interested in mysticism in Sumatra was reported in most popular accounts until he died. Nothing could be farther from the truth, for Davis became a mystic through an experience occurring in New England and through his own inherent disposition. Writing to his close friend, Sanford Gurney, in 1934, Davis explained his ability to contact a higher power:

> Since the crack that let in the light, I never have prayed for success. I think the biggest thing that we can do is to "tune in" with the Creative Force. That alone I believe is the only true basis for success and when we try to bend that Force to our wills, we get terrible static.[43]

Close friends could not help but joke that the crack that let in the light came from the blow to the head in the great train wreck.

Throughout the whole of his stay in the East, there was no time when Davis became interested in any occult or mystic religion.[44] But since most people recognized something of the spiritual in Davis, it was typical for journalists to make an association with geographical religious stereotypes. The label was applied and the legend grew.

Davis' antics added to legend, for he took unique chances in Sumatra to prove his faith. He had an utter loathing of serpents, but on inspection trips into the snake-infected properties, he refused to use protective leggings worn by all other white planters.[45] Instead, "he strode forth in his immaculate linen suit and white shoes without any leg protection."[46] Davis simply refused to take precautionary measures against snake bite.[47] His abhorrence of vipers caused him much unhappiness, and he saw more reptiles than anyone else; however, each safe passage through the jungles strengthened his belief in his destiny. He had many narrow escapes, such as stepping within striking distance of the deadly rice snake without harm. As a result, Davis sincerely believed that "this work in the East was a Triumph of Faith in God and no credit to me, for I Believe He was Guiding me all the Way."[48]

Perhaps Davis really believed the legend that followed him from the East: "When his time comes, he will go; he knows that a few leggings won't stand in the way of Fate."[49] Davis did advise friends that if a man had a close brush with death and survived, it was significant. Four years before his death, he wrote concerning some accident which a youth had survived:

> Thanks for your letter of December 3rd., with its news of Sam's very narrow escape from death. Thank God his life was spared; and in my Philosophy, that means that God has something of Importance for Sam to do. It just seems a Miracle performed under natural laws that Sam's life was spared.[50]

In addition to snakes, another hazard of the tropics was jungle diseases, such as malaria. Davis suffered less from these various tropical disorders than usual for the average white man,[51] and as he continued to defy the elements with impunity, the legend grew.

Davis' religious philosophy (unless he was transacting business) continued to modify. For instance, he pointed out that one never came upon a church named "St. Rahab's,"[52] and he emphasized that Jesus mixed socially with a wide range of people: "He pointed out that the first person to see Christ resurrected was Mary out of whom he cast seven devils. He recalled that in Christ's ancestry was Rahab the harlot."[53] Davis could not accept Jesus as a meek person; "he believed that Jesus was 'a regular fellow' and 'would take a drink with the boys' if in doing so he could accomplish his purpose with them."[54] Obviously, he entertained some beliefs which would have been condemned by orthodox Christians of his day. Ultimately, he came to believe that everyone would be saved,[55] as revealed in his poem, "Omnipotence," written aboard ship on Antipodes Day, September 25, 1917.

Omnipotence

Whence and why comes the germ
That makes the blood in its courses burn--
That sets the heart and brain afire
Leading to dreams which consume or tire?
What is thy nature and what thine aim
To hold one so mercilessly in chain:
To baffle minds both strong and keen:
To force one on his God to lean?
Art thou Devil or Angel fair?
Leadst thou to Heaven or to Despair?
The questions asked--I pondered well
This riddle of life, is this our Hell?
The earthly prizes we seek to win:

The lures of life the world calls sin:
War and strife--
This struggle of life,
Is this our hell?
In a maze of doubtings my soul I found
And no peace was mine when I looked around.
So knowledge seeking I learned full well
That God is GOD BOTH OF HEAVEN AND HELL.
And in century-spans,
All's well! All's well![56]

One of the most obvious lines illustrative of Davis as a man of vision is, of course, "in century-spans/ All's well! All's well!" There is strong suggestion here that Davis counted on time to resolve all problems. This theme was no idle whim of Davis', for in a later chapter in his life he would spend a fortune backing a play which stressed eventual happiness for all.

In spite of a few remarks to close associates, Davis was never known to criticize churches openly. In a later period in life he even formalized his own worship by reading Derzhavin's "Ode to God" on Sundays.[57] But in spite of his liberal statements, Davis remained a Fundamentalist Biblical scholar particularly in his Puritan devotion to thrift, diligence, capitalism, and the business life.

Davis seems the epitome of paradoxical and dichotomous behavior. Although domineering in business, he was patient, mannerly, and likable. He could be unorthodox in his religious beliefs but was a Christian who lived his faith. Generous to the extreme, he would rarely accept a favor from anyone. A man of high temper, he kept this weakness so subdued that impassivity appeared part of his personality. Davis enjoyed good living, such as expensive dinner parties, but he made no social distinction in his guests or in any association. Considering himself divinely led in life, he would impose his will any time he felt something interfered with his mission. He was an extraordinary but authentic eccentric. Long time friend Joseph Machin, felt it necessary to inquire, "To whom am I speaking, the Yankee or the Mystic?"[58]

A man in such powerful position would influence many people in the course of a lifetime. Many men whom he employed through the plantation business were associated with him off and on for the rest of their lives. Walter B. Mahony, though never an employee of his, was later involved with him on various ventures. George Seybold became a friend for life. After making the inspection trip to the East with Davis, John Warren Bicknell never lost touch and later became a stockholder in Davis' oil company. A forester, Kelts C. Baker, played a large part in developing the Luling Oil Field with his old employer in the rubber business. Nor were all those who came under Davis' influence his employees in the East, for Charles B. Rayner, another man who played a part in the Luling development, was a former representative of the Standard Oil Company as manager of the Singapore office.[59]

The longest and closest associate of Edgar B. Davis over a half century was the talented and versatile David M. Figart. A native of Altoona, Pennsylvania, Figart had the same limited formal education that Davis received in Massachusetts, but his innate brilliance made up the difference. One was always struck by the quick and keen intelligence of David M. Figart.

Arriving in the Philippines as an employee of the U.S. Army Commissary Department in 1907, Figart soon left this position to become secretary to Dr. Victor G. Heiser, Director of Health in the Philippines, who later became known for his autobiography, *An American Doctor's Odyssey.* Appointed to the U.S. Consular service in Singapore in 1910, Figart met Davis and John Warren Bicknell through that office.[60] Davis was building an organization and was on the lookout for good men and was evidently drawn to Figart, for, "later, he made a suggestion that I took to be an invitation to become his secretary; but I did not follow this up until after resigning from the consular service near the end of 1912."[61]

Another story involves George Seybold, who was hired aboard ship as he sailed to his position with the Philippine Constabulary. This unique account serves to shed more light on the dominating aspects of the Davis character.

> Seybold had first heard of Edgar B. Davis in Manila from friends who described him as a rather large but "fabulous character" who managed plantation. Returning from his leave to the states in 1916, Seybold and his wife chanced to travel on a ship with Davis and Figart. "I played bridge with them a couple of times," explained Seybold, "and about two days out of Honolulu my wife told me that these men were asking her very peculiar questions

> and she suspected that they were going to offer me a job. I told her to listen and say nothing."[62]

Shortly thereafter, Figart approached Seybold with an unusual question: "If you stretch a string around the equator and assume the earth to be a perfect sphere, it will be 24,000 miles long. Cut it and add three feet to the length and assume it to be stretched tight again. How far will it be away from the earth?" Seybold replied that he would have to get a pencil in order to figure with pi. Figart suggested that he use three for pi. Seybold figured the problem in his head and gave the answer. "Right. Quickest anyone has ever done it," said Figart, leaving immediately.[63]

The question probably was designed to test a man's presence of mind. On the other hand, the use of the mystical number *three* might have appealed to Davis. At any rate, it was an unusual hiring procedure and part of the reason that Davis impressed Seybold "from the very beginning as a very unusual character."[64]

For whatever his reasons, Davis must have been satisfied with Seybold's answer. As the ship left Nagasaki later on the voyage, Edgar Davis approached Seybold at ship rail and formally asked him to join the United States Rubber Company. Seybold accepted, later becoming head manager of the plantation in Sumatra.

Thus, George Seybold became a part of an efficient working organization which had been built by Edgar B. Davis, and which was largely the result of the application of scientific methods[65] and meticulous planning in all levels of operation. The successful farming procedures which were applied suggest that Davis could rely on the counsel of trained men, although only a few years later he wildcatted for oil repeatedly against the advice of competent professional geologists.

"The important factors," Davis believed,

> in the Success of Hollandasche Amerikansche Plantage Maatschappij or HAPM as the Plantation Company popularly was called, were the formation of an Advisory Board, the scientific Work, the able body of planters, principally Dutch, and the care of the laborers.[66]

Davis does not mention that he was primarily responsible for establishing these principles which developed this unique American farming venture. Even in old age Davis maintained considerable modesty concerning his leadership in this venture. In a letter written in 1948 to John Warren Bicknell, "one of the very few left whom I knew in my U.S. Rubber Days," Davis stressed the importance of the scientist:

> I think you are most generous in your reference to me; but as I remember it, the real Inspiration for scientific and research work came from Raymond Price and was given a real boost by the group of men he sent out under the leadership of Ed Pound.[67]

In truth, Davis not only stimulated research and technology but he also led it with his own ideas. The common methods used to space trees before Davis' reign was to set out seedlings in a row, and after a few years of growth, to cut down every other tree. This seemed unscientific to Davis,

> so he made a card index and kept a case-history of all the seedlings. Just as he surmised, the system of cutting down seedlings 2 and 4 or 1 and 3 often resulted in indiscriminate killing of many fine producers and leaving duds. It took Davis a long time to break up an old Dutch custom, but he finally succeeded and his method made a fifty per cent more efficient plantation.[68]

The largest rubber company in the world, United States Rubber maintained a scientific research department in the estates. W. J. Gallagher, the former Director of Agriculture in Malaya, stressed investigation as a part of development and the vice president in charge of the rubber company's research department in New York sent a group of his men East to work with the experienced British and Dutch scientists. Consequently, the new American plantation spent much more for scientific development than did the older British and Dutch establishments.[69]

American technological advances were both rapid and profitable, resulting in tremendous increases in yields of raw rubber from the trees. An average yield of 300 to 400 pounds of dry rubber per acre was increased, through expert care and tree budding, to a production of from 1,000 to 2,000 pounds per acre.[70] Americans were not selfish with their knowledge, as the British noted in the *R.G.A. Bulletin*:

> H.A.P.M. has been one of the pioneers of rubber research, and their recognition of the value of scientific research has done much for the plantation industry as a whole. Besides being supporters of the R.G.A. and the A.V.R.O.S. Experiment Station, the H.A.P.M. some years ago established their own Scientific Research Department, of which the Director of Research is Mr. J. Grantham.
>
> Every planter today recognizes what the H.A.P.M. Laboratories and staff have contributed to our knowledge. Whether it be bud-grafting, tapping, manuring, investigation into diseases, and the other important problems affecting the industry, the H.A.P.M. organization has been in the forefront. For example, who has not heard about the Keuchenius method of treatment of brown bast, or Mr. Grantham's experiments in manuring, let along the pioneer work in bud-grafting. The contributions to the Archief and other scientific publications by members of the H.A.P.M. Research Staff are read by all interested in the well-being of the industry, and the broad-minded view of the administration in giving free access to their laboratories and records is an example which might be followed by many other organizations.[71]

Davis' plantations became known as the "Mecca of the rubber growing world" after a noted British authority on rubber, Herbert Ashplant, described a tour through HAPM:

> Of all the rubber areas visited, none produced so much useful information as the plantations of the General Rubber Company in Sumatra, Kisaran. The headquarters of these plantations has become the

> Mecca of all planters who wish to keep abreast of recent rubber research.[72]

It is not surprising that Davis remembered this scientific development with pride. "It always has been a great satisfaction to me," he reflected years later, "that HAPM became the first concern that spent real money on research and ultimately became the Mecca of the Plantation Rubber Industry."[73]

Not only were the trees given undivided attention but the men who tapped these precious plants were also cared for attentively. Upon arriving in the tropics, Davis found that death by disease was considered a natural event, for "every morning, Davis told me, he heard the funeral dirge for someone taken off by the cholera."[74] Afterwards, a competent medical staff was established to care for all workers. In time, it became beneficial for the Javanese to go to Sumatra to work, where their health improved under scientific care. Due to the excellent medical attention, by 1927, the death rate out of a population of 22,000 plantation people had fallen below that of New York City.[75] Even plagues were controlled. Davis remembered a cholera epidemic breaking out on a plantation of 12,000 workers. The available medical facilities prevented all but three employees from dying.[76]

Contending with disease was only one problem which Davis was called upon to resolve, however. There were other evils of which the Yankee businessman became aware. "I was shocked," Davis recalled, "that half of the world worked for eight or ten cents a day, and for three years people came to us signing contracts to get 25 cents a day."[77] The nationalism had begun to melt in the swelter of the tropics, and the man who considered himself a future President of the United States began to develop a universal conscience. He would later conclude, "that we haven't given enough consideration to the other people," and

> we either have to make a scientific study of building these people up or they will bring us down, and the great need in this is that we can not hold the spirit of Christianity up to them with one hand, and grab their lands and beat them in trade with the other. The great need of the world today is a practical Christianity; and to sing lustily "God Bless America" doesn't go far enough. "To live and help to live" must be the motto of the future.[78]

To be sure, Davis learned much about handling all sorts of men. By 1916, he was able to pass along some sound advice to Figart who was taking on a bigger job in the system. "You are now to enter upon a new work--the training and management of men," advised Davis.

> No two men are alike and each must be studied separately, but all will yield to a kindly brotherly interest in their welfare, if that interest be sincerely and persistently maintained. Your success in this field--which is the highest business life affords, will be in direct proportion to the spirit of sacrifice and unselfishness you are able to bring to bear upon your work.[79]

Clearly, Davis recognized the individuality of persons, and he had settled on a pattern of treatment which inculcated rather high ideals. A deep understanding of personality was shown by his stress on sincerity as a necessary virtue in personal relations. It is indicative of Davis' innate desire to be the leader that he considered the training and management of men "the highest business life affords," but it must be observed that the leader must evidence a "spirit of sacrifice and unselfishness."

Probably, Davis was training himself for the direction of a whole country of men when he attained the future fulfillment of the divine prophecy that was so much on his mind. From the start, he had received suggestions from the advisory board he had created to coordinate efforts. Composed of heads of the various departments, the board met regularly, permitting "free and frank discussions of all important problems and was of vital importance in the development of the business."[80]

All indications are that the plantations were run on a level of high efficiency, including scientific care of men as well as of trees, and a working organization of both coordination and cooperation. Behind it all "... was Davis who, as managing director of plantations from the beginning through 1918, brought the estates along from the idea stage to the greatest coautchouc development in the world."[81]

In his job as managing director, Davis naturally made many trips home to report to those whose interests he was developing. Travel became commonplace through these many transoceanic voyages, and he encountered many striking experiences which enriched his life and gave spice to his later abilities as a raconteur. World travelers of the early years of this century still met unique hazards through some of the primitive ship accommodations. Davis' keen sense of humor is visible in his following description of conditions on a trip from New York to Singapore:

> Mr. Frank Henderson, a rubber dealer of New York, and Mr. Featherston, his Singapore agent, were fellow-passengers. Mr. Henderson is one of the best storytellers I ever met in my life, and he furnished a great deal of amusement to all of us. He is greatly afraid of rats, and one night, after one had crawled across his face in his berth, he decided that he would turn night into day and day into night, and, for the rest of the trip--some 4 or 5 days--he slept day-times and stayed awake nights. As so often occurs, if a rat were seen, it would be under his chair, or near him in some manner; we told him he seemed to attract them. To cap the climax, the night before we reached Singapore we cornered a rat in the captain's cabin, and, armed with old shoes, descended upon it, and the captain, finally, with a good approach shot, struck it on the head and put it out of business, much to Mr. Henderson's relief.[82]

Other voyagers on the same ship also caught Davis' eye; these extra "passengers" included "two Japanese spaniels, a very cunning chow puppy, some ducks and a lot of lambs besides numerous rats, mammoth roaches, etc."[83]

Although conditions on other ships were even worse than those described above, at least they were always interesting, as David Figart recorded in his diary September 3, 1915, commenting on the *S.S. Dunera*: "the world's worst--infested with rats and cockroaches, uneatable food; we lived on sardines and biscuits."[84]
There was a a theatrical troupe aboard, however, to add to the "glamour."

The three to four weeks it took to sail between New York and Sumatra gave Davis time to stress his passion for bridge and good conversation; consequently, his love of cards and his habit of always making transportation connections by a matter of minutes resulted in one of his most fondly remembered experiences. On a particular trip, a Frenchman had become attached to Edgar Davis as a member of a dedicated bridge foursome. As he so often did, Davis missed the boat in Honolulu and had to be taken out in a launch. To the humor of the situation, as Davis used to tell it, one must imagine this huge figure laboriously climbing a rope ladder leading to the rail of the ship where the Frenchman paced nervously on deck, fearful that the bridge game would be broken up with the absence of his partner. When he saw that the missing party might make it up the precarious ladder, he was overjoyed. As Davis approached the top, two crewmen stood ready to assist him into the ship. By this time, however, the Frenchman, now in an emotional state, almost knocked Davis back in an attempt to greet him. Although the crewmen were unable to keep the excited Frenchman away, they did succeed in pulling Davis onto the ship. As Davis came over the rail, the Frenchman graciously kissed him on top of his bald head.[85]

Close calls with timetables brought Davis other misadventures. Once missing a ship connection in Saigon, Davis was saved the climb up the rope ladder by Figart and Briggs, the American consul, who helped him through a cargo door in the side of the ship.[86]

These were exciting times, for the tropics has always been an area of adventure, and the first world war heightened the intrigue there. Davis was once picked up and questioned as a suspected gun runner in Hong Kong in 1915. He had cabled a message to United States Rubber to arrange for the hiring of George Seybold. The reply just happened to be signed "Colt and Hotchkiss." (Colonel Samuel P. Colt was a nephew of the Colt of revolver fame.) Upon seeing two names which were linked with firearms manufacture, the British brought Davis ashore on a police launch for questioning. He was able to convince the authorities, however, that the signatures were only coincidental.[87]

Other world-wide adventures and the resulting stories augmented the Davis legend as the plantation director circumnavigated the globe many times. Briefly, his travels between 1909 and 1919 went something like this: his pleasure trip of 1907 was closely followed by the 1908 voyage to acquire more information on plantations. In 1910, he and John Warren Bicknell made the trips east to purchase property and to further report on the rubber industry. Davis was back in New York in 1912 when Figart became his secretary. Leaving for Singapore in January, 1913, Davis and Figart did not return to New York until

March of 1915.[88] The director and his secretary left San Francisco in July of 1915 and toured Tokyo after docking in Yokohama in August. September of 1915 found them in Singapore and the rest of the year involved detailed "island hopping" to inspect the growing plantation system.[89]

In addition to one trip back to New York in 1916, Davis traversed the islands constantly to carry out his duties as managing director of the concern.[90] Finally, Figart and Davis returned to New York in August of 1917, after Davis had been home for a short visit in June of the same year.[91] It was after this trip that Davis became engrossed in the efforts to win the war.[92] He did not dock again in Singapore until a year later on august 22, 1918, only to return to New York shortly after Armistice Day.[93]

Frequent trips home from rubber plantations were certainly desirable and almost a necessity, for the white man led a rigorous existence on the equator. "That life," explains a detailed article in a 1934 *Fortune* magazine, "began for Americans rather more recently, when in 1908 a Mr. Edgar B. Davis happened to land in Sumatra."[94] As managing director, Davis probably avoided the drudgery met by those in supervisory jobs, but he still experienced the many discomforts of equatorial living "...for a job on a rubber plantation is not an easy job. The hours are long, the work is hard and monotonous, the pay is low. And the climate is, after all, an unnatural climate for the white man, who is continually a fish out of his own kind of water."[95] The heat was always a difficulty, but malaria, in those days, was a menace in spite of quinine.

One of Davis' habits, or rather lack of a habit, according to *Fortune*, was a handicap to him as a tropical resident. He did not drink. He and Oscar Davis signed "the Pledge" as boys, and, as in all their undertakings, they took it seriously.[96] Although probably not the best alternative,

> it is advisable in Sumatra where all water must be boiled, to be a steady consumer of alcoholic beverages. Beer--good, strong, German beer--is the natural and universal European thirst quencher, and the consumption is terrific. The champion beer drinker used to drink twenty-four liters (twenty-one quarts) a day, but all Sumatrans would be outstanding beer drinkers in any temperate clime. Beer drinking is not a matter of alcoholism, it is a

> matter of necessity. The system needs an abnormally large liquid content and you need the beer to provide the water. The teetotaler is at a ruinous disadvantage since it appears impossible for anyone to consume more than two or three successive glasses of lemonade or other soft drink; and the non-alcoholic finds it hard to hold the attitude in Sumatra.[97]

"Teetotaler Davis" had something stronger than alcohol to maintain his equilibrium in the alien land, however; he felt that God directed his moves and that the work was part of his future mission. Moreover, he disliked alcohol and beer particularly.

In considering the difficult conditions of the early days, one wonders how Davis, only recently recuperated from a complete breakdown from overwork, stood the rugged life as well as he did. He had all the burden of responsibility, and it is quite obvious from the following description of a typical work day of one of Davis' white assistants how trying a single day could be:

> From sunrise to sunset the new man toiled at monotonous, exacting work in tropical heat, for white supervision was necessary every step of the tedious way to a finished acreage of growing Heveas. When the evening tom-tom sounded and the natives filed slowly back to their quarters, the white man was not always through with his day's work. Costs to compute, wages to count--work with pen and paper occupied part of his evening. After a bath and change of clothes, he might eat or try to eat an unappetizing meal--butter melted, bread doughy, condensed milk spotted with ants or flies, half-cooked pancakes, questionable steak. Then, with his head buzzing from quinine, he would sit under a smoky lamp and try to work or read, being too tired, often, to do either. His house, a rude box-like affair on piles, was, of course, only temporary. New houses, usually of cement, were built for all white employees as soon as the sections were completed. But in the meantime the pioneers lived in their ramshackle wooden bungalows, tended by slow, inefficient servants, fighting malarial fevers

> with daily doses of bitter drug. Importations they were, all of them--man, Hevea, cinchona--set down in the steamy little islands and peninsulas of the Indies.[98]

Davis did break down again in the tropics, but the cause could hardly be attributed to a lack of consumption of beer. More than likely he had a relapse of the original disorder, brought on by strain of work in a rigorous environment. This second breakdown, occurring in Java either the latter part of 1911 or in early 1912, was most serious. Greatly depressed, Davis even contemplated suicide. During these dark days, a woman of some Javanese blood who was the wife of a manger for Standard Oil, was very kind and attentive to him as she helped to nurse him back to health. Eventually, he spent some time in Switzerland recuperating.[99] Here, he composed the song "Melancholy Days in Switzerland" as the music came to him in the night hours.[100]

Stability came again, and some time in early 1912 he was back in the islands, this time to finish the job. There were scores of problems involved, but Davis met them all with his unwavering faith, continuing his efforts until HAPM, originally located as a Sumatra system of farms, spread to various other areas. Through this development work, Davis was a twentieth-century pioneer.

As a relatively new way to produce raw rubber, the plantations remained in the development stage a good many years, for there was much to be learned. However,

> As the plantation gradually took shape and the trees grew ready for tapping, living conditions improved. Good roads were built, railway lines were pushed through, better offices were constructed and a regular life took form out of the chaos. Yet in that regular life, there are many drawbacks. Nothing can change the enervating effect of the weather. The working hours are still long and tiresome. Up at 5 a.m. checking the gangs of coolies, watching them trudge out to begin their operations. Eternally checking them. Walking through the never-ending lines of Heveas, inspecting each tree to see whether the tapping has been properly done, keeping records on the yield and health of each one, noting the need of

> pruning and weeding. Eternally inspecting--cups, pails, factory equipment, coolie quarters, buildings, yards and latrines. Always the necessity of keeping everything clean, not only to achieve good crude, but to keep the workmen in good physical shape. Disease, both human and plant, has to be guarded against. Bark, stem, root and leaf of the rubber tree may be attacked. And the assistants must learn to recognize brown bast which appears in the tapping out, pink fungus on the forks of branches or at the junction of limb with trunk. These two are bark plagues. The rotting of leaves and fruit indicate leaf disease. Such pests as white ants and boring beetles also inflict themselves on the Heveas. But of them all, some planters think the root troubles are the worst. Spreading underground as they do, wet rot and the other forms may destroy a whole group of trees almost before the workers realize it. Speed is the essential point in curing sick trees. Therefore daily inspection in important.[101]

There must be a relief from so much monotony, so the white man took some of his "civilized" ways with him to lighten the heavy load of the "white man's burden." Kisaran, headquarters to HAPM and the largest plantation settlement, had extensive facilities for social life. For those who were athletically inclined there were tennis courts, a swimming pool, a bowling alley, and a baseball diamond. Center of social life was the Kisaran Club, housing a dance hall, a stage, and a bar.[102] It seems that even an American atmosphere prevailed, for

> though there have been many parties and much drinking at the Kisaran Club, there appears to be nothing eastern about its gayety or Oriental about its views. During the boom days, when the rubber was high and bonuses enormous, everyone had money and everyone signed endless chits and the planters who gathered at the clubhouse were Good Time Charlies all.[103]

Although a non-drinker, Davis used the club for his lavish parties, and the tennis courts were much to his liking. He was quite good at tennis (he said he had "a fat man's stroke") and even had difficulty getting competition. His friend John Warren Bicknell, Sumatra East Coast champion, was one of the few who gave him a good match. Once, playfully, to prove his athletic prowess, Davis, with racket and tennis ball, accidentally stroked out a ceiling light in his suite in the Manila Hotel. The next day a note in the room requested quiet between 2 and 4 p.m. because it was siesta time.[104] Davis engaged proficiently in many billiard games in the Raffles Hotel in Singapore as a second sport.

Times to enjoy leisure living were only interludes, though, for in reality, life on the plantations was fatiguing and monotonous. Yet, Davis was making steady progress, both in farming and also in status with United States Rubber. From an obscure figure who had stood before a board of directors trying to sell them the germ of an idea in 1907, he rose to become a member of that same body of men. On March 21, 1916, stockholders of the United States Rubber Company elected him to fill a vacancy on the eighteen-man board of directors.[105] People were beginning to pay attention to Edgar B. Davis. The following month, Colonel Samuel P. Colt invited him to accompany a group to inspect a modern sawmill in South Carolina. Senator Lebaron B. Colt went along and made a stirring speech about "some of the difficult questions of the day." Davis was greatly impressed by the tour.[106]

In the following year, 1917, Davis arranged what he considered the most brilliant piece of work he ever did. J. P. Morgan and Company and the First National Bank of New York were financing United States Rubber at six percent interest in 1917.[107] By getting in touch with certain New York banks through his friend Walter B. Mahony,[108] Davis instigated a change in financial arrangements by selling Kuhn, Loeb and Company $60,000,000 worth of five percent bonds.[109] In a letter to Colonel Colt on March 11, 1918, Davis outlined Mahony's part in the negotiations. As a neighbor of Frank Vanderlip, the influential financier, Walter Mahony interested Vanderlip in the vast possibilities of crude rubber in the East by presenting the facts supplied in a lengthy report prepared by Davis. Mahony was also able to arrange friendly interviews between various officials in Vanderlip's home. Eventually, these informal talks led to dinner parties and later to strictly business meetings in which the sale of bonds was arranged.[110] Davis gave much credit to Mahony's efforts. "I want to bring out the fact," he wrote,

> that although you had known Mr. Vanderlip well for a great many years, and probably Mr. Kahn and Mr. Kies also, yet it would have been very difficult for you to have taken the initiative in this matter, which came about gracefully through the kind intervention of Mr. Mahony.[111]

Behind all arrangements, of course, was Davis, who, already established as a valuable plantation manager, proved himself just as able as a company director. Colt was most satisfied with this bond issue.

By this time, Colt and his associates had begun to rely heavily on Davis as the key man in the profitable overseas empire, but after the United States declared war on Germany on April 6, 1917, Davis believed that he should devote his energies to selling a plan he and Figart had devised to win World War I for the Allies. Throughout early 1918, in an emotional frame of mind over his own ideas to end the war, he had little time for HAPM because of his efforts to see various influential political figures and war leaders. United States Rubber officials, however, were urging him to make another inspection trip to the plantations in Sumatra where a company biologist had issued an unfavorable report on certain soil conditions.[112] Davis, because of his activities to promote his war plan, was not only opposed to a trip east but also wanted to be dropped from his company's board of directors. He stated his reasons to Colonel Colt:

> But as I have told you repeatedly, I feel that I have a God-given opportunity to be of service at this time to my country and the world. Splendid progress is being made here, and I feel that it is the most effective service that I can render our Company; but I would like to proceed with as free a mind as possible, and ask that you will be so kind as to drop me from the United States Rubber Company and General Rubber Company directorates this year. The wonderful work which Mr. Tompkins is doing in the detail of the plantation department--and I have never seen greater devotion to the Company or higher efficiency than he is showing--and the fact that I am sure we are profiting to the full extent from the

> various criticisms, leads me to the feeling that no one need to go to Sumatra at this time; but as I have written Mr. Leland, I think it would be very desirable if he could go to the East, investigate fully the conditions there, and convince myself that the case in which I find my mind in contemplating the Sumatra situation is justified.[113]

His activities toward the war effort and his work done in America for United States Rubber will be discussed in detail in the next chapter; his attitude toward the United States Rubber Company at the time was that he could best serve all interests concerned by helping to win the war. Further comments bring to light his deep love for his pet project in the Far East as well as the monetary extent to which he was involved. "Please be assured," Davis continued to the president of United States Rubber,

> that apart from the consideration of my financial interest, I would be most miserably unhappy not to finish my work in the East. I have but recently returned from a visit to the properties. With a greater financial interest than any other individual, and with a moral responsibility that overshadows my financial interest, I am not worrying. Why should you?[114]

In a postscript to his letter to Colt, Davis simply but forcefully stated his theme, and the underlining shows the determination which had brought him where he was in life. "Will appreciate greatly if you can help by dropping my name from the USRCo and the General Rubber directorates," he added. "I will not fail you as to the fulfillment of my proper responsibilities in the East."[115]

Colonel Colt and his associates did not share Davis' relaxed attitude about Eastern investments, however, and they continued to press him to direct his able services to the rubber trees once more. By May of 1918, Davis had reluctantly consented to return to Sumatra, but he had an ulterior motive because of his war plans, to which no one of high influence had listened. He had taken it upon himself to plan a trip to France and present his plan to General Pershing. When arranging his passport to the East, therefore, Davis tried unsuccessfully to go via France.[116] Forced to take a westward route by way of Japan instead of through Europe, he went ahead with the plans to return to the plantations, arriving in Singapore in mid-August of 1918. There, he found that Colt had been partially right in his concern, for business really was not well, as Davis confided to Figart on the eve of his trip with Gordon, Gallagher, Bicknell, and Seybold to the advisory Board meeting in Sumatra. "Never have I had so many difficult questions to decide," wrote Davis,

> and I shall do my best to restore order from the partial chaos which has resulted from the neglect of my routine responsibilities because of the work in Washington. Even the system of management itself, which I felt was, perhaps, the greatest achievement of our work out here, was tottering, and Messrs. Gallagher and Bicknell were almost ready to throw it over. But I am more convinced than ever that it is right, and faithfully will present the facts to the consideration of the others, believing that when they have all been taken into consideration we will find ourselves in agreement.[117]

Davis stayed only long enough to get matters running smoothly again. Arriving in New York on November 16, 1918,[118] he did not again return to Sumatra in a supervisory capacity, although he remained a director of United States Rubber for another year. But with the completion of his work as managing director of the plantations, he had created on of the most romantic stories in American business history, and the impressive financial success he had made for himself was minute compared to the profits the United States Rubber Company reaped over the ensuing years. As an article in *Fortune* magazine in 1934 observed, few adventures in integration have been more profitable.

> The U.S. Rubber Co. carries its investment in the rubber plantations at $18,000,000. From them it has already collected profits of $37,000,000. From 1930 until the spring of 1933 the price of rubber was below the cost of production but losses in bad times never approached the profits of previous years.[119]

In other words, as Howard and Ralph Wolf concluded, "It is, then, the best investment the one-time rubber trust ever made and by far its most important single asset."[120]

It is remarkable but true that during the post-World War I slump in rubber prices, the plantations were a lifesaver for the United States Rubber Company. "As I remember it," Edgar Davis recorded,

> the plantations had paid for the upkeep and development of the growing rubber trees, and had amassed a surplus of approximately $19,000,000, so that in 1920 and '21, when there was a drop in the price of rubber from 53 cents a pound down to 13 cents, the losses of the American rubber companies through stocks on hand and forward contracts were enormous, and this surplus was an important factor in helping the Company out of serious financial difficulties. Irenee Dupont told Walter Mahony and me when we visited him in Wilmington that the principal reason for their going into the United States Rubber Company in a large way was due primarily to the plantation situation.[121]

Much other evidence substantiates Davis' memoirs as correct. To prevent overall losses and to pay dividends, United States Rubber took the $6,000,000 surplus for 1926 and the $4,000,000 which the plantations earned in 1926 and 1927 and kept the company in a position to show a profit.[122] Howard and Ralph Wolf further explain that

> by helping itself to the profits of the plantation subsidiary, tapping the plantation surplus and postponing the writing down of inventory from year to year, it succeeded in regularly paying the eight percent dividend, however. And to the casual eye it presented a not uninviting picture. So right at the end of 1927 and beginning of 1928 the du Pont Estate invested and into U.S. common went $16,000,000 of the munitions millions of Pierre, Irenee, Lammot and those other boys old Charles Ranlett Flint hardly could have recognized as being in the same line of

> business. It was a logical investment, considering the du Pont interest in General Motors and chemicals and synthetic rubber experiments, and it looked like a good enough one at the time.[123]

From the foregoing information, it is not difficult to conclude that when an associate of Kuhn, Loeb and Company told Davis that "the plantations saved the United States Rubber Company from receivership,"[124] he was not exaggerating. Today, as the result of Davis' foresight of sixty years ago, the United States Rubber Company plantations are still operating in Sumatra and Malaya.

Davis emerged from the East at forty-five years of age as a somewhat powerful and influential person who had to his credit the creation of a small but lucrative empire of American capital. Furthermore, as a partial reward for his success, he had been made a member of the board of directors of the largest rubber company in the world. As an executive in big business circles, he had made certain contacts which would influence him for the rest of his life. Moreover, Davis had shown himself to be a man of vision and adaptability. He had made a reality of the single Emerson sentence which captured his fancy, "The ancestor of every action is a thought." Viewing the British and Dutch rubber plantations while on a voyage for his health in 1907, he envisioned rows of Hevea trees as a possible product of American capital and he turned his idea into actuality through persistent effort. After selling his dream, Davis showed himself to be a man of remarkable adaptability; from a background in the New England shoe world, Davis, as managing director, developed the most efficiently run rubber plantation in the East. More than anything else, this ability to fit himself successfully into a completely foreign situation illustrated his genius for American capitalistic enterprise.

Although a recurrence of the original nervous disorder marred his Eastern sojourn, he apparently recovered fully through the kind attention of an Eurasian woman in Java and through professional help in Switzerland. On the other hand, Davis was a powerful man physically; a supple strength lay beneath the massive frame which tended toward obesity. In spite of the seemingly awkward size, he was quite skillful at such games as tennis and golf. Although he did not perform the arduous tasks of the immediate supervisors in the field, as head of all operations, he had to toil long hours in the unhealthy tropical climate. That he was able to maintain the demanding pace required by his job is evidence of great physical stamina.

Partly because of his extraordinary health, a legend began to grow about the Yankee businessman in the East. He suffered little, it was said, from the usual jungle maladies which plagued the white invaders, and he gained the reputation of being the only white man to walk the snake-infested jungles without protective footwear. Since he cut all ties with organized religion shortly before departing eastward, legend mistakenly would have it that Davis adopted his mystical attributes by association with occult religions of the East. Like all fables, the Davis legend was founded on little fact and much fiction; but the truth is that Davis did, for whatever his reasons, take unnecessary risks in the jungles with impunity, and whereas he was mystical in thought, he remained a tough, Yankee businessman in action.

Davis initiated sound business principles, relying heavily on science, advice from experienced men, and hard work. Although stressing secure business measures in all the Eastern operations, he had taken great chances in the beginning, for in a way Davis was a gambler. To those of ordinary perception, his desire to do things in a "big way" without an experimental trial run was certainly a venturesome plunge. He considered himself divinely guided and was inclined to look for a "God-given" opportunity. Once he sensed that a business situation was possible, he staked everything he had on it.

Davis realized the chances he took, even though he never admitted it while taking the risk. A few years after the Eastern sojourn, he had some interesting reflections on his philosophy about opportunity and luck.

> I think that nothing worthwhile is gained without sacrifice and as I have journeyed over the world, and because I have lived my life so differently than I expected and have traveled much, I have come to the conclusion that there is not a difference in men's abilities; that what we think of as the differences is more in a willingness to play the game, to go through to equip himself, and then to wait with patience. Opportunity, as I see it, comes from God and God

> alone, and I believe that if we saw big enough, that luck is only another name for God. I know it is so easy after a person has been successful in a material way to say: "He is lucky." I think of Kipling in "Mary Gloucester" where he shows that the responsibility is with us to do our part: "I took my job and I stuck, /I took the chances they wouldn't, /And now they're calling it luck."[125]

Appropriate indeed is the Kipling line which Davis chose to describe his good fortune, for he had carved his success from the jungle himself after the idea "came to him." Bruce Barton, a writer and personal friend, concluded that Davis was lucky, "but without his dogged determination he would never have lasted long enough to realize on his luck."[126]

Davis even took a sort of pride in the one thing he did not accomplish on the plantations. At certain times during each year Davis ran the work schedule seven days a week rather than the usual six. Here he ran into trouble with the elephants, creatures whose exploits fill his family letters back home as Davis marveled at the grace and strength of these noble beasts of burden. When Davis tried to get the elephants to work on Sundays, they refused to budge. Having had the Sabbath off for years made force of habit too strong. The elephants would not perform, no matter how determined the head man.

Determination was a salient feature of his character, but what many failed to realize was that something deeper burned within the man who worked so diligently to succeed in business enterprises. Personal faith in his destiny drove Davis to succeed, and his faith in his abilities was enhanced through his achievement in the Far East. An already strong belief in mysticism, which he vaguely termed "Faith," was solidified by accomplishments which Davis concluded were fulfilled because "the Good God Guided me, as I said before, in doing things way beyond my natural ability."[127]

Davis' own natural abilities had been greatly enhanced through building the successful plantation system. Leadership was foremost in the many capabilities which became evident during his Eastern experience. Men followed him, both those in his employ and those with United States Rubber who furnished the money. Under his guidance was created the "mecca" of the rubber-growing world, and several of his able assistants were impressed enough with his ability to leave the security of a big corporation to follow Davis in his next venture. As a director of the United States Rubber Company, he instigated a change in financial policy which resulted in a huge savings from reduced interest rates. Edgar B. Davis was partially responsible for the pioneering of employee benefits such as pensions, profit sharing plans, and stock purchasing options that made the United States Rubber Company the first major business firm in America to take such steps.[128] The highest compliment awarded any associate of United States Rubber was paid him when he was offered the presidency of that company. Why he refused this high office will be discussed in the following chapter. Davis wanted to leave the United States Rubber Company, but he did not want out of the rubber business. He wanted instead to develop an international plantation industry. Moreover, because of his recent triumph in the rubber industry, he was confident of one thing: no matter what the task, he believed he was able to handle the job either with his own abilities, by God's will, or through the combination of both that had become his "Faith."

Chapter IV
THE INTERNATIONALIST

For I dipt into the future, far as the human eye could see,Saw the Vision of the world, and all the wonder that would be

Alfred, Lord Tennyson

As an international businessman, Edgar B. Davis began to visualize plans of worldwide cooperation for the good of mankind, but his visionary ideas failed mainly because the international schemes he devised were too broad in scope. Furthermore, he was rarely content to pursue a single plan at a time but instead became enchanted with several schemes of large dimension which gradually pulled him from his plantation back to the bustle of New York City.

Davis was a man who used each successful enterprise as a stepping-stone. A large-scale speculation had paid back larger dividends to both Davis and the company he represented, and his future with the United States Rubber Company was secure had he chosen to remain with that corporation. He had become an internationalist, however, who decided to forego the security of a permanent position and to pursue independently other ventures of a global nature.

Davis had listed the smugness of British planters gloating over the large profits made by selling their crude rubber to American markets as one of his reasons for desiring success in the rubber industry. As a novice to the business, he came to rely heavily on advice from the experienced British and Dutch planters who unselfishly shared their knowledge with him. A British agricultural scientist, W. J. Gallagher, and a Dutch planter, H. Ketner, hired by Davis, became his close friends. Involved as he was with various nationalities and in traveling over different areas of the world, Davis gradually began to acquire a cosmopolitan point of view. He began to sense a need for world-wide planning to stablize the rubber industry as he became firmly convinced that many other industries rode upon the back of that particular business. Realizing that the automobile business depended exclusively on the availability of peumatic tires and that the petroleum trade was interdependent on the number of cars in use, Davis grasped the extent to which various industries relied upon that product. Just as he had realized that American capital could profit from rubber growing, so he began to sense that so important a business could not be left to the unsteady hand of chance. Instead, he reasoned, the leading nations of the world should unite in order to maintain a stability in a venture upon which so many other manufacturers depended.

Davis began to act, and as early as June 17, 1915, he had at least tentative approval of an approach regarding some type of cooperation to British and Dutch interests by the directors of the United States Rubber Company.[1] Less than a year later, he was explaining to various American capitalists the essentials of his scheme to stabilize the industry through a far-reaching system of international cooperation. "I will probably have an opportunity within a short time to talk with Mr. Stone, President, and Mr. Vanderlip, the Chairman, with respect to the extension of our International plan," Davis explained to his friend and associate, John Warren Bicknell. He continued:

> On the 29th I took lunch with Mr. Nicholas Brady and the two financial advisors of the Brady Estates, Messrs. Murray and Flook. Mr. J. C. Brady planned to be there but disappointed us. They are all very much interested in the International plan and Mr. Nicholas Brady has invited me to go with him to present the case to Mr. Stone.[2]

Davis also explained his plan to Bernard Baruch upon meeting him on his South Carolina plantation. "Mr. Baruch," according to Davis,

> showed a keen interest and asked me to expatiate on the subject, and before I was through inquired as to the amount of money which would be required to finance the scheme, and stated that he felt that we would have no difficulty in raising all the money we would need. I am really gratified at the progress we are making and believe it will be only a short time before we can go to work here in New York with a definite end in view, for as soon as the Directors of our company have given their consent, it will only

> mean a short time before we can establish the confidence of the Capitalists.[3]

Just how far Davis had progressed with his plan before the United States became involved in World War I is difficult to say, for peaceful cooperation among nations between 1915 and 1916 became lost in the trenches of Europe. He did lay the idea aside during the war, but he did not abandon it. In the meantime, he felt duty-bound to do his part to stop World War I as soon as America's entry into that conflict became unavoidable. L. D. Tompkins, an associate in the rubber business who had once been employed in an airplane factory, had interested Davis in the future possibilities of the infant aircraft industry.[4] Upon the United States' entering into the world conflict, Davis and Figart conceived a strategy to end the fighting through the use of aerial warfare. The plan, in its simplest form, was to cut all lines of supply and communication by a thorough bombing of railway and road bridges and a constant harassment of all transportation. So sure was Davis of the feasibility of the plan that he felt the winning of the war literally rested on his shoulders. This strategy, he also felt, would enable him to succeed Woodrow Wilson as President,[5] thus fulfilling the prophecy lurking ever in the back of his mind. Davis went to Washington in the fall of 1917 for the purpose of stimulating the government to upgrade the airplane industry with more and better planes;[6] he hoped to present his plan to Wilson personally. That he never got an audience with the President probably came as a shock to Edgar B. Davis after his success in big business circles.

Davis' involvement in a plan for a decisive blow to transportation networks to disorganize the enemy distribution of production was geared to mass production of aircraft necessary to modern warfare. Davis, who became one of the dollar-a-year civilians who contributed their business talent toward the war effort, traveled to Canada to investigate the possibility of acquiring large quantities of lightweight spruce wood for plane construction in the United States.[7]

David Figart, assisting Davis in the objective of greater airplane production, assumed that the planes could be mass produced with advanced U.S. technology, but he began to think ahead as to the best use of hundreds of planes in warfare. As Figart was riding a train between Washington, D.C. and Baltimore, he noticed that at that time there were only two connecting lines between these cities. In a flash he discerned that a few well-placed bombs could disrupt major traffic between these two centers, whereas a heavy bombing raid, even directly on the central railway yards, in either city could be subject to immediate repairs by the readily available crews and equipment.[8] The concept of strategic bombing was born here.

Figart discussed this idea with Davis, who straight away embraced the concept, and the two men set to work on a strategic bombing plan. Research at the Army War College in Washington convinced them that communication and transportation lines were the keys to victory. The American Civil War had illustrated that national production could only serve the war effort if delivered. Even the distraught South had some areas of high food production at the close of the war but could not transport these needed supplies to the troops. Figart and Davis became particularly imbued with the consideration for the direction of destruction against rails and bridges rather than the taking of human lives. Their first inclination was to hit railroad bridges exclusively, but they abandoned this approach upon reading that the Germans had installed nets which were effective in catching the small bombs of the time. They next targeted isolated railway points, particularly vulnerable spots where high embankments would require large earth-moving equipment for repairs. The president of U.S. Rubber Company, Charles Segar, formerly a director of Union Pacific Railroad, provided valuable information about where a few bombs could do the most damage to unprotected railway lines.[9]

Equipped with a layout of maps for their strategics, they began the job in the fall of 1917 of convincing someone in authority to incorporate their project into government policy. Davis insisted on speaking directly with Woodrow Wilson, but he was never able to gain an audience with the President, although he got as far as Joseph Tumulty and Colonel Edward M. House on several occasions. He explained the tactics to be employed to key figures in the war program including senators and members of the House of Representatives and the Cabinet. He sought out ex-Presidents Theodore Roosevelt and William H. Taft and other prominent citizens such as Admiral Robert Peary and Louis Brandeis who would listen to him. Despairing of seeing Wilson, Davis finally attempted unsuccessfully to get a passport to present the plan to the British and French leaders.[10]

In May of 1918 Figart went into the army as a first lieutenant. Davis arranged for him to be attached to the Statistical Branch of the General Staff on the basis of the studies of numerical data he had done for the United States Rubber Company. As Davis continued in his quest to speak directly to Wilson, Figart, who was able to tap many new sources on the power and potential of bombing, produced a professional study for the military.[11]

Figart's report, "A Statistical Analysis of Aerial Bombardments," came out in its final form a few days before Armistice Day 1918.[12] This study was lying unread when World War II opened in 1939. History has proved Figart correct, but the Air Force learned strategic bombing in the last years of World War II by the more difficult lesson of bitter experience.

Meanwhile, Davis was able to see a great many influential people because of his various business contacts, but the intellectual climate in Washington was just not right to accept aerial warfare on the fantastic scale Davis envisioned. Possibly because he did not want to have his energies restricted or perhaps because his ideas had not been accepted by anyone, Davis even abstained from joining the limited airplane building program which was in operation when the chance came to him through Stuart Hotchkiss, a United States Rubber Company executive who worked with one of the air sections in Washington during the war.[13] The chairman of the aircraft board in Washington, Howard Coffin, wanted Davis to join the airplane building program in some capacity, for Davis sent him a resume containing facts relevant to his business career in December of 1917. He made no definite commitment, however, and stressed this point:

> I desire to reiterate the statement made to you that there is no position in Washington that I want or would take; but I am greatly anxious to see a clear, broad, definite war policy inaugurated by our country and adopted by Great Britain, France and Italy, to coordinate the resources of the nations to effect a speedy ending of the war.[14]

In characteristic fashion, Davis continued trying to go to the top, and a meeting with President Wilson remained his goal. He did get several notes from Wilson in response to his many entreaties,[15] but a formal meeting was never granted.

Appointments with other national leaders were unfruitful. A visit to Colonel E. M. House on December 21, 1917, was followed by a stormy conference with Theodore Roosevelt on January 8, 1918.[16] Roosevelt, doing little other than criticize Wilson, got into an argument with Davis, who was able to quiet the ex-President only with a quotation from the Bible.

By early 1918 it was becoming increasingly evident to Davis that he would be frustrated in his efforts to get in direct touch with the President. Senators and representatives had granted interviews, but nothing concrete had come from these talks; consequently, Davis decided to appeal directly to the military leaders in America and in France. His most positive result was a wire from a General Brown stating that the Davis war plan had received approval; the information elated him but nothing further came of the incident.[17]

Finally, on February 3, 1918, Edgar B. Davis sent the following wire to President Wilson:

> With the greatest respect for you as our President and the intellectual leader of the Allies and in the belief that you desire to have everything brought to your attention which might prove of benefit to our country and our Allies in the conduct of the present war permit me again to point out the possibilities of intensive air warfare as the most humane economical and speedy means of victoriously ending the war Period Wonderful preparatory work has been done by the Aircraft Board making a splendid nucleus for a much larger program than that at present authorized Period After a careful analysis of conditions I am convinced that by properly mobilizing and coordinating industries not now being used for war purposes such as piano furniture pleasure motor car manufacturers etcetera at least five times as many airplanes as at present authorized could be built and maintained Period When it is realized that the War Department has been called upon to manage a business twelve times as large as the steel corporation the largest single industrial concern in America did in 1914 it would appear that viewed from a business standpoint the War Department should not be saddled with this additional burden but that a Department of Aeronautics should be created superseding the Aircraft Board with its technicality purely advisory powers Period I shall be glad to furnish exhaustive

> data on this subject if desired and am sending along this constructive suggestion in the spirit of most cordial friendliness and co-operation in the hope that it may aid in the realization of your great vision of a Federated World.[18]

This was perhaps Davis' last attempt to reach Wilson, for it brought no results from the President or from other American authorities. The message itself is typical of Davis' insight into large scale problems. He realized the vast possibilities of turning the private business of assembly lines to the war effort. Of even more importance, he saw the need for creating a separate department of aeronautics to concentrate and facilitate organization, a proposal which was too advanced to be accepted at the time.

Unsuccessful in his efforts to reach the President, Davis tried to get in touch with General Pershing and other Allied military leaders. If getting through to Wilson was difficult, getting to Pershing was an impossibility. Furthermore, Davis' supporters at home began to advise him to cease his efforts. Older brother Oscar Davis was most emphatic in his condemnation of his brother's proposed overseas endeavor,[19] and he raised some interesting points in advising his brother to drop his plan.

> This for your consideration. For you, even with a passport, to go over Pres. Wilson's head with a plan to which he has refused to listen leaves you in a state of insubordination to your elected Commander-in-Chief. In the passport you ask for the protection of your flag and in your very next step refuse to acknowledge as chief the man who signs it, and would in principle be a "man without a country," and you acknowledge no allegiance.[20]

Commenting in a confidential letter to Figart on Oscar's remarks, Davis asked, "...why am I not free to approach whom I will with a plan for the benefit of humanity, not as a citizen of America, but of the world?"[21]

The man who placed himself in the dual role of a "citizen of the world" and the future President of the United States would probably have carried on in his quest for a sympathetic listener to his war plan had he not been side tracked to Sumatra by his own very intense efforts. As narrated in the preceding chapter, Davis returned to the far East at the close of the summer of 1918 but was back in New York shortly before Armistice Day. The war was over, ending his attempt to present his plan of modern techniques for battle, plans which were still in advance of the military preparedness for mechanized warfare in 1939.[22]

With the war over as well as his self-imposed duties as an aircraft authority, Davis redirected his energies to his earlier concern of how to make the world of business a better organized operation. He returned to United States Rubber for a short time, resigning in 1919 to open an office in New York as a business consultant.[23]

Davis probably left the United States Rubber Company for a number of reasons, but a lack of financial gain was not one of them. The original contract with the company had given Davis $12,000 a year plus expenses, together with a percentage of the total plantation value at full production. This royalty proved larger than had been anticipated, and Davis had to threaten a law suit to get his due profits. But Colonel Colt supported him, and the plantation manager was paid in full. This decision seems to have been concluded with good will, or at least the tone of the minutes of the executive committee in January of 1917 would so imply. Davis offered "to reopen the matter of the compensation to be received by him" and then retired from the room. The committee had agreed "to express to Mr. Davis the appreciation of the committee as to his statement and that this Committee desire Mr. Davis to receive what is called for under the terms of his contract with the General Rubber Co."[24]

According to most newspaper accounts of the time, his financial settlement with the company amounted to over $3,000,000. George Seybold's notes, however, set the sum at considerably less.

> After the plantation was in full development the Commission valued the Plantations in 1918 at 3 3/4 times par. The United States Rubber Company had put in at that time eighteen million dollars. Mr. Davis' 8 2/3 came out at a million eight hundred six thousand dollars. They paid him in shares of the Plantation Company, which he sold or traded for US Rubber shares. He gave it to everybody that helped him make it, including the maids at the Belmont Hotel, New York, the bell boys, to everybody. He

> didn't reserve anything. He gave away what he thought everybody ought to have and what was left was his--it happened to be a little over $600,000. To the top men in the East he gave $100,000, $100,000, $100,000. He then scaled down through the lower ranks.[25]

By the standards of the times, Davis, as a capitalist, had been overly generous, but he was still a wealthy man considering the half million dollars Seybold credits to his account. Davis probably reserved something approximating a million dollars, for he sank this much in unsuccessful dry holes in a quest for oil a few years later.

He states in his memoirs that he completed his "work with the rubber company on December 18, 1919, and returned as a Director in April, 1920, after having twice refused the offer to be President of the Company."[26] There may be some truth to a suggestion by Seybold that Davis' strange acts of generosity caused a split in the company. Although he had proved himself both on the plantations and in the sharp world of business circles, he had refused the company presidency once before and exhibited some eccentricity in giving away large sums of money. "He gave it all away," explained Seybold, "and by that time he had become so impractical in the minds of U.S. Rubber Company officials that they could not see eye to eye with him, so there was a kind of mutual agreement that he had better get out ... and so he did."[27] Davis and the company parted by mutual agreement, and he remained in the good graces of retiring president Colonel Samuel P. Colt, who asked him to submit, before he left, his ideas for the future course of the company.

Meanwhile, by a strange twist of irony, Davis had paved the way for Charles B. Seger to be the company president. Davis had saved the company a large sum of money by refinancing its loan with Kuhn, Loeb and Company, and by 1919 the funded indebtedness to them was $71,600,000. When Colt stepped aside, Kuhn, Loeb officials, in order to protect their bonds, influenced the selection of Colt's replacement. Charles B. Seger had risen from office boy to the presidency of the Union Pacific Railroad, in which position he had become friendly with officials of Kuhn, Loeb and Company. He was a strange choice to head the largest rubber company in the world, since rail transportation had been his field and he had never worked in manufacture or production. Furthermore, he was somewhat of a tyrant who would permit no one else on the elevator with him as he ascended or descended from his twentieth-floor offices.[28]

Davis did not intend to get out of the rubber business altogether but instead planned to promote his international rubber plantation scheme. He wrote Figart in 1925 discussing his dream for a world-wide rubber company, indicating that he had some regrets about leaving United States Rubber. Davis explained that the future of his plan for the rubber industry was based upon his "control of the United States Rubber Company which, in the evidence of God, I believe is a part of my Mission to do."[29] In 1919, however, it seemed best to Davis to leave the corporation and strike out on his own with his various business schemes.

Davis' business moves remained tied to his political ambitions. He did not receive recognition for his war plan, nor did he succeed Woodrow Wilson as President. Since he had hoped to gain national recognition from his war efforts, he was working indirectly to gain the Presidency, but he chose always to work in this roundabout way. Some time between 1904 and his permanent return from Sumatra, Davis made a strange decision about his "Mission": he would not "lift a finger" to gain the White House and would thereby "demonstrate one of the greatest miracles since the time of Christ."[30]

The passive quality of Davis' political philosophy is something about which David Figart did much thinking:

> He made the statement many, many times that he would never "lift a finger" to bring about his Mission. Now, many men-- and women--have felt they had a mission, or Mission, in life; and if my limited reading of history and uncertain memory do not mislead me, many such people have accomplished their mission by great personal sacrifices devoted to that end. And so if God tells me, in a Voice, that He has a certain job for me to do, I suspect it would be my duty to devote all my energies to preparing for that job and setting in motion the forces which would bring it to fruition. Mr. Davis was equipped mentally and spiritually for the Mission for which he would not "lift a finger." Was that perhaps one reason, at least, why he never achieved his Mission? In the 1920's he was well known in the top financial and business

> circles. Men like Bernard Baruch, Litchfield (president of Goodyear), Otto Kahn of Kuhn, Loeb, Harvey Firestone, Cy Eaton, and many others, used to come to our offices at 366 Madison Ave. They had great respect and admiration for Mr. Davis.[31]

Davis, however, refused to tip his hand; and Figart's explanation may be as accurate as any is likely to be. The rubber historians Howard and Ralph Wolf came to much the same conclusion in 1936 when they wrote:

> ...for all news concerning Davis is second hand. He refuses to be interviewed and dislikes being photographed, which may account for the fact that one or the other of the great American political parties has overlooked the best bet in its history by failing to nominate him for the Presidency.[32]

In the meantime Davis was busy enough, even if he were not trying to gain the presidential nomination directly. As a business consultant, he had a few irons in the fire. Only one story of his business experiences of the times does he include in his memoirs, but it is an intriguing anecdote:

> Subsequently, I opened an office in New York and, as Henry Ford was having difficulties with his minority interests, I went to Detroit supported by Otto Kahn, Esq., of Kuhn, Loeb & Company, with the idea of trying to purchase the Henry Ford majority interests in that Company. Fortunately for the automobile industry and the country, I failed in this attempt.[33]

During the same time he crystallized the business philosophy that had been developing in his mind for some time, theories including some novel concepts and reform ideas. Davis set forth his plan for the corporation of the future in a letter requested by Colonel Colt and the board of directors of United States Rubber in the spring of 1919. This proposal is not so important for the methods suggested for making money for the company as it is for its concern for the public and its interest in the common man.

> The world is undergoing a radical political change, and inevitably the basic change in the principles of Government will be accompanied by a corresponding industrial change. I would see the United States Rubber Company of the future the first among the great corporations to interpret the Spirit of the times as its ideal of service to the country, the public and its shareholders. I believe that the great work done by Theodore Roosevelt will last and that monopoly is dead in America, but the big corporation which cooperates with the Government and serves the public has come to stay, because the large industrial unit rests on a sound economic basis. And the general public never begrudges wealth to those who serve it well, and whose services it understands. The large corporation can render services to the country, the performing of which is impossible for the small business.[34]

Abreast of the "Spirit of the times" himself, he surpassed most contemporaries in his vision of the future corporation.

Pointing out the inequality of America's output of crude rubber when contrasted with American consumption, he made suggestions for international cooperation to stabilize the price of rubber, a theme he would espouse off and on for the rest of his life. He made further suggestions to Colonel Colt, including a "conservative" expansion in foreign manufacture, the application of modern advertising techniques, a streamlining of the chain of command for efficiency, and the investment of large sums of money for research. Finally, Davis expounded his share-the-wealth plan, remarkable for the second decade of the twentieth century, which "should incorporate a profit-sharing or bonus plan, so far-reaching that the woman who washes up the office floor, or the man who sweeps out the factory, would be interested in the success of the Company and their undivided loyalty to it be encouraged."[35]

Davis' advice to the company he had left contained no theoretical schemes: the rubber plantations which he had built had blossomed under the exact conditions which he suggested be applied to the entire corporation; moreover, Davis had set the example of profit sharing by distributing his own wealth to those who were employees of United States Rubber but were directly under his supervision.

Suggestions to a single corporation were one thing, but Davis had other ideas of larger scope. In 1920 he espoused a business revolution for the whole nation in an eight-page pamphlet. *The Dawn of a New Day: Containing Suggestions for the Introduction of a New Industrial Order.* The theme of his three-point program was a noble one: he proposed to "construct a new economic system in which Capital, Labor and Management mutually are recognized and have their just and full share of the proceeds of industry."[36] The first point stressed that workers be given an opportunity to buy stock. The argument was the same as that outlined to United States Rubber executives: no matter how insignificant a common laborer's position, if he owned a part of the business, he would be inclined to work so that the business might prosper.

As a second point, Davis suggested the formation of a $100,000,000 corporation, the American Cooperative Association, "to promote the interests of justice to Labor,"[37] by coordinating and utilizing the potency of wage earners as investors. Davis considered this proposal a safeguard of industrial life, and he believed his outline to be a bridge between Capital and Labor:

> Should not every up-to-date corporation have its vice-president in charge of industrial relations? And should not the American Cooperative Association have representation on the directorate of any corporation in whose affairs it is interested? With mutual confidence established, who better is equipped for this work than the men who for years have had the fullest confidence of the workers?[38]

The money for such an undertaking would be raised through a drive similar to the Liberty Loan drives of World War I in which bonds were sold through an intensive campaign.

For his third point, Davis, to coordinate all suggested efforts, recommended that the President and Congress create an Industrial Relations Commission to investigate and advise on a division of surplus profits between Labor and Capital. This commission would have no powers other than to advise, and the American Cooperative

Association would invest only in businesses recommended by the Industrial Relations Commission.[39]

Davis realized the inherent weakness in his program: the unselfishness of influential men was a quality not found in abundance within the rough-and-tumble business community of the 1920's. Oscar Davis, a humanitarian in private life but a realist in the competitive business world in which he was successful, called it the poorest thing his brother had ever written.[40] The new industrial order which Edgar Davis had suggested was not a final solution to business problems, he admitted, but a workable plan for improving the current situation. In Davis' own words, the greatest weakness in his plan--or anyone's plan--lay not in the design but in the men who had to operate the machinery: "...the ultimate solution only can come when the great mass of men see that there is something better in life than materialism, and when a Spirit of Love dominates men generally in their relations one with another."[41]

The world of business was not ready for a new day, for there was too much money to be made before the twilight of the 1920's. With the dawn of the thirties and the depression, the Davis plan might have found support, but the pieces had to be picked up before anything could be done, and Davis' plans for an economic new deal were forgotten.

In any concern for business development, Davis' heart lay with the rubber industry. Although the war had interrupted his attempts within the United States Rubber Company to unify the rubber business on a world-wide scale, Davis, as an independent business advisor, printed privately *A Proposal For the Organization of an International Rubber Company* which outlined his plan to stabilize the industry. When most people had been content just to count their profits during the rubber boom, Davis was looking ahead to the inevitable problems of supply and demand which usually grow out of any boom conditions. Free to operate widely after his break with United States Rubber, Davis found a post-war rubber business in dire need of some plan to raise the low price of crude rubber. The 1919 price of 50 cents dropped to 11.5 cents in July of 1921, a vast change from the top 1910 boom price of $3.00 a pound. The 690,000 tons of crude rubber produced in 1922 was countered by a 250,000 ton demand. Trees maturing from the heaviest planting years were only ripe for the post-war economic slump, and the new cord tires of the 1920's greatly outlasted the old fabric tires.[42] The clamor grew, especially by British and Dutch planters, for some sort of restriction.

British planters, producing seventy-five percent of the world's crude rubber production, attempted a partially successful voluntary restriction plan from November 1, 1920, to January 1, 1922. This experiment was dropped for the remainder of 1922, for only fifty-five percent of the planters felt that they had benefited enough to continue.[43] It became clear, with the immense drop in prices, that a mandatory governmental policy would be required. Edgar B. Davis had warned rubber manufacturers in America, who used seventy percent of the British supply, that they might be at the mercy of British planters if measures were ever taken to regulate the price, but his advice was not followed by those outside his own company. Although British restriction was only partially responsible, the big rise in crude rubber prices in 1926 left the United States Rubber Company in an excellent situation with their own large stock of crude supply.[44]

In October, 1921, the British Rubber Growers' Association had requested Parliament to look into the downward trend in crude rubber prices. A committee, mainly represented by members of the Rubber Growers' Association and headed by Sir James Stevenson, produced the Stevenson Plan, which became law on November 1, 1922.[45] This plan called for a proratable acreage for each planter based on top production years and a graduated tax for going over limited production.[46] But the Stevenson scheme was doomed at the start because of its own rigid inelasticity. Also, the crude rubber market continued to fluctuate violently through changes in supply and demand: a new balloon tire required thirty percent more rubber than the cord tire, new developments for reclaiming rubber were found in America, and the Dutch improved scientific techniques and encouraged natives of the Dutch East Indies to produce rubber from their own property. By 1928, British planters sensed that they would be surpassed by the unrestricted Dutch and native planters; consequently, in November of the same year, all British rubber restrictions were removed.[47]

Although the Stevenson Plan failed, drastic need for restriction remained. Perhaps another plan would have worked. Edgar B. Davis had presented his own plan prior to that of Stevenson, and although it had glaring weaknesses it was elastic and contained ideas of merit.

Walter B. Mahony, Davis' friend from his first venture in rubber, and Davis' assistant, David M. Figart, helped to present the project,[48] which was printed in pamphlet form some time in early 1922. *A Proposal For the Organization of an International Plantation Rubber Company* was typical of Davis' vision. Briefly, he called for amalgamation of the British, Dutch, Belgian, and American rubber companies, along with American financial interests, to stabilize the industry. This grandiose scheme was outlined with simplicity. The giant corporation, Rubber Plantations, Ltd., to be incorporated with at least fifty million pounds sterling, would receive interests in various estates in rubber growing areas. These properties would be managed from funds provided through a syndicate open to investment from citizens of any nation and any reshuffling of employees was to be done with the interest of each person's economic security in mind. One point required advisory councils, which were the regular meetings of the heads of all departments, meetings that Davis considered important to his own success in the business. The last two points of the program outlined meetings between plantation rubber officials and American rubber manufacturing interests to determine future guidelines for crude rubber production.[49] The obvious advantages in such cooperation was attractive:

> ...international market for securities; formulation of policies affecting output and surplus stocks; scattering of risks from diseases and pests, winds, floods, deterioration of trees, etc.; reduction in costs through economies of large-scale management; centralized administration of labor; benefits to manufacturers and planters through large-scale production of a uniform product under new processes as developed; organized campaign for extension of present uses of rubber, and stimulation of new uses; maintenance of efficient research and statistical departments to secure accurate knowledge of progress in all phases of the industry; and stabilizing influence in the industry.[50]

Accompanied by Walter B. Mahony and David M. Figart, Davis lent weight to his plan by carrying it personally to the Dutch planting interests at the Hague and to the British Rubber Growers' Association in London during the spring and summer of 1922. Figart spoke to the Dutch at the Hague, while Davis spoke at three meetings with the British.[51] Davis stressed that the idea was not brought about by the current crises in the rubber business but had grown out of years of concern and love for the business; and he spoke the truth when he declared that

> the proposal for the organization of an International Plantation Rubber Company represents the crystallization of ideas held by my colleague, Mr. Mahoney, and myself for a period of over fifteen years, aided in a most important manner by an intensive study of the industry by Mr. Figart. What we are proposing is a single and economically sound plan which would be of great benefit to the industry, and a profitable venture to all concerned.[52]

Attempting to dispel the usual fears that Americans had greedy designs on plantation interests, Davis spoke of the new American corporation brought about by the breaking of a few giant trusts during the Roosevelt administration. "The Corporation with a soul has arrived," he said,[53] run by an intelligent self interest which considered doing the "right thing" an essential part of good business. Crediting the development of the plantations solely to the British, Davis maintained that the American motor car industry had kept the sinking plantation industry alive.[54] Thus he came to his point for the need of an *organized* corporation and he presented his proposal for the organization of an international company.

One of the main weaknesses in Davis' presentation was that he had only token support from American financial interests. He had merely spoken to numerous American capitalists, including Bernard Baruch, the financier, and Frank Seiberling, the tire manufacturer, who had expressed an interest in the scheme. Davis had no definite commitment from these businessmen. Howard and Ralph Wolf may be correct in the assertion that most American manufacturers were at that time too wrapped up in their own post-war economic problems to generate any interest in investing in a corporation designed to solve the problem of a surplus in overseas crude rubber.[55]

It appears from the available evidence that Davis was quite sincere, believing genuine collaboration and mutual good will feasible on a world scale. There were already international agreements of this character in existence, and during the 1920s cartels were often viewed in the United States as a European weapon to combat American corporate might. Skepticism, when so many diverse elements were involved, was inevitable, and history has shown that international trade agreements to deal with world-wide overproduction were generally unsuccessful. But Davis believed his scheme had a higher sanction and he never wavered in his devotion:

> I represent no great corporation now, nor am I the emissary of any group of financiers. But I am able to assure you that if the leaders of the industry, or a substantial portion of them, are able to get together here, they will receive ample and potent support from our side. We have gone as far as we can go with financiers and manufacturers until we know that the plantation interests desire to support this Cooperative International plan.[56]

As might be expected, Davis' speeches met with much criticism, which was largely negative. The main argument against the proposal was based on the belief that any action by the Rubber Growers' Association, such as appointing a committee, might complicate the then present action of the government's study of a restriction plan.[57] After a touchy discussion, an amended motion passed "That this meeting is unable to proceed further with the consideration of the scheme until the recommendation of the Colonial Office and the decision of the Government thereon are known."[58]

Immediately before the final question, Davis, sensing a negative vote, passionately spoke on his international philosophy which contrasted so sharply with the narrow patriotism of many men after World War I. Speaking for members of his group, Davis stressed that they "were seeking the permanent success of the industry, and ... of this plan."[59] The true love and fascination he felt for the industry are revealed in his next remarks:

> For my part I have come over here imbued with the idea that international cooperation was of far greater benefit than any individual interest. It was a great cause to serve, and in doing so I was actuated by the sense of responsibility which I had for a number of men I see here and many men who are not present and some men who are no more. I am here to pay my bill to this industry and I am going to cancel that

> obligation here and now; but it is quite within your power to say here, "We want none of this thing."[60]

In saying that he had canceled his "obligation" to the industry Davis had spoken in haste, for he would believe in his plan for the rest of his life. He closed his remarks by denying the charge that American manufacturers had profited from the slump in rubber prices, pointing out that manufacturers had lost heavily because of huge stocks of rubber and cotton which they had purchased and maintained at the high price before the decline. He then charged that no one should be losing because all could benefit through cooperation, and he warned against excessive nationalism:

> ... if you men think you are doing the best for industry by merely consulting your own immediate interest in a blind and near-sighted patriotism you are entirely wrong. Out of this will come men with the long viewpoint, and you will see that our countries need each other, and in none more than in this industry. We have brought to you the fairest proposition it was in our minds to bring forward. Whether you accept it or not is your responsibility. Thank you, gentlemen.[61]

The men were impressed enough by the closing remarks to pass by acclamation a vote of thanks to Davis and his efforts, but the proposal failed. In November the Stevenson plan, with all its drawbacks and without Dutch cooperation, was passed.[62]

It was later alleged by some members of the Rubber Growers' Association that the prices suggested by Davis to plantation owners were too low.[63] On the other hand, David Figart thinks that the matter of prices was a minor factor in the failure of the scheme, for throughout the many informal talks he had with plantation directors, the subject was rarely mentioned.[64] A major reason for the failure of the scheme, he contends, was the sheer epic proportions of the project; the novelty of amalgamating so many different interests with the breaking up of traditional organizations was just too much for the established directors to accept.[65]

Moreover, the Stevenson plan was in everyone's mind and many were engrossed with the details of this conception when Davis arrived on the scene.[66] Figart gained the support of the ex-editor of the Ceylon *Times*, and he obtained courteous hearings from all companies, but he never found any group really prepared to go along with the plan.[67] One English politician later used Davis' proposal as the basis for an argument for government intervention to keep Americans from taking control of the troubled British plantation industry.[68] The following 1925 speech to Parliament by J. H. Thomas referred to the Davis plan:

> In 1921 and 1922 there was an effort to bankrupt our rubber producing concerns, so that people in America could have bought up the whole lot, wiping out the investment of British small shareholders, and exploiting the situation.[69]

But Davis' intentions were not base; he still clung to his dream to coordinate and stabilize the rubber business even if he had to finance it himself. "I am expecting a tremendous success," he wrote Figart in 1923, "which will make possible the carrying out of some of my other ideas, including our International cooperation scheme in cultivated rubber."[70] He continued to feel that his group could carry out the proposal. "Do not doubt," he wrote later in the same year. "I have Faith to believe that it is our destiny that we--you, Walter and I--should do a great constructive work together along the lines of international cooperation."[71]

At the time he financed his trip abroad to present his proposal, Davis was operating on the tail end of the fortune made in Sumatra, the bulk of his money having been sunk in the dry holes of an oil scheme which he had begun to pursue with an increased passion between 1919 and 1922. He intended for this oil interlude to be temporary, for all profits he planned to devote to promoting his international scheme. Once sidetracked into one successful oil venture, though, he continued exploratory drilling, always hoping for the bigger strike which would enable him to return to the rubber industry with enough capital to operate on the broad scale of his dreams. No matter how his fortunes rose and fell in the future, he never lost his dream of some day realizing his vision of an international plantation rubber industry.

If one balances the successes against the failures of Davis' life, there is an approximate balance between the two. Like so many men of genius, Davis had an abundance of talent, the most obvious of which was the ability to adapt to any business venture where there was profit to be made. Of no small credit to his character is that he was generous with his own financial gain. A man of foresight, he was a progressive idealist, but he was also an extraordinary eccentric who would be remembered largely for his idiosyncrasies.

He does have to his credit the achievement of the American system of rubber plantations in the East. And he is still remembered by the few remaining who knew him in his prime. Godfrey E. Coombs, a retired English biologist who once managed the plantations in Sumatra, has paid tribute to the lasting work of Edgar B. Davis, remembering him as

> one who to me was a great gentleman and to the Natural Rubber Industry a positive genius. Who, but a person of such outstanding personality and vision could conceive the large scale planting of rubber involving the assemblage of various races and nationalities and technical talents. It really is an epic story.[72]

Chapter V
THE DISCOVERY WELL

I took the chances they wouldn't an' now they're calling it luck.

Rudyard Kipling

Fifty miles east of San Antonio and forty miles south of Austin lies Luling, Texas, across a geological fault known today as a natural oil trap in both the Edwards lime and the Austin chalk formations. Topographically, the area is noticeably uneven. Westward, five miles from Luling toward San Marcos, the poor mesquite pasture holding a concentration of oil wells drops suddenly into rolling blackland farms. Similarly, north to Austin, broken terrain slopes into level cotton fields near Lockhart. One can stand on the main street of Luling and survey the rugged sand hills making a semi-circle on the east and south side of town. Looking southward, his gaze crosses the San Marcos River, marking both the boundary between Caldwell and Guadalupe Counties and the city limits of Luling.

Early seekers after oil attempted to read these surface signs on the earth's crust, trying to imagine what happened far beneath to make the surface area so rough and broken. At Luling there was a shift or break which sealed off the natural movement of oil through the earth, confining it for collection for thousands of years. Oil migrates, usually with water and gas, by seeping through the layers of earth. The internal barriers near Luling caused reservoirs in layers of gas, oil, and water in that order with the water underneath and the lighter gas on top. Great pressure builds as these minerals steadily accumulate.[1]

Oil and Texas have been inseparably linked in history. Survivors of the abortive Hernando de Soto expedition repaired their leaky barks with the ooze from the earth near present Beaumont in July, 1543. Local Indians skimmed ointment from these oil seeps for generations, and later Spanish and Anglo settlers used petroleum medicinally as the Indians did, and as a lubricant[2]. Though petroleum was well known, the story of oil in Texas remained limited until the nineteenth century. Commercial production began in 1866, when Lyne T. Barret produced petroleum from a shallow, steam-drilled well near Nacogdoches. Barret never profited from his discovery, for Pennsylvania oil could be imported to the area for less than his own production costs.[3] In 1871 natural gas escaped from a well drilled in Young County, although no commercialization came from this discovery either. By 1874, some petroleum signs materialized in eighteen separate counties across the state, but these sources existed mainly as topics of conversation. Various oil "showings" encouraged Standard Oil to drill two exploratory wells in Bell County in 1881, but the company abandoned both as unproductive.[4] The first major field resulted from the efforts of Edgar Farrar and B. F. Hitchcock near the Barret find in Nacogdoches, where their Petroleum Prospecting Company brought in thirty producers between 1886 and 1890.[5]

The first actual "boom" dates from 1894, when the Corsicana Oil and Development Company began a drilling campaign in and around Corsicana that led to three hundred producers by the close of the century. The city even boasted a refinery, but much of the oil served mundane purposes such as laying the dust in the streets. This field produced 800,000 barrels of crude in the first four years of peak production.[6] A more sensational discovery at Beaumont on January 10, 1901, flowed this same amount of oil in only ten days!

Spindletop made the connection between oil and Texas and fused into one phrase, "big oil money," as both millionaires and new petroleum companies sprang up at Beaumont. Stories of instant wealth sent wildcatters scurrying to all parts of the coastal area. Successful strikes proved new fields at Saratoga, Sour Lake, and Humble by 1904. Even though dwarfed by Spindletop, the Humble Field produced 2,900,000 barrels a month in 1905.[7] Soon natural gas became another great resource of tremendous reserves to be tapped. Chartered and organized in 1909, Lone Star Gas Company took advantage of the vaporous substance that so often accompanied the production of oil, profiting from sales to both domestic and industrial users.[8]

Texas oil output continued to reach high levels as individuals and corporations brought in million-barrel-a-year fields in various locations around the state, bringing booms, speculation, and prosperity. Petrolia, in Clay county, was a find of extra dimension, for not only was the field rich in natural gas, but the shallow wells provided inexpensive production. At this same time, Electra, only thirty miles west of Petrolia, a field of phenomenal production, in folklore is the basis for rancher Tom Waggoner's legendary complaint that his oil discovery ruined the water well he was drilling.[9] One of the wildest booms in the state occurred at Burkburnett between 1913 and 1918, when one gusher after another turned the site into a forest of derricks and produced forty million barrels of oil in this five year span.[10] Rivaling Burkburnett for roaring boom conditions was Ranger, rampant with oil fever and discovery throughout 1917, when a surge of growth boosted the town's population from 1,000 to 30,000 in twelve months. Ranger was a tough oil town, but profits skyrocketed as the high-grade crude from this field found a ready market during World War I.[11] The next year, 1919, Edgar B. Davis entered Texas in search of the black gold that would make his name legend among wildcatters in the Southwest. His search for oil was prolonged and costly.

It is easy today to point out the revealing surface features of the fault line that traps the oil in the Luling Field, for the many oil wells along this structure map the course. Before the discovery, however, when the rough land west of Luling was cotton fields, mesquite clumps, or post oak groves, it was quite a different matter to believe there was oil somewhere below the surface. The decision, based as it was upon the rudimentary knowledge of the time, to conduct exploratory drilling marked a courageous and pioneering break-through in oil exploration. Early searchers for surface indications of oil at Luling were thwarted because the most common oil-bearing formation was the more easily recognizable salt dome; and, since there usually was oil somewhere under such domes, experienced men looked for any hill or mound to produce.[12] The Luling Field contained no such domes or mounds. Consequently, the discovery there is largely a story of trial and error drilling based on 1920 scientific knowledge, early wildcatting techniques, hunches, hard-headed determination, and just plain luck. Luling and Edgar B. Davis were made for each other.

Davis was not the first to try for oil in the area. John A. Otto of New Braunfels arrived in Luling in 1879, looking for a dam site to erect a water mill. He had drilled a costly dry hole in an attempt to find oil in Comal County the year before, and he was going back into a more stable business enterprise. As he rode across Salt Flat, a waste area just north of Luling where salt water seepage from some underground source stunts vegetation, he had a flash of intuition that he had found an oil field.[13] He decided to establish himself in the water-power business before wildcatting again, and he founded the village of Ottine seven miles down the San Marcos River from Luling in Gonzales County. Here he prospered with his water mill and from a toll bridge he built across the river.[14]

As Otto developed his business and his town, he continued to observe the surroundings for possible signs of oil. He had found places at Ottine along the river and back on the Salt Flat at Luling where a kitchen match could briefly ignite gas escaping from cracks in the earth and he dreamed of wildcatting again.[15]

While Otto was experimenting with peculiar gas phenomena near Luling, John E. Shelton of Lockhart took out the first oil and gas option in Caldwell County on May 18, 1901, leasing 900 acres in the northeastern part of the county. Shelton, who never followed this up with any drilling activity, was possibly motivated by the widely circulating news of the discovery of the Spindletop Field at Beaumont in January of that year.[16]

The next year John A. Otto began wildcatting. He leased over 2000 acres at Luling and Ottine and began to put down wells. Although he made the first drilling location in what later became the Salt Flat Field, limited funds and faulty equipment caused Otto to abandon his project at 1000 feet. He did not doubt his intuition about oil and drilled other holes near Ottine. Although he found no oil, he brought in a gusher of hot artesian water which eventually became the location of Warm Springs Hospital, later prominent for success in treating polio victims.[17] Today, the hospital is a modern rehabilitation and physical therapy center.

Meanwhile, other local residents began to believe in the possibility of oil under the Salt Flat north of Luling. Thomas Wilson, originally from Rosedale, England, arrived as an emigrant agent for the Southern Pacific Railroad. He brought settlers to Luling in 1880, staying on himself to become a notable businessman and town booster. Wilson drew a curious map of the area in 1903, predicting with remarkable accuracy the site of the future discovery well in the Salt Flat Field a quarter of a century later. The Wilson sketch shows a system of storage tanks and a gravity flow pipe line to the railroad through Luling. Though Wilson formed a small oil company on May 21, 1903, he never did any drilling.[18]

News of the Luling oil activity attracted other speculators who engaged in more intensive exploration. The most energetic, Morris O. Rayor, a 1911 engineering graduate of the University of Colorado, in 1914 enlisted a number of Austin residents in the Mozell Oil Company.

This group drilled on several locations near Luling and on one attempt samples taken from the hole showed enough traces of oil to sustain interest in further drilling. Rayor sought to interest others and induced two Fort Worth lawyers, Carl Wade and Norman Dodge, to look into possibilities in Luling. These men entered into a partnership with him separate from the Mozell Oil Company and agreed that Rayor would lease promising acreage while they drummed up more capital.[19]

Rayor's competition included R. L. Yound of Lampasas and George H. Cook of Austin, who in 1918 put down the deepest test in the Salt Flat area before abandoning the well at 1200 feet.[20] At this time Dodge and Wade became involved with another speculator, William F. Peale of Des Moines, Iowa, a real estate broker, who, on yearly business trips to Forth Worth had become interested in the oil business. These three men formed a new organization in March, 1919, named the Texas Southern Oil and Lease Syndicate. Peale also bought out Rayor's interests, since Rayor had depleted his cash resources and needed to raise money.[21] Peale's strategy in Luling was to lease large blocks of acreage. By controlling numerous leases Peale hoped to benefit by reselling properties after an oil showing by his company boosted prices. In this way, one could profit even from dry holes.[22]

Meanwhile, Morris Rayor sought investors for further wildcatting at Luling. He found more capital in Detroit, Michigan for the Detroit Texas Development Company, eventually discovering more oil signs around Luling, but he never hit real paydirt.[23] Rayor tried all of the angles. Like many another early twentieth century wildcatter, he did not rely entirely on the infant science of geology but broadened the means of his search for elusive oil by employing spiritual techniques, methods not necessarily as scientific as geology, but as old as the oil industry itself. As a student of Theosophy, Rayor placed some credence in the belief that the dead could aid the living in certain missions in life. He brought a medium from Detroit to Luling, where friends gathered to hold seances,[24] ostensibly to locate oil. In this small town, new faces attracted attention, and Luling-ites took notice of Rayor's visits to well locations with strangers. Consequently, the legend persists to this day that Rayor consulted the eerie residents of the other world in order to find the wealth of this one. He is remembered as a wildcatter, petroleum engineer, geologist, and spiritualist, and the description is fairly accurate as far as his career in Luling is concerned. He never made the big strike, but he was always around, pointing the way to the gushers yet to come.

While Rayor went his independent way, Peale, Dodge, and Wade broadened fund-raising efforts for the Texas Southern Oil and Lease Syndicate. At the time, businessmen looking for big money went to Wall Street, so Carl Wade, in the spring of 1919, treked to New York for Eastern investors. He got in touch with a former fraternity brother at Harvard, John Warren Bicknell, an executive with the United States Rubber Company. Bicknell introduced Wade to Edgar B. Davis.[25]

Bicknell, of course, knew first-hand of Davis' phenomenal success in the world of business, but he was also aware of his brother Oscar Davis, one of the top men in the Massachusetts shoe enterprises. Oscar reflected the same strict New England Calvinist tradition of his younger brother and had followed the same formula to the top. Even though their working class family lacked wealth and prominence, if they conducted themselves properly, worked hard, saved their money, and risked their funds only after careful consideration of the investment, they would succeed not only in business but also in life. Applying these lessons well, both became millionaires in shoe manufacturing: Oscar with the George Keith Walkover Shoe Company and Edgar with the Charles Eaton Shoe Company. Both fit the mold of the Horatio Alger figure and the description of the legendary folk-heroes of American business, self-made men who had achieved success on personal merit alone.

A gamble in oil did not appeal to Davis' business instincts, so he arranged for Wade to meet Wall Street bankers, who turned out to be equally disinterested in speculating in black gold. Davis refused a second offer, but his two assistants--former employees of the Far Eastern rubber venture-- Kelts C. Baker and Arthur Peck, looked into the situation in Luling on their own initiative, later reporting to Davis that the area looked favorable and recommending investment. Still unmoved, Davis put the matter to his brother Oscar, the successful shoe manufacturer who was more inclined to speculate than Edgar. Oscar agreed to invest $75,000 on the condition that Edgar manage the Davis portion for a third of the profits.[26]

Edgar Davis sent K. C. Baker to Luling to direct management of the Davis investment. A forester by trade, he sought advice from his brother who worked for City Service Oil Company in East Texas. Baker's brother recommended employing a former City Service geologist, Vern Woolsey, to inspect the property for possible drilling sites. Acting on this counsel, Baker found Woolsey, a 1916 graduate of Oklahoma University, stationed at Fort Sam Houston, San Antonio,

Texas, where he had been since going into the army in 1918. In late spring, 1919, both Baker and Woolsey failed to get the army to release Woolsey for a few days work at Luling, but upon receiving his discharge June 1, 1919, Woolsey came directly to Luling as consulting geologist to the oil company. Texas Southern Oil and Lease Syndicate had been having its geological work done by a mining engineer with whose findings Woolsey thoroughly disagreed, and his initial examination rejected all existing recommendations on drilling locations. In July, 1919, Woolsey made oil field history when he discovered the surface fault that crossed the San Marcos River and roughly walked out the structure of the future Luling Field near the site of the discovery well, about five miles northwest of Luling. Woolsey's advice was to the point: "The fault was there, and when I find a structure, I recommend drilling."[27] The subsequent discovery well marked the first time oil was found based on a fault line clearly visible on the earth's surface.

Baker wired Davis the information. Davis, always the man of action, recommended that the company put down a test well on the basis of Woolsey's advice. Oscar received the news of the Woolsey discoveries calmly, resolved either to the success or failure of his gamble, but in September, 1919, Edgar made his first trip to Texas.[28]

Davis stepped from the Southern Pacific passenger car into the center of a town of 2000 in the grip of the post-war recession that not even harvest time of the staple crop, cotton, could brighten. Little else promised to add to the economy except pecans and scattered cattle sales until the next spring. Luling needed an economic boost, one Davis intended to provide as he researched the possibilities of wildcatting for oil.

While Davis established himself there, the townsfolk "sized this newcomer up." A 350-pound Yankee in a white suit with a trunk strap for a belt was bound to stir attention, but first impressions were positive. His cosmopolitan manners struck many as the most polite they had ever experienced. Here was a Northerner who possessed none of the brash forwardness often offensive to the Southern culture. He bore all the marks of a monied person in his initial dealings and was accorded in turn the deference the world gives to the wealthy. In no time he was a social lion, easily a stand out in any crowd at recitals, parties, bridge games, and other limited fare. But his main business was business, and this he tended to thoroughly.

Davis looked over the properties, discussed the first drilling site, and returned East. The Mozelle No. 1, located seven miles east of Luling was drilled in the late fall of 1919 and did nothing but exhaust Oscar's $75,000 by the end of the year. This left Oscar debating whether or not he should advance $25,000 more to start the new year. He took his loss with amazing good humor, decided not to invest further, and gave Edgar complete interest in what had been spent if he cared to go on.[29] Edgar's intentions were that Oscar would get his money back if the oil came, even though Oscar offered to write off his investment as a loss.[30]

To close out 1919 and begin the new decade, the Texas Southern Oil and Lease Syndicate began the Thompson No. 1, six miles northwest of Luling. By April, 1920, W. F. Peale, reporting on the progress to a depth of 1928 feet could not have been more discouraging. The driller had made mistakes in the log as to depth; bolts had worked loose from the rotary table, and had fallen into the hole, necessitating time-consuming fishing operations; special pipe had had to be located in Beaumont in order to reduce the size of the hole for a better chance to find oil; the boiler had been ruined by a new helper who did not check the water level before firing it. Hoping to get to the test depth of 2500 feet by mid-May, Peale was selling surplus materials from the Mozell well in order to continue drilling on the Thompson site, where expenses were running over $5,000 a month. Peale was optimistic, though, mainly because established oil companies were beginning to send noted geologists into the area. Exploration had increased, with eight competitive wells being drilled at that time and a ninth rigging up. Peale predicted a discovery well by someone within six months.[31]

In Peale's own operation, there were just enough signs to justify continuing work until the end of the year. He uncovered oil showings at 150, 700, 950, 1700, and 2020 feet but abandoned the well December 12, 1920, at 2040 feet with only a total production of 80 barrels of oil. K. C. Baker shuttled back to New York with a first-hand account of the well for Davis. The two men mapped out future exploration.[32] Dodge and Wade left business decisions to the Davises, who had now financed the syndicate for over a year in the form of loans against the entire company as a lien. Edgar had augmented Oscar's original investment with his own $25,000 in 1919 and $41,500 through 1920. He sent $2,000 more in January, 1921.[33] Oscar, who still good-naturedly joked with his brother about the losses (Oscar said the Thompson well was like his dancing--he "had it in the head but could not deliver in the feet"), opposed Edgar's desire to risk personally $15,000 more but still insisted that Edgar go on with no debt to him if he so desired.

Infected with the wildcatter's dream, Edgar wanted another try, but he did let leases expire that were not quite near the fault line Woolsey had discovered, for Edgar was feeling the pinch of dry holes. He was having to renew some of his own notes involving other enterprises. "I hoped to be able to pay this with oil proceeds," he wrote his brother, "but up to date I will have to 'say it with flowers.'"[34]

Davis sent Baker back to Luling at the close of February, 1921, to locate another well site. He had made his money by sticking to a business situation in the past and determined to do it again:

> We may or may not get oil. It is an act of faith with me, but I would not feel that I had played the game without another trial and I cannot figure too nicely on what failure would mean. I feel that as a retailer of lemonade I played the game right up to the hilt; likewise in the Eaton Company; likewise in the Rubber Company; and I want to do the same in oil and feel that if we lose out, I will be the gainer from having played the game to the limit.[35]

The decision to go on also included going it alone. Davis organized, directed, and assumed the risk of a new enterprise when he incorporated the United North and South Oil Company on March 1, 1921. He became president; Baker, vice-president; Peale, treasurer; and Arthur Peck, secretary. The name was a Yankee's gesture toward easing old animosities of the Civil War.[36] The Texas Southern Oil and Lease Syndicate had lasted exactly two years but had become indebted to the Davises much more than the total company was worth, and Edgar Davis bought out the syndicate by canceling the notes.[37]

Within sight of the Thompson well and closer to the fault line, the United North and South Oil Company began drilling the Cartwright No. 1 and by mid-April were down to 1,780 feet.[38] Davis spent the summer in Luling, attending to his oil business and suffering from neuritis. He made a sad journey back to Massachusetts to join his family in burying their mother, whom they adored and respected. It was she who had instilled the Protestant work ethic and placed the emphasis on getting ahead into the two boys. Back in Texas, he noted signs that drove him on. "I can see too many rainbows around those drilling rigs to quit," Davis insisted.[39] Escaping gas around the drill pipe and traces of oil on the surface of the mud in the slush pit often sparkle and shine as small "rainbows."

And more than fumes escaped Cartwright No. 1, for in early August oil gushed nearly to the top of the derrick for over fifteen minutes before sulfur water flowed with no further sign of oil. The organization hired experienced oilman John E. Mowinkle, who was leasing lands in the area for the Somerset Oil Company of San Antonio, to attempt to make the well a producer.[40] The well sputtered more sulfur water, and Davis returned to New York, leaving Baker and company to put down Cartwright No. 2 and abandon No. 1.[41]

Some time in 1921 a singular oil exploration crew landed in Luling composed of a young businessman, David Kahn, and his "clairvoyant" friend Edgar Cayce. To locate oil, Cayce went into a trance, spoke in detail of the underground oil structure, while Kahn took notes. In this manner they supposedly located first Luling and then the shallow oil reservoir they sought through psychic experience. With three thousand acres under lease, the pair entered upon frustrating drilling operations that depleted their funds. David Kahn met Edgar Davis shortly thereafter in Forth Worth and New York, where Kahn related his psychic information to Davis.[42]

That Davis put much stock in this chance conversation is doubtful, but he was interested in psychic phenomena. In 1929 he was attempting to get in touch with Edgar Cayce, and he did meet Cayce in the thirties and had several interpretations of his life related by Cayce while the seer was in his trance.[43]

In 1921-1922, Davis was faced with the sharp reality of his exorbitant drilling activities, not dreams. In New York, he busied himself with plans to form a rubber cartel, and to develop air cooled engines as a way of forgetting dry holes in the Southwest. Before his summer trip south, he had confided in friends that one of his New York projects looked gloomy:

> Not only was the year 1919, in which you were interested, unsuccessful, but I have had another year in which I have gone in the hole badly. My main constructive interest in that year was in the development of a big transportation scheme upon which I have received five distinct setbacks. I intend to have one more trial to put it through, yet the outlook is not propitious.[44]

Davis' first love was the rubber industry, anyway, and he put much energy throughout the fall and winter of 1921 to create his proposed amalgamation of British, Dutch, Belgian, and American rubber companies, supported by American financial interests, to stabilize the industry.

An international scheme required world travel to put it across. On the last day of February, 1922, Edgar B. Davis and Walter B. Mahony sailed for London, where they joined Figart and began approaching British rubber growers. Mahony and Davis carried the plan to the Dutch in Holland, and there Davis received the news that his beloved brother Oscar had died suddenly of pneumonia on March 19, 1922. Davis and Mahony returned to London, spent two days in busy conferences, and sailed for New York on March 25.[45]

Mahony and Davis developed their rubber plan voluntarily at their own expense and it cost them in time, travel, living expenses, and advertising. Whereas Mahony's business interests were prospering, Davis' fortunes were on the decline. In addition to having to forward money to Texas to keep the United North and South Oil Company punching in dry holes, Edgar bought out Oscar's investment from the estate. To keep going, Davis had to sell his British War Bonds prematurely at a substantial loss.[46]

Reduced to selling his office furniture and his Packard to finance his trip to Luling, Davis learned that Cartwright No. 2 was a costly duster.[47] He decided to use what little money remained and what further credit he could get to put down three more wells simultaneously. During the first week in July the United North and South Oil Company set up a derrick for Cartwright No. 3, along the surface fault mapped by Woolsey and near the other two failures on the same tract. Drillers also began rigging up the Ghormley well across the river in Guadalupe County near tiny Sullivan, Texas; but Davis encountered a legal problem with the lease in making a third location.[48]

The rig was set up on the Meriweather tract, but Peale had not secured a clear title to the lease because of a technicality involving an illegitimate child in the ownership of land. Davis wanted to move to the nearest clear lease, in this case the Rafael Rios farm about five miles northwest of Luling and a mile north of the San Marcos River. The consulting geologist advised him not to move. Davis had his mind made up, had the rig skidded a mile, and the location became the Rios No.

1.[49] This well set the stage for oil field lore with the original site proving dry and the fateful move becoming the lucky break.

With the exception of Woolsey (who had gone to work for the Atlantic Oil and Refining Company after his brief stay with Davis), no geologist supported further drilling in the area, believing that the numerous dry holes had graphically illustrated that oil did not exist in paying quantities; furthermore, the Edwards lime and Austin chalk, the two strata that could produce liquid, were obviously water producers.[50] One recognized geologist summarized that "in an ordinary wildcat well, you have one chance in a hundred. Here in this situation, you have but a small fraction of one percent of a chance."[51] The company treasurer's report condenses the situation:

> We are drilling three wildcat wells against all geological advice, the enterprise being continued solely by one man who has faith in it.
>
> On March 19, 1922, the company owed this man (without interest) $94,600 and the total assets of the company on the same date were about $20,000.
>
> On July 1, 1922, the company owed this man (with interest) $177,633.99 and had assets of about $35,000.
>
> The company's stock never has had any market value.[52]

Davis' financial condition was bleak indeed. Operating on credit, owing not only his employees but also business firms, the Luling bank, and private individuals, he was never hesitant in asking for credit, nor did he solicit loans in an obsequious manner no matter how insufficient his funds. He balanced this character trait with his own generosity when he had the money, but if broke he had a strange habit of requesting credit from anyone on the shakiest of collateral. At these moments he remained a Calvinist when spending, not borrowing. In this way he kept going, even though he had not met a payroll since June, 1922. He spoke individually with the employees, and his one secretary, Miss Kate Nugent, and the men in the field stayed on. One scorching August day, he revealed to the roughnecks on Rios #1 a fifty-cent piece as the only cash he had in the world. This earnest man, dressed in his tropical white suits, somehow inspired confidence as he spoke in terms of "When I strike oil," not "If I strike oil."[53] Certainly Davis' faith was strong here, but these theatrics also reflect the acting ability of the master promoter. From any perspective, it shows a lot of nerve.

The situation worsened. When the bank returned Davis' $285 check for insufficient funds, his insurance agent had to tell him that he could extend credit to indemnify for only a limited time. Davis could not work his men in the dangerous oil field without insurance. Searching his mind, he remembered that he had $300 in municipal bonds in his safe in Brockton and immediately wired his secretary to cash them in. The secretary had discovered more British War Bonds Davis had forgotten he even had, enough to finance a few more weeks. Davis, who always impressed others by his bulk, had Luling laughing as he brought the news: "He almost--not quite, but almost--broke into a trot as he came across that railroad track from the telegraph office, waving that yellow paper."[54]

Back on credit by August, he still owed outstanding bills all over town and backpay to a crew operating without salaries. He studied his Bible. He read and reread Kipling's "If" (which he felt had been written especially for him), found a rare beauty in the Texas wildflowers and cactus (his one "dividend" during his trying times), and never lost his faith. To complete Rios No. 1, Davis mortgaged for $4,000 his pumping equipment which he used to get water from the river to his wells for drilling purposes, but the bank informed him that this was the last loan.[55]

With Davis at the end of his financial rope, on August 9, 1922, the Rios No. 1 struck an oil sand at 2,161 feet and began producing 150 barrels of oil a day.[56] Davis had reinforced two truths of oil exploration: "Luck was present at the birth of the oil industry, and the role it has since played has been both factual and legendary;" and ". . .the only reliable geologist was Dr. Drill."[57] But luck, chance, or whatever, Davis, of course, would call it "faith."

With the victory of a discovery well, Davis was not yet in the clear. Money was still short. Then there was always the possibility of a well drying up. Even a gusher can suddenly cease flowing as quickly as it began. Davis had to demonstrate a productive property with subsequent exploration. Therefore the immediate problems of disposing of the oil, maintaining and enlarging lease holdings, and drilling more producers were pressing. Could he develop production quickly enough to finance his needs? One thing was certain: he would keep on. A man well qualified to analyze Davis' drive is fellow wildcatter Morris O. Rayor, who has recorded that "the first oil, the Luling Field, resulted from the amazing determination and persistence of Edgar B. Davis."[58] In the meantime, Davis had drilled "as wild a wildcat as one ever encounters"[59] and had secured a place for himself in the history of petroleum exploration. Moreover, just as he had pioneered new techniques of rubber growing and production in the Far East, Davis had established important new precedents in the United States oil industry. This was the first instance in Texas where an obvious geological fault had been the main cause for sustained exploration, and this was the first oil production from the Edwards Limestone formation. The importance of this shallow find is obvious. Luling became a major field, reaching the 100,000,000 barrel record in the next quarter century.[60] At the point of discovery, however, Davis had not time to rest on his laurels. He instead launched what he always styled his "toughest fight,"[61] the development of further production to "prove" his field.

This photograph captures both the spiritual and intellectual sides of Edgar B. Davis. (From author's private collection.)

Even Edgar B. Davis and H. Ketner, both 300 pounders, are dwarfed by this huge tree stump in Sumatra (1911). (From author's private collection.)

Davis finds the glare off his bald head a little too bright under this rubber tree in Ceylon (1911). (From author's private collection.)

Here Davis remembers those time forgot. The 1926 gift to Sir Henry Wickham. Left to right: Editor Grange of the Ceylon *Times*, Crosbie Roles, Sir Henry Wickham, and David M. Figart. (From author's private collection.)

In this photo Davis is seen at his desk in his Luling office (1950). He never retired. (From author's private collection.)

Scene from *The Ladder*, a big flop on Broadway. (From author's private collection.)

In addition to his executive talents, Tommy Caylor was a great wit. Here he tells a good story at a Luling office coffee break (1950). Left to right: Hazel Muenster, Tommy Caylor, Catherine Davis (no relation), Edgar B. Davis, Inez Griffin, Bruce Pipkin, Lorraine Crockett. (From author's private collection.)

Davis spoke at discovery well Rios No. 1 for the Silver Anniversary of the Luling Oil Field (August 9,1947). (From author's private collection.)

Here Davis remembers the black citizens of Luling's segregated society (1947). (From author's private collection.)

Here Davis shares a jovial moment with his long-time secretary Inez Griffin in the Luling office (1950). (From author's private collection.)

Chapter VI
CASHING IN

The general area seemed good. If he could only locate the exact spot--

William A. Owens

To keep wildcatting for oil in Texas, with its risks always inviting financial ruin, while at the same time tending to the details of fund raising, meeting payrolls, arranging further exploration, and handling a hundred other concerns that filled Davis' mind, required a very high level of business ability. As entrepreneur, his challenge was to make the best use of shaky operations as they stood in hope of gaining some advantage to reward him for his efforts. This period from the discovery well on August 9, 1922, until he was able actually to deliver paying quantities of crude oil to market was the wildcatter's second uphill battle in the oil game, and Edgar Davis was unable to free himself from financial stress until the middle of 1923. With the completion of Rios No. 1, Davis had no money to drill another well. Without capital of his own, the only way he could demonstrate a proven oil field was to trade or sell small tracts to other oil men who could afford to drill immediately. One of these arrangements with a competitor paid off; the completion of the Prairie Lea Production Company Merriweather No. 1 in mid-December of 1922 on land acquired from Davis made one hundred barrels a day, without water, from penetration of only a few feet into the Edwards limestone formation.[1] Based on this success, Kelts C. Baker, vice president of United North and South Oil Company, announced future large-scale drilling operations. At this point the United North and South needed a timely gusher of its own.

Davis weathered out a bleak December in 1922, his credit cut off by the local bankers after a $12,000 overdraft, while facing a monthly $5,000 payroll. To carry on, Davis arranged to sell new production to Magnolia Petroleum Company, which advanced him loans on future oil, enabling him to hang on to his leases and begin the new year drilling on the Merriweather No. 2.[2] The end of March, 1923, found Davis promoting two drilling operations, the Merriweather No. 2 and the Hardeman No. 1, without results. The irony was bitter: after months of sacrifice he had made an important oil discovery in a new stratum, but he was now further in debt and struggling to hold on to the many acres under lease which he believed would ultimately prove profitable. Then came the dramatic moment in the spring. On Saturday, April 14, Davis wrote to Magnolia that he could not meet the Sunday deadline for a $25,000 loan from that company. His own words preserve the flavor of the situation:

> As we had been waiting for either the Hardeman or the Merriweather well to come in, in order to raise money to meet a $25,000.00 loan from the Magnolia Petroleum Company, it was with a very depressed feeling that I felt compelled [sic] to write them that it was impossible for me to meet the obligation, when due April 15. But I wrote them Saturday morning showing appreciation for their kindness, and stating that they were free--that is, morally free, as of course they were legally free--to take any steps necessary to protect their loan. In other words, the law could take its course and we would take our medicine.
>
> On Sunday afternoon Mr. Peale took Miss Manford of Luling and me out to see the well [Merriweather No. 2]. When we arrived we heard that it had been gushing, but we were not prepared for what happened. In fact, we had entered the motor car to come away, despairing of any immediate action, when I chanced to look up and saw clouds of what looked like thick black smoke coming out of the hole and shooting up the derrick in increasing force. We hastily got out of the automobile and beheld one of the sights of our lives, for the oil was thrown clear to the top of the derrick, a height of 112 feet. As this was unexpected and we were to the leeward of the well, we soon literally were baptized in oil, –baptized by sprinkling. The automobile was covered.

> The well is a fine one and Mr. Baker has just telephoned that it will give a minimum of four or five hundred barrels of oil per day, whereas yesterday a conservative estimate was three hundred barrels. This should add millions to the value of our property as soon as we can cash in. I today had made satisfactory arrangements with the Magnolia Petroleum Company for a continuation of our loan for sixty days. I have Faith to believe that a wonderful miracle has been done although along entirely natural lines.[3]

It is the above narrative that has become a part of the folklore of the oil industry, but it is usually incorrectly told in connection with the Rios No. 1 well. Making Rios No. 1 a gusher does enhance the legend of the important discovery well. Obviously, though, high drama sprayed over the derrick of Merriweather No. 2; the difference between success or failure depended on such a strike, for Davis would have lost control of his operations without this dramatic blow out. For the sake of folklore, however, the gusher is better related to Rios No. 1. Few raconteurs want the truth to get in the way of a good tale.

Davis wired Magnolia executives that he would speak with company officials the next Monday in Dallas. At this meeting he convinced Magnolia officers to advance another $25,000, which he used to renew leases that expired that month in Caldwell County. He arranged additional financing by selling Magnolia future production at fifty cents a barrel, twenty-five cents less than the then market price; Magnolia Petroleum Company began advancing $100,000 a month.[4] Greatly concerned about borrowing money to operate in early May, Davis correctly predicted an improved situation by the end of the month.[5] Luling Field production figures for May, up six times that of April, encouraged Magnolia to make an improved offer of a $250,000 advance for unrecovered oil. Already, Magnolia was making plans for storage tanks and a pipe line.[6]

The Rios No. 1, the discovery well, had paved the way for eight additional producers by June, 1923. All were flowing wells (not requiring artificial pumping), and by the end of the month there were fifty derricks standing in the Luling Field. The boom was definitely on. At summer's end, United North and South Oil Company, Grayburg Oil Company, Magnolia, and six other companies had produced 235,335 barrels of oil. Drilling by rotary method required much water to wash the cuttings made by the spinning bit back out of the hole. United North and South had installed an efficient water plant with two powerful engines at a cost of $55,000 to pump water throughout the field. Ever the businessman, Davis was selling water to anyone who wanted to drill; he made $8,500 from this sideline in the month of July alone. The proximity of the San Marcos River, the source of drilling water, aided significantly in the development of the entire field. Additionally, Davis had a third interest in a pipe line to the Southern Pacific Railroad line where he could sell oil to companies that wanted to ship by tank car. These entrepreneurial accomplishments provided Davis a badly needed breather as he whittled down the risks of his oil venture in a continued drive toward the wildcatter's dream of unlimited private profit.

An independent engineer who did appraisal work, reported to Magnolia in positive terms:

> I have investigated, in my experience in the oil business, a great many oil properties but will say frankly that the United North and South Oil Company, judging from present developments, have an outlook before them to make one of the greatest producing properties that I have ever seen.[7]

Midsummer 1923 was the most comfortable period Davis spent in the oil business since his entrance into wildcatting in 1919. In July the Luling Field produced 170,500 barrels of oil (as contrasted to only 12,000 barrels the previous April); the weather was unseasonably mild for a Texas summer, with frequent cooling rains keeping alive a few of the wild flowers that always gladdened Davis' heart during his quest for oil; and he journeyed East to mix business with pleasure in the comfortable surroundings of New York City, reminiscent of the high-finance dealings of his United States Rubber Company days. "Have had quite a respite from the anxieties of the winter and spring," he wrote, "and have seen quite a number of ball games, played <u>at</u> golf, tackled John at tennis, attended a number of championship bouts and generally have had quite a holiday while putting thru [sic] a deal for the development of another part of our property."[8]

Davis still faced uncertainty, for he lacked sufficient funds to hold onto all his leases, especially the ones across the San Marcos River in Guadalupe County where the strategy of finding oil in new territory plagued him once again. In New York he bargained for resources with officials of the Atlantic Oil and Producing Company as he had earlier dealt with Magnolia Petroleum Company executives. Atlantic directors provided their geologist, Vern Woolsey, discoverer of the fault line in the Luling Field, and loaned United North and South $100,000 for drilling four wells. Another $100,000 was to be advanced monthly beginning the fifteenth of whatever month followed the discovery well in Guadalupe County. As with Magnolia, the repayment was to be in oil at fifty cents a barrel (after Magnolia had collected its million barrels).[9]

Leaving New York August 1, Davis resumed his promoting efforts in Pittsburgh, talking the Oil Well Supply Company out of $200,000 credit for six months. The company threw in a free pass in its stadium box where he enjoyed New York's three to two victory over Pittsburgh. From there he journeyed to Cleveland to check on the development of an air-cooled automobile engine in which he had a small financial investment. Here at the Hotel Statler he read of President Harding's death and determined to suspend work in his oil field on the day of the funeral. Traveling south, he stopped off to swelter in the St. Louis heat and to cheer Boston's defeat of the local team. Back in Dallas, Sunday, August 5, he was still in the big-league oil money, yet he found time to enjoy a Texas-League ball game with Dallas taking Ft. Worth two to one in the ninth. He dined on the roof of the Adolphus Hotel and then steamed to Luling on the night train. Good oil news greeted him, with wells coming in on Monday and Tuesday. Daily payments of from 15,000 to 20,000 barrels of oil to Magnolia were to commence shortly.[10]

Back in Texas, Davis appraised his opportunities and deployed his resources toward the challenge of striking oil on his improved leases. He had discovered Rios No. 1 against scientific advice, and he continued this trend by insisting that the Luling Field would deliver greater production on the Guadalupe County side of the San Marcos River. On the other hand, he placed some faith in those trained in geology for development work by employing Ernest W. Brucks as chief geologist and utilizing the consulting services of George C. Matson and Davis Donoghue. Sam H. Rabon brought his excellent field supervision experience to the United North and South. Thus Davis applied his considerable management skills to pioneer work in the first field in Texas to produce from the Edwards lime. This Edwards reservoir of petroleum nestled against impervious shale along the fault displacement geologist Vern Woolsey had discovered as it outcrops on the north bank of the San Marcos River. Few of the wells in the Luling Field were spectacular gushers, although one blew in at 3,000 barrels a day to keep up interest, and another blasted oil off the crown block of the derrick, making 11,500 barrels daily for several weeks. An average of 900 barrels a day per well was evident in early 1924.[11]

In spite of this success on the Caldwell County side of the river, the area of the discovery well, Davis was still susceptible to losing his many unproductive leases on the Guadalupe County side of the field, an area Davis maintained would out-produce the rival producing half of the field. Geological opinion was contrary and seemed the correct assessment, for the first three holes were dusters. For the third time in his wildcatting career Davis faced a delicate and trying situation; he had to bring in oil for Atlantic Oil and Producing Company or else lose many of his precious leases. Atlantic officials were pessimistic, but Davis placed his typical faith in the fourth attempt, the Marines No. 1, and optimistically departed Luling for Massachusetts to celebrate Christmas with his sisters. Marines No. 1 came in on December 27,[12] the first of many successes in Guadalupe County; this strike preserved all of the United North and South leases; and 1923 marked the last year of financial strain with the Luling Field. Starting with the new year, Davis could develop his properties at a style and pace more conducive to the temperament of a capitalist who had known the security of sound financial backing.

Davis had played the game to the hilt, as he so often reminded himself and others, and he had won. The victory has been viewed from several points of view. Oil field historian Walter Rundell, Jr., sees the success as a combination of determination and good fortune: "Davis' experience documented the rewards that could follow a bold gesture. Since he entered the oil business a complete neophyte, it was fortunate that the bold gesture was also coupled with considerable luck."[13] Bruce Barton believed that the opportunity was only realized through tenacity: "He had been very lucky, people say; but without his dogged determination he would never have lasted long enough to realize on his luck."[14] The wildcatter himself usually ruled out the role of chance, seeing rather the hand of providence that he believed had guided his destiny since his mystical experience of December 1, 1904, when he believed that he heard a voice calling him to be President of the United States:

> On the Guadalupe tract across the creek, we had drilled three wells, all dry holes, and were drilling the

> fourth. The Atlantic people paid for the exploration work. December twenty-first I was preparing to go North to be with my sisters on Christmas Day. I went to see the Atlantic people and advised them although we had three dry holes on this tract, I knew we would get oil in the fourth. If we got oil before the end of the month, we could pay them for $100,000 which they were to pay by the fifteenth of the following month. On December twenty-seventh the Marines well came in, enabling us to carry on here. We drilled just on the border line. On one side, the land was useless for anything but farm land, and on the other it was eventually covered with derricks. Why did we drill where we did when one foot away the land was worthless? How did these things happen the way they did? Can you explain it? I tell you I am as sure of getting oil today as I was of that fourth well on the Guadalupe tract coming in. This is something that is bigger than all of us.[15]

Davis' United North and South Oil Company maintained offices on the outskirts of Luling where he, as president, and Kelts C. Baker, vice president and general manager, administered affairs. William F. Peale still operated as land man, and Charles B. Rayner, formerly manager of the Singapore office of Standard Oil and later a director in the New York office of Standard, became treasurer of United North and South. John Mowinckle and Sam Rabon were the two experienced and practical oil men. Davis owned eighty percent of the stock, or 213,000 shares out of a total of 266,250 shares. The balance of the shares was owned mostly by the above management committee.[16]

To match the experienced men making up the management committee, the United North and South equipment was the very best. Dehydrating plants on both sides of the San Marcos River processed thousands of barrels into clean pipeline oil per month at a cost of one cent per barrel for delivery to Magnolia and Atlantic. These companies used railroad tank cars to transport the oil, but in 1924 Magnolia constructed an eight-inch pipeline from Luling to its main line near Houston. By mid-1924, United North and South boasted eighty-one producing wells in Caldwell County and thirty-two in Guadalupe

County. Development had been steady but impressive, and the Luling Field began to rank in the national standings. In January, 1924, twenty-four fields in the United States produced at least fifteen hundred barrels daily. Luling first produced this amount in February, 1924, ranking twenty-sixth nationally at that time. By March, Luling's output of 20,750 barrels a day ranked it eighteenth in the nation. The next month it was one of the dozen largest fields in the United States, averaging thirty-two thousand barrels a day. By December 31, 1924, exactly 391 producing wells had a cumulative production of 14,500,000 barrels, with a daily output of forty-three thousand barrels.[17]

Fortune continued to be with Davis, for even what appeared at first to be a ruinous condition of the oil field actually proved beneficial. Sulphur water began to appear more and more, either encountered prior to striking the oil formation, mixed in the petroleum itself, or just underneath the oil level; but the water eventually proved helpful to the recovery of oil, for ultimately oil rises to the top of water. Thus, production increased, even though wells ceased to flow and were recovered by mechanical pumps.[18] When water emerged with the oil, it was piped to a great earthen tank south of Luling where it still remains as a local landmark, the "salt lake."

The production level was the Edward lime at a depth of about two thousand, one hundred feet with the pay strata in approximately forty feet of this formation. Controlling over sixty percent of the Luling Field, the United North and South left little room for competition in 1924. Magnolia made three thousand, five hundred barrels daily; Grayburg Oil and Refining Company, three thousand, five hundred; The Texas Company, one thousand, five hundred; Rio Bravo Oil Company, one thousand; and J. K. Hughes Development Company, one thousand. The relatively low cost of drilling in the Luling Field was linked to the shallow oil. Completing a well cost an average of $14,000. When the natural flow of black gold ceased, pumping expenses were six cents per barrel. These costs still returned Davis a high margin of profit even as he fulfilled his fifty cent a barrel contracts at less than the going price of between seventy cents and one dollar.[19]

Economic and social factors in the city of Luling changed rapidly with the development of the oil field that bore its name. In the 1870's, as the rail head point for freighting operations into Mexico and when a branch of the Chisholm Trail ran by the town, Luling had been known as "the toughest town in Texas." By 1920, it resembled the set for Lum and Abner movies, complete with dirt streets (usually dusty), and one main street where store buildings fronted the Southern Pacific Line connecting Houston and San Antonio. The census counted at least fifteen hundred citizens. The lovely San Marcos River meandered by as the southern city limits, turning the wheel that both ginned the local cotton crop and generated the town's electricity. Two miles to the east, Plum Creek slipped into the larger stream of the San Marcos. Ed Burleson and Felix Huston had routed the Comanches in the 1840 Battle of Plum Creek seven miles to the north, and the Indians who had camped for generations north and south of Luling had moved on, leaving only lost arrow heads, which continue to crop up in plowed fields. Rogers' Springs, once well known for producing drinking water especially recommended for rheumatism, diseases of the liver, and chronic disorders, no longer drew crowds to annually sip the thermal liquid.[20]

Post-World War I depression had hit Luling hard, and it reflected an environment of economic decline. However, the train still stopped there. It brought Edgar B. Davis to town, and his discovery roused the drowsing village. The small settlement quickly filled with the typical boom town types, people who heeded the call of a new field and tried to get there early before the riches were all taken. Oil field work was dangerous, rough, and generally followed by tough men; but the character and personality of the oil field workers was as varied as any group, notwithstanding the stereotyped image. Competent in moving heavy iron in often impossible situations, he had to be somewhat indifferent to danger, and it is this trait that has created the public image of a tough character.

A drilling crew in action on a rotary rig is a poetic scene to watch, a ballet of deadly proportions, for one miscue can mean maiming or death for one and all. Over one hundred feet in height, the derrick twists three sections of thirty-foot drill pipe into the earth by means of the rotary turntable on the floor of the derrick. Two or three roughnecks guide the pipe into the hole and add new sections of pipe as needed by unscrewing a joint of pipe at the rotary table and coupling on another piece of pipe to follow the others down the hole the drill bit makes. This and all operations must be coordinated perfectly with the actions of the driller as he spins the rotary against the roughnecks' pipe tongs and raises or lowers the pipe in and out of the hole with cable and draw works. High above on his monkey board, the derrick man attaches the top end of the drill stem into the traveling block or uncouples it if the operation is going the other way. The beauty of this team work is best seen when the crew makes a round trip to change a worn bit. With the precision of an orchestra, the players pull all the pipe from the hole, change the bit, and then run it all back in to drill again and make more hole.

The driller does the hiring and firing and the roughnecks and derrick men do the hiring on and the quitting. Independence and individualism is second nature to such an organizational structure. Then there is the mutual respect always evident when dangerous work requiring great skill of the participants links all who do the job well with an unspoken bond.

Always the aesthetic, Davis appreciated the symmetry of the drilling operation, and he liked to watch a top crew in action, but he never understood the operation in a mechanical sense. Just as he could never learn to drive a car, he could never quite grasp what was going on below the surface. This is what made him so different from most wildcatters. Usually the oil finders had the ability to visualize and understand at least the rudimentary elements of all phases of bringing in a producing well. Davis seemed to think that you drilled down and the oil came up. It was this naivete that led to so many mistakes Davis made as an oil man. There is nothing like success in the oil business, though, no matter how it comes, and Davis hit oil and the oil characters began to hit Luling. So the geologist, the oil promoter, the shooter, the driller, the roughneck, the teamster, and the land man made their way to Luling. Then came the criminal element, seeking profits not directly from oil but indirectly from the men of honest toil. The con man, the pickpocket, the gambler, the bootlegger, the thief, and the prostitute, also flocked to Luling.[21]

The pressure of a population explosion was more than the community could handle. Inhabitants of Luling climbed from fifteen hundred to ten thousand in only a few months. Luling was overcrowded, but neither the town itself nor Caldwell County was necessarily "lawless." In the early 1920's there were many in the area whose memory spanned back to the Luling of the frontier when the notorious western gunmen John Wesley Hardin and Ben Thompson passed often through the town. The community had boasted its own gunfighters, and Luling had and needed a "boot hill" in its heyday.[22]When the oil boom hit, the toughest fellows around town and county were the local law officers, a group known to be able to become just a little rougher than any opposition wanted to get. Consequently, disorder never blossomed openly in Luling. As a result, the section of town usually catering to vice in a boom town was absent from Luling and instead sprang up across the San Marcos River due south from Rios No. 1, in Guadalupe County, where it was isolated from the nearest town in that county.[23]

This unique settlement had a distinct name. The hottest drilling activity in the Guadalupe County side of the Luling Field was on the Allen Farm, and when buildings sprang up along the county road that passed the farm, John Allen put up a sign, "Allen Town." A newly arrived blacksmith quickly placed a sign "Gander Slue" (he meant slough) on his side of the road. Sloughs abound in the area and Allen did have a gander on his earthen stock tank. The smithy won out, and although the town is gone, the lane has been Gander Slue Road to this day.[24]

In the town of Gander Slue, sin flourished twenty-four hours a day. Here the disorderly elements congregated. Gamblers, bootleggers, and madams operated openly in the hastily assembled city. Thieves conspired to rob drilling crews going to and from work, causing shift changes to walk single file with enough space between each man to watch for ambush. Texas Ranger Frank Hamer led a raid on Gander Slue, wrecking gaming tables and scattering the unruly element. Yet, within a matter of days the town of vice was back into full operation.[25]

One other encampment of citizenry made up the boom area of the Luling Field. Up the road, across the river, and into Caldwell County dwelled the very poor of those who comprised the boom town population; their tent and lean-to city was Ragtown.[26]

Back in Luling, living conditions became more crowded, if not more lawless. Streets filled with laboring animals pulling heavy loads, for although steam power twisted the rotary bit into the earth, trucks had not replaced the mule for moving supplies and equipment. For instance, United North and South got along with one hundred teams of mules and seven trucks. Often ten teams of twenty animals each pulled the pipe, drill stems, and other heavy equipment through the town to the oil fields. The extra traffic of mules, horses, automobiles, and trucks raised new dust from dry streets and made them a quagmire on the rainy days. One could actually catch a ride across muddy main street "piggy-back," carried by a man in rubber boots.[27]

The ingenious could, therefore, profit from the boom even without lease or land. For instance, it was impossible to supply the demand for sleeping space. Private homes became rooming houses. Cots set up in tents rented for fifty cents for twelve hours.[28]

In the press of numbers, the Luling School System went to two shifts for students, morning or afternoon. Funerals were frequent, for oil field accidents were numerous, and choirs assembled to sing for a departed soul whom they had never known.[29]

If the city of Luling omitted the lawlessness from its boom town image, it also strangely lacked the Coal-Oil Johnny types, or rather, those landowners who throw away in wasteful spending their fortune from oil. Instead, many Luling residents viewed their sudden increase in income as money to be used wisely. Examples of conservative reaction include Leopoldo Marines, who bought more farm land; and John Allen, who divided half his wealth among his large family of eleven and invested the rest in safe securities. Many others in Luling showed similar good judgment in handling the windfall.[30]

Davis stood to gain the most, and vowed that great wealth would not go to his head, particularly since he believed his success providential. He explained to friends that Rudyard Kipling's "If" and "The Explorer" explained his actions of courage in the face of difficulty as well as these acts could be described. But all of Davis' inherent Calvinism impelled him steadily toward cashing in on a grand scale.[31] On the whole, Davis' Puritan character constituted the mainspring of his intense desire for profits, although by this stage of his career nonpecuniary motives also influenced him. In addition to the incentive of financial gain, the need for power to promote his rubber cartel played an increasing role in his life. Even more importantly, the belief in the mystical winning of the Presidency was tied in his mind to the prestige accorded to the rich and famous. In May and June of 1924, he placed advertisements in *Oil Weekly, Wall Street Journal, Journal of Commerce,* and other similar media explaining that he would fulfill oil delivery contracts by July 1, 1924, and that he was ready to enter into negotiations to sell his one hundred twenty-one wells on his twenty-one thousand acres of oil and gas leases strategically following the seven miles of fault line structure running north and south through Caldwell and Guadalupe counties with the San Marcos River as the dividing line.[32] Eventually, representatives from three major companies looked over his property, but they made no definite offer to buy at this time.

Throughout the oil boom Davis lived in the Wilson Hotel (Luling's finest but a far cry from his suite at the Belmont Hotel in New York City.) He was therefore quite pleased when Kelts Baker went on an extended vacation and left him the use of his house complete with maid, house servant, and piano. The piano enabled him to write new words to the hymn "Abide With Me, "whereas the home provided him a place to entertain the office force. Then there were always his bridge games, played to win with a vengeance. Davis and his management committee, composed of many old friends of the Far East, pursued their pastimes. Golf matches and skeet shooting were two favorite diversions of the executives. Usually the management committee got along famously.[33]

Strangely, in spite of all his concentration on the fascinating oil business, wildcatting was still secondary to his plans to re-enter the rubber business as an international leader to stabilize the world price of rubber through united cooperation of the largest corporations. Petroleum money represented a means to a different business end. He developed unusual and vague ideas about deep oil at Luling; these vast reservoirs would make the earlier strike pale into insignificance, and he maintained for years that greater reserves lay some four or five thousand feet below the paying horizon of twenty-two hundred feet. Meanwhile, he got some "bites" on his offer to sell. Humble and Magnolia representatives toured his property, and Roxana (the Royal Dutch) sent inquiries.[34]

Suddenly, Davis changed his tactics, withdrew his offer to sell, and postponed all action in anticipation of the deep oil he became increasingly certain he would strike. He determined to retain his property until he proved the lower level one way or another. The fifty million dollar fortune that he imagined he would need to buy controlling interest in the United States Rubber Company and some other rival company of approximately the same size could not be met by disposing of his field at that time.[35]

At this point in his wildcatting career Davis began to rely more and more on his intuition in the search for oil and to ignore the scientific evidence that did not back up his perception. He had made a name for himself with the United States Rubber Company by scientifically managing a rubber plantation. In the oil industry he gradually abandoned science altogether and became obsessed with the unsound equation that the deeper the oil strata the greater the productivity.[36] This monomania cost him dearly!

Other company officials expressed their skepticism that the extreme expense represented by the drill bit spinning so deep underground would ever gush to the surface as profits; rather, the deep search for oil would amount to ever-increasing losses. Then, when

Davis began to exceed eccentricity past all geologic evidence, and at great cost, friction mounted.

The two test wells where both the expense and tempers rose were Kelley No. 1 and the Tiller No. 2. Luling Field production was definitely in the Edwards formation, generally 730 feet thick, with fifty to one hundred fifty feet of this structure producing oil. Here average production was at twenty-two hundred feet below the drilling rig; but profit was a sure thing at this productive, shallow level. Yet Davis insisted on going further, even below the 3,900 feet in an early test well, Chester Byrd No. 2, where small traces of oil quickly turned to flowing salt water. Kelley No. 1 encountered an oil-stained sand at 4,600 feet which also turned to salt water, exciting Davis to bore deeper and depressing everyone else in the company. Both the Kelley and the Tiller bit into a schist formation of uniform hardness at 4,723 feet and 4,807 feet respectively.[37] So Davis closed out 1924 in a mixed situation: one hundred fifty wells showing a budding profit; and two rigs drilling expensively--and, according to scientific opinion, uselessly--toward the unknown.[38]

On New Year's Day, 1925, Davis contemplated his deep tests from his Massachusetts office with equanimity and further resolved to withhold selling until the lower horizon, wherever it was, produced.[39] When informed that the Kelley and Tiller wells, turning through schist formation at $50.00 per foot, could only expect to hit solid granite, Davis sent instructions to carry on: "Faith is the bridge over the river dispair [sic] at the end of the road called knowledge which leads into the promised land. Let's find the granite."[40]

The next month, Humble officials disclosed a desire to buy out Davis but made no definite offer. To Davis' relief, the oil men indicated no interest in his quest for deep oil; they only wanted to purchase the Edwards production. Davis wanted to reserve the deeper oil that he believed to be at Luling for himself. The latest news on the deep tests was that drill bits were being changed *for each inch* made in the hardest part of the rock formation![41] To the professional man in the field, this operation was madness.[42] Davis' comment was that "good things come hard";[43] this reflected his New England Calvinism. Remarks in Luling ran along the debate over which was harder, the crystalline rock or Davis' head.[44]

Davis' correspondence does reveal a concern for the frustrations of those who could not understand his policy, and he felt obligated to explain in detail his actions to those closest to him:

> You write "it was a great disappointment to learn that yours [my] rubber plans were dependent upon this [deep oil tests]" and I am sorry that you feel that way. However, when I survey the immensity of the work I have visualized to do in rubber and other lines I cannot see how this property, wonderful as it is, can be capable of furnishing me with the capital to carry out the work to be done; consequently I must keep on. The deep tests do not look encouraging; in fact they look nearly as badly [sic] as they possibly could look. We are down to 5,231 feet and 4,938 respectively and are in what is called a schist which never has been known to produce oil.
>
> In a talk with our geologist the other day he said that he expected that we would get into something worse and the organization here, while carrying out my instructions in perfect good faith, has recommended me to quit. In fact I came down here feeling it would be necessary to break with our entire organization on this matter of deep tests in the pursuance of my Vision. I am glad to state that Mr. Baker, who has done a great work here, is going to play the game to the limit and I look for the others to fall in line although I sympathize with them in their fear that I will dissipate a considerable amount of our present winnings in this search for deep oil.
>
> I hope this may enable you to see I must keep on.[45]

Professional opinion was starkly realistic, as revealed in this report by company geologist Ernest Brucks, whose assessment has been borne out by time:

> As far as production from deeper sands is concerned, I am firmly convinced that none can be expected and that the tremendous cost of deep sand exploration must be borne ultimately by the income from the Edwards production. I claim, therefore, with

> the utmost sincerity and perfect confidence, that further expenditure along that line would be futile from the standpoint of sound business policy, and that the only good that might come from the expenditure of funds for this purpose would be in its service as a gratuity to landowners profiting through the high bonus paid for the acreage, to the employees directly concerned and to the supply houses that furnish the material used. Incidentally, some geologic information of doubtful utility might be disclosed.[46]

Brucks, possibly from frustration, left United North and South for a job in Mexico with Standard Oil.[47] As for Davis, "Something implores me to go on. Read Kipling's 'Explorer.'"[48]

The mystery of the "something" that drove Davis succumbs easily to psychological analysis. One of the most deeply rooted characteristics of Davis, his self confidence, sprung from his Calvinism: the greater the struggle, the greater the reward. Had not the Luling Discovery well and two later timely strikes proven this? Now the Kelley and Tiller wells, following the same pattern and requiring even greater effort, would proportionately crown the seeker with the ultimate prize. A man called of God to be President of the United States could hardly be expected to falter. He need only screw his drill bit to the sticking place and he would not fail. In short, this was Davis' "Faith." But somewhere Faith and self assertiveness merged into the egoism of Edgar B. Davis that became an end in itself. To conclude that these character traits were a form of madness is to oversimplify. To write his actions off as mere eccentricities is equally an elementary conclusion. Davis was a man of extreme self confidence and ample courage, an Emersonian individual to the core whose self interest was the valid end of all action. Besides, Davis was celibate. He had no wife or mistress nagging him about his follies. And he somehow rationalized the thrift condition of his brand of Calvinism; unless he was making a business deal or borrowing money at interest.

Davis left the drilling crews to do the actual exploration work in the search for subterranean riches while he himself heeded the call to travel again. For a time he operated out of his Massachusetts office, with frequent trips to New York to keep in touch with both oil and rubber executives. Between 1924 and 1925 oil output in Texas increased by ten million barrels, boosting the Lone Star State to first place in oil production in the nation while temporarily depressing the price of crude, but the news in April, 1925, that oil had fallen by twenty-five cents a barrel did not dampen his spirits nor did the reports about making only inches a day at great financial outlay in the Kelley and Tiller wells. On the bright side, while pursuing the elusive dream of some fabulous store of oil in the vast depths of the earth, he owned a company in sound enough condition to pay him a spring dividend of $25,000; and Davis could certainly breathe easier as he described his financial standing:

> Today we have liquid assets enough to take care of all liabilities, and own our property, splendidly equipped, with every necessary well drilled, and important reserve acreages, free and clear, but there is something bigger yet:[49]

As he contemplated the future, rubber, not oil (unless it be vast streams of petroleum to finance ultimate control of the giant world rubber industry), remained uppermost on his mind as he mapped out his future from the Hotel Belmont in New York City. He was obviously shaken and mentally nostalgic as so much was brought back to his mind of the exotic days of plantation rubber when he learned of Huibreght Ketner's death. The giant Dutchman and he had pioneered the entrance of the United States into the Far East twenty years earlier.[50] Davis decided to embark on a journey to study the international rubber situation firsthand, not only in his old haunts in the Far East, but also in new ground in the Philippines. He would travel with his old friend David M. Figart, then in London. His send-off was a giant fireworks display blasted off for the Fourth of July at the Davis summer home on Buzzards Bay, Massachusetts.

Sailing from New York in September, 1925, Davis arrived in London on October 8;[51] the next day he and Figart departed for Naples, from which they left for Colombo, Ceylon, by way of Port Said, arriving Sunday, October 25.[52]

Leaving Ceylon, Figart and Davis sailed to Sumatra the first of November, where they were at home touring the United States Rubber Company plantations with old friends such as John Warren Bicknell. The eighth of November they went to Java to depart for Singapore. Keen tennis matches were added to bridge games and fine dinners at Raffles with rubber planters, consuls, and journalists. The next jaunt was to Borneo, where they arrived for Thanksgiving, only to be back in Singapore by mid-December after a tour of the Zamboanga area of the Philippine Islands. They sailed back to Colombo, Ceylon, and spent Christmas two days out at sea heading back for Suez and the West.[53]

Figart had made a thorough study of the rubber industry for Secretary Herbert Hoover, and Davis sought to inform the Commerce Secretary further. The conclusion of this communique reflects Davis' continued fascination with the rubber industry in which he played such an essential role:

> The British policy of restriction will enable rubber growers to take several hundred million dollars out of the American people this year while the high price of rubber cannot fail unfavorably to affect the prosperity of oil, automotive and rubber-manufacturing industries; and as such continued expenditures by the American people for a necessary product must be a matter of grave concern to our Government, might it not be well to sound the Philippine Government as to its attitude toward a system of cooperative development in plantation rubber?
>
> The position of America as regards her future supplies is so critical that I have felt it possibly was my duty as a pioneer in the investment of larger American capital in plantation rubber, to reenter the industry in the interest of those great American enterprises which are dependent directly or indirectly upon it...[54]

Back in the United States, Davis began what was to be his biggest year financially, 1926, the beginning of the sixth decade of oil exploration and production in Texas. Although the 1925 total production of the Caldwell County side of the Luling Field of 9,371,922 barrels was slightly down from the 10,699,178 of 1924, the cumulative total of 22,500,000 barrels was impressive and cause to expect a future steady yield. Also, during 1925, United North and South installed electricity on pumping wells; this proved much more efficient than the old gasoline-powered pumps for maintaining the high level of daily production. It was during this period, 1925-1926, that

Texas began forging ahead from second place behind Oklahoma among producing states toward the first place, achieved in 1928; in 1925, Texas increased its production by 10,000,000 barrels; in 1926, by 22,000,000.[55]

High recovery of oil in Davis' field led to extended search in Texas for similar production from the relatively shallow Edwards structure.[56] Resulting success had not only greatly increased Texas output of oil but had also made important changes in the economic situation, as later pointed out by John R. Sandidge, geologist for the Magnolia Petroleum Company:

> The discovery of oil in the Edwards formation of south-central Texas opened a chapter in the history of the oil business which was as important locally as were the great discovery at Spindletop for the Gulf Coast, Yates for west Texas, and "Dad" (C.M.) Joiner's No. 3 Daisy Bradford well for east Texas. It lifted a large part of the population from marginal farming and subsistence living in the towns to positions of comfort and in some cases to luxury. After the excesses accompanying the boom days had subsided, cultural improvements and general progressiveness characterized the community life, and both the countryside and the urban centers have continued to become more attractive. The economic impact has been of major importance throughout the main productive area, extending from Calwell to Webb Counties, a distance of 165 miles, and over a period of thirty-six years.[57]

With the Luling Field definitely "proved" and with the inches made per day in the deep test wells even more doubtful, Davis decided to formally put his property on the market again. He and Walter B. Mahony went to Florida in March hoping to make a sale there, and at the same time they were able to discuss their future plans in the rubber industry.[57]

Unsuccessful in Florida, Davis again placed advertisements in leading newspapers and oil journals. Several offers did not meet his expectations, for some Mexican Fields of similar make-up had begun to dry up at the time. Magnolia, already familiar with the field and equipped to take the oil out, was able to make the best offer of $12,100,000 for the Davis properties: 215 wells pumping out 17,000 barrels daily from leases comprising sixty percent of the Luling Field. On June 11, 1926, Magnolia officials presented Davis with a check for $6,050,000; the other half of the payment would be paid on installments out of the future production. Davis retained all oil below three thousand feet. The United North and South Oil Company had already realized $4,000,000 in profit from the field, and Davis still had $2,000,000 of this in the bank.[59]

Edgar B. Davis had consummated the largest oil deal in Texas up to that time. As a millionaire United States Rubber Company executive he had discovered the deference accorded the wealthy of the world. Now he was truly rich, one of the business elites, and he cut quite a swath with his doings reported from the Luling *Signal* to the *New York Times* and, for world consumption, in the London *Times.* But for a man destined to occupy the White House he trod the wrong path, becoming legendary as an eccentric rather than strengthening his reputation as the knowledgeable entrepreneur who could emerge from behind the mythical figure when serious business needed to be tended to. In the meantime, Davis had a real good time.

Chapter VII
MINE TO SHARE

I may go broke again but it looks as though I would have the fun of giving away several millions of dollars before I do so.

Edgar B. Davis

Edgar B. Davis had planned to divide and distribute a part of his oil fortune even before Magnolia purchased his property for the $12,100,000 record sum. Previously he had set a standard for altruism when he gave away a third of his fortune made in the rubber industry to employees, friends, and associates. Davis' generosity stemmed in part from an experience in the Eaton Shoe Company in Massachusetts. When a relative of the owner of the firm received the promotion in the company Davis had applied for, Davis suspected nepotism, and his brooding over this incident resulted in a nervous breakdown in 1904. When he recovered, he vowed that if given the opportunity he would be scrupulously fair to his own employees. The loyalty of his work force at Luling when the secretary and drill crew worked for two months without pay to bring in Rios No. 1 strengthened Davis' commitment to make an equitable distribution of his riches.[1]

Davis staged the world's biggest free picnic to announce his profit sharing at Luling on June 5, 1926. Invitations were directed expressly to the residents of Caldwell and Guadalupe Counties, but with the understanding that the celebration was open to the general public. Blacks attended their picnic north of town on the Negro school grounds, whereas whites lunched on 100 acres along the San Marcos River south of town. It was so well attended that when parking space ran out along the river, Davis quickly purchased an adjacent field, and late arrivals drove out on the corn crop. At least fifteen thousand guests consumed 12,200 pounds of beef, 5,180 pounds of mutton, 2,000 fryers, 8,700 ice cream sandwiches, 85 gallons of ice cream, 7,000 cakes, 6,560 bottles of near beer, 28,800 bottles of soft drinks, and unknown quantities of beans, potato salad, pickles and coffee. A San Antonio Negro jazz band entertained for blacks, and the Alamo City Municipal Band played for the whites. Davis arranged for a special concert by three New York opera stars: Ruth Royer, soprano; Isadores Luckstone, pianist,; and Edward McNamara, baritone, performed for both gatherings. Then the guests settled down to light up 7,500 cigars and 100,000 cigarettes while Davis described his scheme of philanthropy, charity, and almsgiving.[2]

He had already notified each of his four hundred and fifty employees by letter that he would pay them a bonus of up to 100 percent of their total earnings, depending on their length of service. The management committee, comprising a group of employees headed by John Mowinckle, would receive a special bonus. After explaining this plan to the crowd, he announced that the picnic site would become a city park, complete with a community club house and an endowment fund for upkeep. The white center would have a golf course and swimming facilities on the river. For the blacks, he spoke of an 80-acre recreation park complete with club house on a site to be purchased. Luling would have a one million dollar model demonstration farm to serve Caldwell and Guadalupe Counties. In closing, he announced the sale of his oil properties and made positive statements about the high standards of community support and good will on the part of Magnolia Petroleum Company and its relationship with Luling.[3]

On July 1, 1926, Davis distributed bonus checks to all employees who had been on the payroll as of June 1 of that year. He based the formula for the premium on a percentage of total earnings: one year, 25 per cent; two years, 50 percent; three years, 75 per cent; and for four years or more he matched dollar for dollar. By the standards of the time these men and women became rich overnight. Individual checks ranged from $500 to $20,000. There were no unions and no overtime in the oil field in those days and the hours were long and the work, "slinging iron" on a drilling rig, was both hard and dangerous. Drillers made $12.00 for a twelve-hour day, whereas their derrick men and roughnecks drew $7.00 and $6.00 respectively for the same tour. Roustabouts put in a meager eight-hour day but picked up only $3.00 for their daily efforts; their gang pusher, or boss, took home $5.00 a day. Tool pushers received both $300 a month and a company car. Men who had not saved a dime suddenly had money to burn. One roughneck boasted an $8,000 check. A young secretary had $2,300 for two and one half years service with the United North and South Oil Company.[4]

Luling's two banks handled the largest sums they ever transacted. Local auto and furniture dealers sold out, for $1,000 would go a long way in 1926. Chevrolet automobiles, that week, bore price tags from $595 to $745; a half-ton truck cost $395; one ton, $495. An adult could see Hoot Gibson in *The Texas Streak* at the Princess Theatre, "Coolest Spot in Town," for 25 cents--children a dime. On the way home one could pick up three pounds of Maxwell House coffee for $1.51 and a can of Carnation milk for 12 cents. There was no sales tax. Willie J. Biggs, a roughneck for the United North and South, took his $1,600 bonus check, added $300 he and his wife had saved, and built their first house. The proud couple moved into this home completely paid for.[5] Davis' gesture made headlines nationwide. And as Howard and Ralph Wolf put it in *Rubber: A Story of Glory and Greed*, "The thing that makes all this important is that here is one share-the-wealth messiah who actually has practiced what he preaches."[6]

Nor did Davis forget those who had contributed to his triumph but were no longer in his employ. To Vern Woolsey, the geologist who discovered the Luling Fault Line, he sent a sizable check; to the contractor who drilled the second successful well in the Luling Field, he mailed $5,000.[7]

Davis' endeavor to repay all who gave him aid transcended those directly involved. Rudyard Kipling, for example, discovered through the mail how he had indirectly contributed to the Luling Wildcatter's success with his poems "If" and "The Explorer." At a rare book auction Davis bid $1125 for Richard Burton's translation of Haji Abu Ed-Yosdi's *The Kasidah* and mailed this to the British poet along with an explanatory letter.[8] In the meantime, there were acts of kindness toward the unfortunate: when a tornado devastated tiny Rock Springs, Texas, in April of the following year, Davis immediately wired $5,000 for relief.[9] There were other gifts of various amounts, and not all can be traced, for Davis was silent on some of his acts of generosity and so were the recipients.[10]

As had been rumored, the largest sums went to the management committee, each of whom had been salaried at $6,000 a year since 1924, but not the $200,000 bonus reported by most newspapers. Their portions, though on a larger scale than other employees, were also prorated. In addition, each member of the management committee, regardless of time of employment, received a $5,000 bonus at Easter,

1926. Kelts C. Baker, who had been with Davis from the start of his oil venture, received a check for $250,000. John Mowinckle, first hired in an advisory capacity in January, 1922, was paid $24,461. Sam Rabon, employed in August, 1923, got $50,000. Charles B. Rayner, who worked for Davis since November, 1924, and William F. Peale, who had been an employee of the original Southern Oil and Lease Syndicate, received $21,650. These payments are listed as "part payment of bonus." Later, each of these men received additional substantial bonuses from Edgar B. Davis for the years 1927, 1928, and 1929, when they made up the management committee of a new oil company formed at Luling.[11]

Apparently, these later payments, in addition to agreed upon compensation, reflected Davis' efforts to reward these associates for their contributions before the sale to Magnolia. Newspaper reporters assumed the bonus payments were larger than they actually were because each of the managers took his stock settlement by separate check in June, 1926. Payments for stock dividends included: Baker, $96,322; Mowinckle, $100,538; Peale, $103,350; Rabon, $3,400; and Rayner, $10,200.[12] As an added treat Davis financed a vacation trip for these five associates to his spacious summer home on Buzzards Bay in Massachusetts, where each man found his bonus check by his breakfast place on the first morning.[13] Total profit sharing with every employee of United North and South Oil Company after the sale to Magnolia was $1,750,000--not too far short of the two million figure headlined by the newspapers from coast to coast at the time.

Money rewarded to individuals had both permanent and transient consequences. Parks and foundations built at Luling, for example, had lasting effects. On the last day of the year in 1926, Davis presented the deeds to the white and black city parks, along with a $50,000 endowment fund, to Luling mayor Calhoun T. Greenwood. Planned and built by San Antonio firms for $60,000, the completed club house for whites was a combination of mission and Spanish architecture, completely furnished at a cost of $7,000 and landscaped for $8,000. The smaller club house of blacks, was to be built for $20,000 on an eight-acre plot north of town. The combined gifts to the people of Luling totaled $170,500.[14]

For over half a century these two recreation centers have seen continuous and positive use. Senior proms, class reunions, private parties, family reunions, and small concerts represent only a few of the many gatherings held at these club houses. For generations of Luling blacks, the Negro club house was a source of community pride. The black residents of Luling now had an available gathering place for the "Juneteenth" celebrations, commemorating emancipation day in Texas on June 19, 1865, the day slavery actually ended in the Lone Star State. It was separate, unequal in size, but exclusively theirs, thank to Davis, who had been forewarned that blacks would be barred from a city park on the south side of town. Whatever his inclinations, Davis could not alter the segregationist pattern of Southern life in the 1920s, but he could, and did, make segregation a less harsh burden for the Luling blacks. The black citizens made up roughly one fourth of the population of Luling, which might explain the smaller structure. This gesture to the Southern black became part of the Davis folklore in the incorrect story that he built a golf course for his servants when they were barred from the local white greens.[15]

It is interesting that as Davis prowled Caldwell and Guadalupe Counties in his quest for oil he became conscious of the blacks tending the numerous white cotton fields. He understood the drawbacks of the one-crop system, for the wildcatter had made his second fortune in scientific rubber farming, albeit with one crop. His Sumatra rubber plantations led in developing modern techniques such as bud grafting, and U.S. Rubber continued experimental programs after Davis' departure. Just as cotton often glutted the market, depressing prices, so had varying supplies of raw rubber caused a wildly fluctuating world market. Whereas rubber was probably the best crop suited for far off Sumatra, Davis sensed that the Luling farmer could better diversify. He was particularly concerned about the many farmers who had no oil under their land. Consequently, although the testimonials of Henry W. Grady and "New South" doctrines had not reached Luling (or had been ignored), Davis resolved to effect economic changes. He had already brought in industry; he now would industrialize agriculture.[16]

The contradiction between his increasing insistence that science be applied to the tillage of the soil and his own decreasing reliance on scientific advice for finding oil provides a dichotomy which Davis never cared to explain. He had made a reputation with the largest rubber company in the world by stern devotion to the application of expert knowledge and technological skill, and he invested a million dollars in trying to establish this precedent in Texas. Curiously, he continually discounted geology and petroleum engineering in his quest for oil and contradictorily expended a fortune on whims and hunches. In short, he became the extreme of wildcatters, one of "the greatest gamblers," one who chanced all in reckless abandon in search of a dream. As so many, who in centuries past came before him looking for minerals in the Southwest, he searched for El Dorado, and he seemed to enjoy taking risks.

His first strike, made by dismissing scientific advice, had rewarded him, and he invested part of his proceeds in promoting scientific agriculture. He bought a two-section cotton plantation with 900 acres cleared for cultivation and established the Luling Foundation Farm. The land runs from the Luling city limits westward along six miles of the winding San Marcos River and is bordered on the north by Highway 90. One of its landmarks is the largest oak tree in Caldwell County. Kelts C. Baker, originally a forester with Davis in Sumatra, immediately began diversification by planting 600 pecan trees and preparing the ground to produce high grade corn and sorghum seed for local farmers.

Baker sought advice from Texas A&M College professors on types of seed, planting, and cultivation. Next, he made arrangements to purchase registered Jersey stock in large lots at bargain prices and resell them to area farmers at cost. Bulls from the farm could be circulated among local farmers for a small fee.[17] Instructors in poultry raising, dairy farming, and horticulture from Texas A&M College began visitations in the summer of 1926 and continued to advise throughout the planning stages, and by January, 1927, the consensus was that proper diversification demonstrations should begin with dairying, poultry raising, and hog feeding. Davis requested that committees of interested area bankers, businessmen, and farmers form to make recommendations for managing the million dollar grant. Committee reports suggested additional programs along the lines already established on the model farm, including "bull circles," "boar circles," seed distribution, hatcheries, pure-bred stock importations, county fair prizes, educational courses, and marketing information.[18]

Kelts C. Baker, acting as trustee for the farm, brought in more practical experience by hiring Jack Shelton, county agent of Cooke County, in March 1927. A native of Coleman County, he graduated from Texas A&M College in 1917, attended officers' training school at Leon Springs, and became one of the youngest majors in World War I. Although a dairy specialist, Shelton had experience with many other branches of scientific farming. He stressed the practical nature of soil improvement, terracing, fertilization, crop rotation, herd management, improved seed, and intensive cultivation. An advisory during the planning stage, Shelton stayed on as general manager until 1935 and was effective in demonstrating how to make a success of farming through the essentials of intelligent management.[19]

Continuing in an advisory capacity during the developmental stage from Texas A&M College were Dean Edwin J. Kyler, head of the school of agriculture since 1920 and chairman of the Department of Horticulture; James C. Morgan, chairman of the Department of Agronomy, Duncan H. Reid, head of the Department of Poultry Science; and A. L. Darnell, professor of dairying.[20] Dean Kyle, who later became one of the original seven trustees to govern the farm locally, was ideally suited for working out the development of the Luling Foundation Farm. After graduating from Texas A&M in 1899, he took two advanced degrees at Cornell University before returning to A&M as professor of horticulture. In 1912 he served on the committee that established the new and expanded extension service at Texas A&M. He served his alma mater not only as a professor and department head but also as a worker for academic excellence and a supporter of the athletic program. His memory lives on in the stadium named Kyle Field.[21] Davis himself acknowledged a debt to Texas A&M by stipulating in the charter of the foundation that if the farm ever ceased to function in its intended capacity, then the title should pass immediately to Texas A&M College.[22]

The document establishing the farm reveals much of Davis' philosophy of life, his wildcatting experiences, and his attitude about material gain:

> That I, Edgar B. Davis, a bachelor, believing that the kind and gracious Providence Who guides the destinies of all humanity, directed me in the search for and the discovery of oil near Luling, Texas; and in our successful management and favorable outcome of the business; and believing that the wealth which has resulted has not come through any virtue or ability of mine but has been given in trust; and desiring to discharge in some measure the trust which has been reposed in me.
>
> NOW THEREFORE, in a Spirit of gratitude to the Giver of all good for His beneficence; and in consideration of the opportunity which the resources of Texas gave me, and of my interest in the welfare of

> the citizens of the City of Luling and of Caldwell, Guadalupe, and Gonzales Counties... have GIVEN... all of the following.[23]

Already aware of the discrimination against blacks, he may have had first-hand experience with occasional animosity against the rich; he was also aware that Texas was ruled by a single-party government. In any event, Davis expressly stated that gifts or favors should be distributed "without regard to the race, party, sex, creed or poverty or riches of the recipient."[24] In the end, those who received aid would be not only area farmers, but also sick and disabled persons or needy orphans. The board of trustees would determine the need.[25]

Davis' gift began with the 1200 acres, complete with buildings and stock (a total property value of $250,000) plus a $750,000 endowment fund which made up his million dollar pledge. June 6, 1927, marked the date of transfer to foundation status. Original trustees were Dr. Sidney J. Francis, Chairman; Dean Edwin J. Kyle; Andrew J. McKean, Sr.; Clarence L. Boothe; Charles H. Donegan, Walter Cardwell; and Edgar B. Davis.[26]

As it developed, the Luling Foundation became more of a demonstration farm than a dispenser of direct charity, although the two aims blended at times. In 1927, the Foundation sent $6,000 in relief funds to victims of a tornado in Rocksprings, Texas, and the same year it sent funds to sufferers along the flooding Mississippi River. It gave $1,000 to the Red Cross in 1930 for tornado relief, followed by another thousand in 1931 during the drought. There have been donations to the nearby Warm Springs Foundation for treatment of polio. (Incidentally, this therapy center was built around the warm waters which wildcatter John A. Otto discovered while drilling for oil and was funded by the donations of successful Texas wildcatter Hugh Roy Cullen.) Also the Foundation Farm gave regular grants listed under educational expenditures, to the boys' and girls' scouting programs, which totaled $200,000 in the first twenty years of operation.[27]

The Luling Foundation was first and foremost a model farm. Davis believed that "all things come from the soil."[28] The petroleum Davis found surely would be depleted, but his Foundation Farm, designed for permanence, should last as long as his "Mecca of the rubber growing world" in distant Sumatra.[29]

The farm undertook an educational program in 1934. Vocational training in the practical and scientific aspects of farming allowed youngsters to live the learning experience. After screening applicants, Foundation officials enrolled twenty men between eighteen and twenty-two years of age in a year's program designed to teach the principles of farming. Students drew $20.00 per month during their work-study year, receiving $15.00 in cash monthly and the $60.00 balance when completing the year. Room, board, and laundry service rounded out the remuneration. The food was good, the cottages comfortable, and the surroundings healthy, with magazines, newspapers, and books available. Trainees spent three months in dairying, three months in poultry science, three months working with livestock, and the last quarter of the year learning agronomy. Two nights a week they heard lectures, usually provided by Texas A&M College through the extension service. At the close of the session, a student could apply to attend one year at Texas A&M and continue to receive the $20.00 per month. From 1934 until 1941 and the outbreak of the war, the Farm educated 130 men in this manner.[30]

After World War II, the Luling Foundation ran a similar school for veterans who financed their way with the G.I. Bill of Rights. The British government sent a representative to attend this operation for a time. The Farm's Agricultural School for Veterans put together a combination of classroom study, individual instruction, and on-the-job training in farm practices and techniques.[31]

Edgar B. Davis, in 1937, conceived of the idea of a large freezer unit, mainly to aid local farmers in marketing their beef cooperatively, but also to provide farm and city dwellers alike with home-type freezing facilities. So many families took advantage of the individual rental freezer lockers that the trustees soon enlarged the entire plant.[32]

The Luling Foundation peaked as a model farm in the 1940's, becoming a scientific show place and an esthetic layout of practical grace an symmetry. But perfection in farming is as difficult to find as Davis' El Dorado of unlimited oil; the perfect farm would require exact weather, cooperative insects, and no new plant diseases. Despite the obstacles, the Luling Foundation for a time achieved the highest possible degree of performance.

At the present, the demonstration farm continues to serve mankind in a variety of ways. Its major resources are the 300-head of beef cattle making up the total livestock. The Luling Foundation continues to sponsor annual field days. Two separate cattle operations, pasture management with various grass varieties, pecan bottoms, and gardening are still featured in the 1992 demonstrations. After a recent barbeque the trustees presented two $1,000 scholarships to high school seniors planning to major in agriculture in college.[33] A Foundation spokesman made this significant point: "It's the closest thing to an experiment station or demonstration farm that we have anywhere near here."[34] Few small towns have had the advantages provided Luling, and the Foundation Farm remains an important adjunct to community well-being, particularly so under the capable direction of Texas A&M graduate Archie Abrameit, the current manager.

Davis called Luling his hometown, and he generously rewarded his adopted place of residence. But his roots were deep in Massachusetts, and he did not forget his city of origin nor his home state in his philanthropy. Upon returning to the Northeast, he announced his intentions of establishing the one-million-dollar Amy D. Pratt and Oscar C. Davis Foundation for charitable purposes, in Massachusetts in general and the Brockton area in particular. As in the case of the Luling Foundation, he affirmed that his own wealth was a special blessing of Providence and that he was merely passing it on to his fellow man. Residents of Brockton would understand Davis' honoring his deceased brother and sister in such a manner, for Amy and Oscar were well-known for their humanitarianism, even though the hallmark of their concern for the fellow man had always been to take no credit to themselves for their kindnesses. Edgar Davis further explained that he had also been inspired to charitable activities by the life styles of George E. Keith and Preston B. Keith of Brockton. To administer the Foundation "without regard to race, creed, or party," Davis named three trustees, George H. Leach, vice president of the George E. Keith Company; Joseph Machin, a retired minister; and Charles P. Holland, president of the Plymouth Realty Company.[35]

During the formalities of applying to the Massachusetts legislature for a charter, Davis and the acting trustees drew up a set of by-laws for the proposed charitable organization and submitted them to the scrutiny of Dr. Frederick Keppel, president of the Carnegie Foundation, and Ralph Hayes, president of the New York Community Trust Fund. These two directors, familiar with the administration of endowment funds designed for perpetuation, suggested that a foundation without a family name would more likely receive future donations to continue the good work.[36]

Davis followed this advice, sincerely believing "that after a lifetime of unostentatious charity, and with the greatest good to the greatest number in mind, that Amy and Oscar, if they were here, would approve of changing the name to 'The Pilgrim Foundation.'"[37] *Pilgrim* suggested the Calvinism and drive of their New England heritage. Also, the Davises traced their genealogy back to the *Mayflower* on both sides of the family lineage. Davis followed a suggestion from Keppel and Hayes that he continue his association with the Pilgrim Foundation as a board member.[38]

On Sunday, February 6, 1927, the wildcatter presented a million dollar check, the largest ever transacted by a Brockton bank, creating the institution and proclaiming "that the funds for the Foundation about to be created for the benefit of humanity came from the Good God Himself. I sign these papers to the Honor and Glory of God."[39] The by-laws stipulated a selection of three trustees chosen by and from a board of seven directors originally organized to include Davis for life; three to be appointed each year by Davis, and three more annual appointments, one by the mayor of Brockton, another by the president of the Central Labor Union of Brockton, and a third by the President of the Brockton Chamber of Commerce. Davis' acting trustees, Leech, Holland, and Machin, were then elected to be official Foundation trustees by directors Davis, H. Lawton Blanchard, Dr. Peirce H. Leavitt, and John P. Meade. Davis was named president; Joseph Machin, treasurer; and the single employee, Mary L. Papineau, secretary. Income from the principal was designated for general charitable and educational purposes, particularly for needy orphans and children.[40]

Immediate aid rather than bureaucratic delays became the guiding principle of the Pilgrim Foundation, as Papineau, who also acted as field worker, investigated cases and quickly distributed cash, clothes, or medical attention as needed. The one million produced $50,000 a year, of which $40,000 annually went to charity. Quick aid carried the risk of rewarding a few undeserving cases, but the trustees preferred a few mistakes to having someone in need do without. One Boston newspaper called the Pilgrim Foundation "the most unusual charity in New England."[41]

This endowed institution has retained its distinctive nature for a half century. In these fifty years, a family member has been associated with directing the trust. Since Edgar B. Davis' death, his nephew Lincoln Davis, who was present at the founding ceremonies and who is a son of Oscar Davis, has been a trustee. In recent history, The Pilgrim Foundation, now grown to two million dollars through careful investments and donations, emphasizes giving assistance to young men and women attending college. Interestingly, recipients are not asked to reimburse The Pilgrim Foundation, but rather to give what help they can to other individuals in the spirit of the Davises of Brockton.[42]

"The man who gave Brockton a million" also made a contribution of two $50,000 swimming pools to his hometown area. One, completed by mid-summer at Campello in South Brockton, was near the old natural "swimming hole" where Davis and his boyhood friends used to cool off. The other, in use by the end of the summer, was in North Brockton at Montello. The facilities included wading pools for tots, large dressing rooms, and a landscaped park area around the pools. Designed to be self-supporting, the arrangement provided for small charges. Originally, children paid a nickel and adults a dime, whereas non-residents of Brockton could enjoy a swim for fifteen cents. Moral standards of the time and place banned "mixed bathing"; consequently, women and girls observed a different swimming schedule from men and boys. Boston newspapers proclaimed the pools the most up-to-date in the United States.[43] They are still in use today, and although time has dimmed their modernity, the group swimming policy conforms to present lifestyles.

Davis made other "minor" donations. A golfer during his younger days, Davis contributed $15,000 toward the cost of a golf course that was under construction in a Brockton park. At this point Davis had bestowed over three million dollars on his fellow man. A Brockton editorial writer, reflecting on this depletion of a fortune, made this incisive observation: "A million trips easily off the tongue. Assembling such a sum, dollar by dollar, represents a goal that but few men obtain."[44] The wildcatter was fast becoming the legendary "Edgar B. Davis, American rubber and oil magnate renowned for carrying generosity to the limits of eccentricity."[45]

The man who did so much for the city which had nurtured him during his youth, and for the Texas town which he had begun to call his home, had already shown a knack for remembering single individuals. There was one other personality whom most people did not recall and, in a way, whom even time had forgotten, but whom Edgar B. Davis did not neglect. The background of this story begins in South America at the time of Davis' birth and in some way symbolizes a synthesis of Davis' philosophy of the interdependence of various capitalistic endeavors in the free enterprise system. According to historian Walter P. Webb, the New World, beginning with the flow of gold and silver in the 1500's, began to enrich the older, "civilized" area of the globe. New

World products soon included an interesting array of material goods. "Scientists," Webb points out,

> brought home strange plants and herbs and made plant experiment stations in scores of European gardens. In South America they found the bark of a tree from which quinine was derived to cure the plague of malaria and another plant which was sent to the East Indies to establish the rubber industry and add to the fortunes of Holland and Britain.[46]

What Webb does not mention is that the "plant," Hevea, was illegally taken from South America, for Brazil forbade the exportation of seeds or plants. Sir Clements Markham, who had purloined quinine plants from South America, tried unsuccessfully to encourage others to smuggle Hevea seeds to England. Later, Sir William Jackson Hooker, director of the Royal Botanical Gardens at Kew, pursued Hevea through correspondence with Henry A. Wickham, an Englishman in the Amazon experienced in extracting Hevea milk. Combining a bold stroke with a run of extraordinary luck, Wickham managed clandestinely to send enough seeds to Hooker to produce 3,000 healthy plants in Kew by 1876.[47]

The British and the Dutch, and ultimately Davis, profited mightily from this illicit activity. However, Wickham did not fare so well. Although King George formally and officially recognized his "work" by knighting him in 1920, Sir Henry's pension of 100 pounds a year still left him in straightened circumstances. He had no other source of income and was burdened by costly medical bills. A Bostonian, Quincy Tucker, long associated with rubber growing in many parts of the world, upon running into Wickham at conventions and rubber exhibitions, sensed the plight of the old pioneer. Tucker launched a one-man campaign to raise money for the Hevea seed hero. Although the British Rubber Growers' Association declined to give aid, the International Association for Rubber Cultivation at the Hague provided 500 pounds for the years 1923 and 1924, and the Rubber Association of America began sending Wickham 100 pounds a year. Funds were still insufficient, however, when Tucker found Davis. He had met Edgar B. Davis in 1909 in Massachusetts, followed his successful career in rubber, and traced him to Luling in 1924. Davis responded at the time that his own fortunes were unsteady but that when the oil came, he would reward Wickham in a handsome manner.[48]

In May of 1926, Davis having decided to send a cash gift to Wickham, determined to raise further contributions from American businessmen, arguing that tire and auto manufacturing, oil and gasoline production and consumption were all dependent upon the plantation rubber industry and all were indebted to Wickham.[49] Davis proved no more successful than Tucker, but, characteristically, he made his own gift a sizable one. Davis sent 1,000 pounds to Wickham on the latter's eightieth birthday, May 29, 1926, and the recipient "was perfectly delighted and quite overcome at the generosity manifested." Wickham also "referred rather bitterly to the fact that the British Government had done nothing for him except to give him a 'blap on the shoulder.'"[50] Sir Henry declared that Davis, a pioneer in his own way, was a fellow who could understand the risks he took a half century earlier some 600 miles up the Amazon.[51] Davis sent 5,000 pounds to Wickham the next month,[52] making his total gift 6,000 pounds or twenty-five thousand American dollars.[53]

Writing from "one pioneer" to "another," Wickham vowed he would "never forget...that most generous gift expression of appreciation of endeavour..."[54] Wickham's return gifts included several souvenir seeds from the actual Amazon caper, as well as a number of primitive art works by the old Hevea thief. These drawings of jungle scenes evoke memories of rain forests and tall, tropical trees simmering in an equatorial heat.[55] Whatever Davis thought artistically of the Wickham drawings the record does not show. But his love of the arts in general--painting, music, the theatre, literature--is on record, for Davis unloaded a vast sum as patron of the arts with, as examined in the next chapter, mixed results.

Chapter VIII
THE PLAY'S THE THING

Edgar B. Davis spent a million dollars trying to keep that turkey running on Broadway.

Walter Winchell

Edgar B. Davis loved classical music, played dilettante concert piano extremely well, and regularly enjoyed cantatas, operas, and symphonies. A true aficionado, he daily discussed opera with his Boston-Italian immigrant shoe shine man. Davis shelled out the exorbitant pre-World War I price of ten dollars a ticket for front row seats for Huibreght Ketner and him to hear Enrico Caruso in New York. That night Caruso hit his flats and sharps to Davis' immense satisfaction, but when Davis turned to beam benevolently upon his guest he found Ketner fast asleep, mouth open, his snores drowned out by Caruso's powerful tenor. Davis treasured this story as much as he revered the arts, and here is Davis the patron in summary. He adored the arts, he wanted to share them with his friends, he was willing to be extravagant, but his pretentions were tempered at times by his sense of humor. While his oil fortune lasted, Davis, from 1926 to 1929, gave vigorous financial support to encourage painting, music, literature, and drama. These contributions, though sometimes admirable and at all times generous, often resulted in more attention for their profuse munificence than for their aesthetic judgment. This was particularly the case in his largest and most unusual expenditure during the time he backed "the biggest flop on Broadway" as angel of *The Ladder*.

A chance conversation with an old home-town friend germinated the project. The story began in the Brockton public schools. Seated next to each other alphabetically, Edgar Davis and J. Frank Davis, who was no relation, became boyhood chums through their association in the classroom. As adults, their careers took them in separate directions: Edgar Davis, from shoes, to rubber, to oil; J. Frank Davis, into newspaper work in Boston. After Admiral Robert E. Peary had discovered the North Pole in 1909, J. Frank Davis journeyed to the Arctic to interview the explorer. While there, he slipped on the ice and seriously injured his spine. Forced to discontinue active newspaper work, he traveled southwestward for his health, eventually settling in San Antonio, where he supported himself by short-story writing for magazines.[1]

In the Alamo City the paths of the two Brocktonians crossed, and they renewed their friendship over numerous hands of bridge. Once in a conversation on the subject of reincarnation, J. Frank pointed out to Edgar the statement that Jesus made about John the Baptist in Matthew 11:14: "And if ye are willing to receive it, this is Elijah that is to come." Edgar, a Biblical scholar, was also steeped in Emerson's essays and quite familiar with the theme of "Compensation." Along with Emerson, he believed that sometime, somewhere, there was eventual happiness for everyone. The oilman challenged his friend to write a play, which Edgar would produce, utilizing the transmigration of souls as a vehicle to illustrate the theme of mankind's achieving a state of well-being and good fortune.[2]

Thereupon J. Frank Davis authored *The Ladder*, which traces a group in four settings over a 600-year time period. In the prologue of the play, Margaret Newell, the heroine, torn between the love of two men in 1926 New York City, falls asleep and dreams three previous existences, beginning in the year 1300 in an English castle. The same characters then successively appear in London in 1679 and then in New York's Bowery in 1844. When Newell rouses from sleep to the Manhattan of 1926 she also awakens to the solution of her problem based on the visions of her earlier lives.[3] Davis selected the title from *Gradatim*, by Josiah Gilbert Holland: "Heaven is not reached at a single bound, but we build the ladder by which we rise from the lowly earth to the vaulted skies, and we mount to its summit round by round."[4]

To enhance the talents of his amateur playwright, Edgar Davis employed a well-known man about Broadway, Brock Pemberton, to produce *The Ladder*, which opened in New York's Mansfield Theatre October 21, 1926. The experienced and established performers Antoinette Perry and Edgar Stehli were surrounded by expensive sets, but the critics lashed out in negative criticisms. Alexander Woolcott rated the drama "a large, richly upholstered piece of nothing at all."[5] Brooks Atkinson, though impressed by the sets and the leading lady, borrowed from Samuel Johnson for summary: "Declamation roar'd, whilst Passion slept."[6] Leading critics were at least consistent in disdain: Percy Hammond complained in the *Herald Tribune*: "it is not with the author's belief in earthly immortality that playgoers will be dissatisfied. They will quarrel rather with the incredible naivete of its presentment--slow, muddled, amateurish..."[7] In addition to the unfavorable publicity, Broadway offered at the same time some heady competition: *Naughty Riquette*, with Mitzi; Florence Reed in *The Shanghai Gesture*; *Sex*, starring Mae West; *Sunny*, with Marilyn Miller; *An American Tragedy*; and *Abie's Irish Rose*, running its fifth straight year at the time.[8]

While theatergoers trooped all winter to the other Broadway productions, *The Ladder* drew an average of thirty persons per performance. Davis livened up the dreary prospects of the cast, crew, and technicians with sumptuous dinners at leading night spots where he lavished gifts on them. When summer's heat oppressed the stage, the oil man eliminated Saturday performances, surprising the cast by insisting that there be no salary cuts. As the play shifted from the Mansfield Theatre to the Waldorf and later to the Lyric, Davis exhibited his penchant for sharing his wealth with all his employees, including maids and scrubwomen.[9]

The speculative Davis, needing a rewrite of his play, bought out Brock Pemberton's contract, formed a new company, hired Brock's brother Murdock, an experienced Broadway advertising figure, and determined to revamp his play. Moss Hart, who later wrote and directed some of the great American stage comedies and musicals, including *You Can't Take It With You* and *The Man Who Came to Dinner*, was ambitious to make his mark on Broadway at this time. He heard of the antics of this "crazy Texan" and toyed with the idea of offering his unproved services in hopes of sharing in the windfall but then rejected the idea of approaching Davis as impractical. Eugene O'Neill turned down a handsome offer, but the current actors jumped into the re-writing. Edgar Stehli and Murdock Pemberton polished the lines, while Margaret Anglin, who had become fascinated with Davis' extravagant and kindly benevolence to her profession, stepped into the role of directrix, and Carol McComas performed as the new leading lady. Robert Edmond Jones, scene director of world renown, redesigned the stage in lovely and costly new sets and decked out the performers in matching costumes.[10]

On the whole, players acted their parts seriously as the established professionals they were, but some were just riding Davis' theatrical train as far as it would take them. Irene Purcell, one of the female leads, explained: "We play the roles in which we are cast. This is no sinecure. We respect Mr. Davis' ideals and we are working our hardest. If he chooses to spend his money this way rather than on a gold-plated motor car and a kennel of poodle dogs, that is his business."[11] On the other hand, Philip Merivale quit after one frustrating year, although he had saved a tidy sum before leaving *The Ladder.*[12]

Publicity-minded Davis offered the startling innovation that one could have his money back if he were not pleased with the performance. A desperate Davis advertised ten weekly $500 cash prizes for the best essay on *The Ladder.* But more people entered the contest than attended the play, for New York lottery laws forbade the requirement of viewing the show to participate in the contest. This led one journalist wag to quip that the meanest man anywhere was one who won the $500 prize, then went to the play for the first time and asked for his money back. In November of 1927, Davis, who had squandered $750,000 on his Broadway dry hole, enlisted an extraordinary advertising gimmick: starting Thanksgiving Day, 1927, he would present the drama free of charge. If a packed house was the goal, the device worked, complete with a queue stretching from the box office down the block and around the corner. A cross section of New Yorkers formed this line, from ticket scalpers (who sold their free tickets to those at the end of the line) to ditchdiggers in mud-caked clothes to neatly uniformed chauffeurs picking up tickets for the executive waiting comfortably in a parked limousine. From this motley crowd, reminiscent of the afternoon playgoers of Elizabethan England, one might catch a conversation much more fascinating than the dialogue inside:

> "I seen this show last night."
> "Yeah?"
> "Sure, and I seen it last week too."
> "But I hear it ain't so hot."
> "No, but what'ya expect for nothing."[13]

The flop packed them in as long as everyone was a guest of the house, and *The Ladder* even set two records: by the last week of February, 1928, the drama completed the longest run of any play then showing in New York; it also marked a new height for Broadway shows as a money loser.[14]

Already a unique figure of known eccentricity, Davis' Broadway antics fit securely into the ballyhoo days of the roaring twenties. "It was a fabulous era," recalled Murdock Pemberton, "and at the time he did not seem to be much more than one of the world-proper citizens. I realize now, how different he was."[15] Among the historic angels of Broadway who had backed theatrical productions over the years for a variety of reasons, the extraordinary impact of Davis carved a niche in the folklore and myth of American theatre annals.[16]

There is a story, probably apocryphal, that at one performance only one man made up the audience, and as the only person in the house, he moved closer to the stage between acts. Mid-way through the second act, a second patron came in, who, as fate would have it, had purchased the lone occupied seat. Not one to miss an opportunity for a little dramatic humor, the usher required the startled interloper to move. On another occasion, the husband of directrix Margaret Anglin, assuming that a rehearsal was going on in front of a few scattered onlookers, startled the small but legitimate audience by noisily strolling down the aisle leading his terrier and delivering her sack lunch from in front of the footlights.[17]

To Murdock Pemberton, the most fantastic event in his association with Davis--overall "the most pleasant, exciting and unbelievable chapters" of his life--occurred when the millionaire packed him off to Europe in response to a conversational whim. Pemberton mused that he had never seen the Louvre. Davis launched into whirlwind preparations, purchased him new luggage, secured a rushed-up passport, arranged a complete letter of credit, and gave him $500 cash for tips. Of course, Pemberton could publicize *The Ladder* on his journey. The startled fellow sailed in three days, touring not only the famous Paris art gallery but also sightseeing in Berlin, Vienna, Budapest, and London.[18]

The play ran into the year 1928 at a loss of $12,000 to $15,000 a week, while Davis, who never lingered on one continent too long in those days, embarked on an around the world jaunt, this time intending to rattle across Russia on the Trans-Siberian Railway. He kept in touch with *The Ladder's* fortunes by cable, instructing the recharging of admissions in June. In August he dispatched a dramatic cable from Moscow directing the closing of the play, if by a certain date it did not become a success.[19] As printed in all New York papers, it read:

> With a decent respect for public opinion, let me give my reasons for putting on *The Ladder*. We see life about us full of suffering, seeming inequalities, and injustices. When we accept the statements of scientists that the universe has been millions of years in the making it seems to me that this brief span of three-score years and ten cannot be God's best plan for the world, but rather than our sufferings, griefs, mistakes, and dissappointments [sic] are but the necessary precedents to our coming into harmony with a Great Plan of Life, in which we achieve our hearts' desires or-- something better. It was Faith in this ultimate universal success that induced me to put on *The Ladder*. It embodied no creed; it promoted no cult. The idea of reincarnation was the motif used to indicate the steps of progress towards this ultimate goal. Theatre owners, players, staffs, and the public have had everything to gain from our endeavor to widen the scope of the theatre; but a play, like any other business, should pay its own way in order to avoid becoming a parasite on the economic body. And while I believe we have a powerful play, as fundamental in its philosophy as the plays of the ancient Greeks and with adequate entertainment value, yet if *The Ladder* in substantially its present form at the Cort Theatre, does not give evidence of being self-sustaining by about November first, it will be withdrawn.[20]

The Ladder is certainly not classical material, but Davis sincerely spoke from good intentions. He would never, however, escape from the image which connected in the popular mind his residence in the Far East with his belief in the theory of reincarnation. In reality the transmigration of souls was simply, as Davis insisted, a theme used to present the concept of a balancing force in life so that the underprivileged eventually got their share. He was closer to fellow New Englander Ralph W. Emerson's expressions in "Compensation" than he was to any Eastern religion. Once caught up in the aura of the theatre, he resorted to his natural instinct to keep on in a venture, particularly where the odds and professional advice were against him. The story of his oil fortune was that of an undertaking that went badly at first and then, when all seemed hopeless, made a dramatic turn-around with a gusher. He could no more call a halt to the play than he could cease the fruitless deep drilling for hidden oil in Luling--as long as he had funds, that is.[21]

The New York run closed on November 10, 1928, with the 47-member cast playing to an audience of 75, who were also guests to the party Davis gave on the stage after the show. There he made a rare gesture for him in accepting a gift. The gold Howard pocket watch from the cast still keeps perfect time after 64 years in his nephew Lincoln Davis's keeping. Each actor's name is engraved on the watch chain.[22]

As a theatrical postscript Davis staged the production for a two-week Boston run, playing to packed and paying houses and to bad reviews in the Boston press. There the final curtain fell on another chapter in eccentricity, adding more to the Davis legend. The account books showed an expenditure of $1,255,384.11, a record loss that should hold its own for another half century even with modern inflation.[23] The extreme waste, so quaintly curious today, appeared shamefully excessive in the 1930's, causing Walter Winchell to make the observation that Davis would have gotten his message across better by wrapping a sandwich in a pamphlet and giving it away.[24]

In his own way, Davis was sensitive to the needs around him. When J.Frank Davis tried to return to short-story writing after a two year involvement with Edgar and *The Ladder*, he found that he had lost touch with editors and had difficulty in reentering the market. Edgar Davis gave his old friend $5,000 in January of 1928 to make the transition back to his craft. When a sinus infection further incapacitated the writer in the summer of 1929, Edgar commissioned him to revise the play for $1,000 and also sent $500 expense money to deliver the altered version to Brock Pemberton in New York.[25]

This was the last time Davis had any great sum of money to spend on his pet project, for hard times were around the bend. In the decade to come J. Frank wrote and edited for the WPA, whereas Edgar found troubles enough in the oil he brought in but could not market profitably. He still talked of making a success of the drama when the next million-dollar field came in. Even as late as 1950, Davis commissioned his long-time associate, David Figart, to approach successful British film producer J. Arthur Rank about a movie version of his pet play. Rank appeared interested at first and inquired how much money Davis was willing to put in. When Figart replied that

Davis meant only to contribute the play, Rank courteously declined.[26]

Whereas *The Ladder* set records of doubtful significance, Edgar Davis promoted art in Texas with a crowning success. Support of oil paintings of Texas landscapes and farm and ranch scenes originated in the most difficult days of Davis' search for oil. When Davis wildcatted in the spring and summer of 1922 with his credit stretched to the breaking point, he found comfort in the lovely wildflowers of the Luling area. They symbolized to him a rebirth of hope.[27] He particularly related to the bluebonnet, the state flower of Texas and the same blossom that inspired folklorist J. Frank Dobie to observe that "no other flower--for me at least--brings such upsurging of the spirit and at the same time such restfulness."[28]

Now millionaire Davis paid tribute to the natural beauty of Texas that sustained him during his lonely quest for oil by financing competitions in art that captured the loveliness and native toughness of the wildflowers of the Lone Star State. Beginning in 1927, he sponsored, under the direction of the San Antonio Art League, a series of three annual contests for oil paintings of the natural scenery of Texas, with prizes totaling $53,000. Davis put up $5,000 for the best painting of Texas wildflowers by any United States artist who had gained national prominence and who held membership in a recognized art organization, but any Texas artist who did not compete in the national contest could enter the $1,000 competition limited to painters from the Lone Star State. Davis arranged to show the paintings nationally and then to donate the national winning canvas to the Lotus Club of New York and the first-place Texas oil to the Whitte Museum in San Antonio. Six thousand dollars, the largest cash award ever offered in the United States for paintings, astonished the art community.[29]

Mrs. Henry P. Drought, president of the Art League, directed the arrangements. Judges Charles C. Curran, corresponding secretary of the National Academy of Design; Henry B. Snell, president of the New York Water Color Club; and French etcher, Edouard Leon, pronounced English-born Dawson Dawson-Watson's "The Glory of the Morning" the best among 350 entries for the $5,000 prize. Drawn from St. Louis for the contest, Dawson-Watson set up his easel and captured a cactus scene in the rugged hill country northwest of the Alamo City. His artistic temperament fit in so well with the atmosphere that he made San Antonio his permanent home. Spanish immigrant to San Antonio, Jose Arpa, took the $1,000 award with "Flower Mead," a scene of

Texas wildflowers nestled in the rugged hill country. The popular show ran a month to visitors numbering 30,000 adults and 10,000 school children, moving Davis to announce a second contest for the next year with additional categories and even more prize money.[30]

In the spring of 1928, Davis set up prizes aggregating $14,500, with the top awards in the national category of Texas wildflowers ranging from $1,000 to $2,500. National artists could also compete in the Texas Ranch Life section or the division called Texas Cotton Fields. Awards in these two areas ranged from $1,000 to $1,500. A Texas wildflower division served only Texas artists with $1,000 and $1,500 awards.[31] Ellworth Woodward of New Orleans and New Yorkers Alphaeus Cole and Abbott Graves judged the ninety finalists selected from the 600 canvases submitted. Artists from twenty states participated, and officials were unanimous in their praise of the show.[32]

Newspaper coverage was widespread since Davis broke his own record for prize money awarded in art competition in the United States. The Texas press heralded Davis' gesture of recognizing both the beauty of the state and the native artist, and some of the national newspapers commented favorably, particularly on Davis' encouragement of Texas artistic genius.[33] But stereotyping of Texana raised its prejudiced head in Manhattan and in the Windy City. The Chicago *News* categorized the contest as third-rate art competing for first-class prize money and rated the champion picture as "indistinguishable."[34] The *New York Times* scoffed at the show, on display at Columbia University's Avery Hall by special invitation of Dr. Nicholas Murray Butler, as unimpressive. *The New Yorker* could not hide admiration for the figure of the cash prize but rated the canvases as assembly-line production, snorting that "These paintings took down $15,000 of some man's money."[35]

Time proved Davis' tastes correct. Southwestern art scenes of the same genre--wildflowers, cactus, decaying oaks, and ancient fences--command high prices today. Furthermore, this medium has held steady on the market for some years. Undaunted as usual by negative criticism, Davis proclaimed $31,500 in awards for 1929 spring's flowering, and as the prize money shot up so did both the number of artists entering and the variety of states they represented. He had created genuine national attention.[36] A pilgrimage of artists descended on San Antonio to authenticate their productions. The outcome was 139 finalists ranging from the modernistic to the traditionalist. Judges Cole and Graves were assisted this year by Herman Dudley Murphy of

Lexington, Massachusetts. These men concluded that Davis had succeeded in making San Antonio the art center of the south. Davis evidently concurred in this judgment, for he ceased his underwriting of the contest and talked in terms of a future national competition to record the whole of the American scene.[37]

Davis definitely left his mark on San Antonio, a city long noted for its cultural charm. Sidney Lanier found it enchanting in 1872, and even to the cynical Larry McMurtry, it remains "the one truly lovely city in the state," maintaining "an ambiance that all the rest of our cities lack." To McMurtry, "it is of Texas, and yet it transcends Texas in some way, as San Francisco transcends California, as New Orleans transcends Louisiana."[38] Appealingly, the city evoked the tradition and the atmosphere that inspired artists to remain, some establishing private studios and art schools. Art colonies have flourished to the present day.[39]

Charm and grace of setting are only part of any attraction to creative persons, and even the most aesthetic artist must eventually gain some funds. Davis' awards stimulated the move of the artist to Southwest Texas, just as in the second half of the twentieth century the booming conditions of Texas, particularly in Houston, attracted the artist by feeding his needs with boom-town profits. In the 1970's *Southwest Art*, one of the most beautiful and costly of all the current publications devoted to painting and sculpture, quite naturally thrives out of new-rich Houston. The magazine perpetuates the beauty of Texas flora and landscape throughout a large percentage of its pages, which are lovingly put together by hand, making the publication a minor work of art itself.

Through contests and art shows, Davis shared the natural beauties of Texas with the rest of the nation. In return, during the three years of the art competition he arranged to provide the San Antonio area free concerts by New York's resident opera talent. For consecutive seasons he bussed professionals from the East to Texas to sing Easter music. Socially, he rubbed shoulders with these same musicians in his private life during this period of the big money.

Hosting gala affairs was an inherent tendency with Davis, and after the oil affluence came he built his spacious A House in the Oaks in Luling. In addition, he renovated an old estate on Buzzards Bay, Massachusetts, the palatial A House on the Sand, largely for the purpose of entertaining. Entertaining was commonplace at both locations, but the New England summer resort became legendary for elegant parties and concerts. At these stylish occasions, highly paid artists performed to select groups who either stayed for a sumptuous dinner party or else adjourned to nearby restaurants at the oil man's expense. At intervals, Davis himself, a fine pianist, accompanied some diva in her number.[40] Davis hosted twenty-one of these lavish musical presentations at A House on the Sand in the summers of 1925 and 1926.[41] These profuse entertainments persisted to the end of the 1920's as Davis continued his individual patronage of the arts. For instance, tenor Richard Crooks resonated through the rooms of A House on the Sand in July, 1927, for $500, with Davis laying $50 on his accompanist. Lesser-known baritone, Frederick Baer, enriched Davis' audience the same month for only $250.[42]

These same artists entertained in the Southwest and at Brockton, Massachusetts, each Easter, courtesy of Edgar B. Davis, who staged "The Seven Last Words of Christ," a cantata by Theodore Dubois. This Scriptural story of the Crucifixion, set to music in arias and choruses with orchestral accompaniment, deeply moved capacity audiences in the Brockton Theatre and San Antonio's Municipal Auditorium. Both cities staged a second free presentation of the famed oratorio to accommodate the large crowds. Seats were particularly scarce in Brockton in 1928, and Davis insisted on standing in line himself to hear the free music.[43]

For the special solos, Davis provided top entertainers who drew $1,000 or $750 for their musical services plus $250 each for travel expenses.[44] The philanthropist also continued his memorable habit of rewarding all who had a part in staging one of his productions. Stagehands, ushers, doormen, check women, and scrubwomen pocketed a $20 gold piece as a momenta of the occasion.[45] Second only to the actual performance in Brockton in 1928 was the live broadcasting of the oratorio through Station WEEI of the Edison Electrical Illuminating Company of Boston,[46] a technological first for the times.

Davis occupied himself in promotion and advancement of the arts erratically. *The Ladder* flopped enormously; the wildflower painting contests blossomed ostentatiously and successfully; and the free concerts hit a high level of sophistication. Edgar Davis' literary involvement grew out of a peculiar misunderstanding between two longtime friends about expenditures for the *North American Review*, one of the most historic, respected, and scholarly journals in the country. Davis believed his outlay of the purchase price to be a one-time disbursement. Because Walter B. Mahony understand the underwriting as a permanent commitment, the association turned into a long-standing financial involvement. That their mutual feeling of esteem remained throughout the ordeal of keeping afloat a floundering magazine is a tribute to the concept of friendship and a memorial to an age that sill produced gentlemen marked by an exclusiveness of manners. Just who was right and who was wrong in their verbal agreement will never be known.

In 1907, on his first voyage around the world, Davis met fellow-traveler Walter B. Mahony, and the two finished the journey together, initiating a lifetime friendship. A lawyer by training, Mahony rarely practiced this profession and instead was a successful bond salesman in New York. On the trip the two men conceived the idea of America's entrance into the plantation rubber industry. Ultimately Davis brought about the United States Rubber Company holdings in Sumatra, and he and Mahony were large stockholders in that company. At one point in the plantation development, Mahony's friendship was indispensable to Davis in beneficially refinancing the U.S. Rubber overseas operations. For years they had worked on creating an international rubber company by a proposal to merge the giants of that industry. In this way they hoped to stabilize the price of crude rubber, a commodity known to fluctuate drastically. Then Davis was side-tracked into the oil venture.

During his free-spending days Davis quite naturally wanted to remember his friend and associate of over two decades of global business. When mixing money and friendship, a spoken understanding seems sufficient for the moment, and yet after the passage of time each party remembers the agreement differently. Here occurred a case in point. In conversation, in the summer of 1926 in New York City, Davis asked Walter Mahony if there were any desire that oil money could make possible for him. Mahony replied that he would like to own and edit the *North American Review.*[47]

This was the oldest continuing magazine in America and, as such, had a distinguished history. Founded in 1815 under the editorship of William Tudor, Jr., the periodical flourished for more than a century with editors of cosmopolitan experience; contributors of prominence in literature, scholarship, and public affairs; and a serious readership of distinguished Americans and Europeans who looked on the journal as an authoritative source of current and past history and a forum for the debate of new issues by the intellectuals of the nineteenth century. Thomas Jefferson was an early subscriber, and ten presidents contributed articles over the years. William Cullen Bryant's

"Thanatopsis" and Alan Seeger's "I have a Rendezvous With Death" first appeared between its covers, as did Mark Twain's "To a Person Sitting in Darkness." The *North American Review* entered the twentieth century as an acknowledged literary influence in the United States and a vital force in politics and general affairs.[48]

In 1899, Colonel George Harvey, whose fortune had been made in electric railways, bought and became editor of the *North American Review*, a position he held longer than any other director of the magazine. During his editorship he was also president of Harper and Brothers Publishers from 1900 to 1915, and from 1921 to 1923 he served as Ambassador to Great Britain. In 1906 Harvey began the original editorial department in the *North American Review*, thus giving the periodical its first personal slant.[49] Harvey mixed an intense patriotism with his editorials during World War I: "Our chief duty before God and Man is to KILL HUNS" he raged in his magazine.[50]

In October, 1926, Davis put up the money for Mahony to buy the *Review*, but the exact nature of the purchase is unclear. Walter B. Mahony remembered the transaction this way: In conversation, Davis stated to Mahony, "I'll buy it for you and back it until it gets on its feet. Whatever price is satisfactory to you would be agreeable to me."[51] Mahony immediately negotiated with Colonel Harvey, who agreed to reduce his $75,000 asking price to the $50,000 Mahony offered.[52]

Davis remembered the incident differently. Davis maintained that he never intended to put in more than the purchase price, unless the magazine began to exhaust Mahony's finances. Furthermore, Davis was certain that he had reserved the option to repurchase the *North American Review* for the price paid to Harvey plus six percent interest.[53] To further complicate the misunderstanding, Davis always believed that Mahony paid too much for a magazine operating in the red. Davis was sure that he could have bargained better with Harvey and reduced the purchase price. Here Davis showed the dichotomous nature of his businessman-philanthropist personality. He never loaned money; rather, he made it a gift. However, in any business deal, he drove a hard bargain. Business was business. "Do you see any green here?" he asked while pulling at his lower eyelid, his favorite gesture when bragging on his own sharp trading instincts.[54]

But Davis met the $50,000 arrangement with Harvey,[55] and Mahony became editor and owner. Though Mahony drew no salary, within two years he had put in $50,000 of his own money[56] and had devoted the time and energy necessary to improve the magazine's fortunes. He changed the appearance of the type, making the format more attractive. He attracted writers with newsworthy contributions: Amy Lowell and Lincoln Steffens commented in the *Review*; Nicholas Murray Butler (Mahony's brother-in-law) and other college presidents shared their views in articles; and the English writers Gilbert K. Chesterton and V. Sackville-West represented two of the several distinguished foreign correspondents. The list ran to political commentators, and from Vice President Charles Dawes to cabinet members, and congressmen. Mahony also sought out new talent both to write articles and to help him plan the publication. He employed as an associate editor the experienced Kenneth Wilcox Payne from *McClure's* in 1929. Mahony's efforts more than doubled circulation.[57]

These exertions revitalizing the *North American Review* caused the editorship to become a physical and financial burden to Mahony. But when Mahony began to entertain the idea of selling out, Davis advised against such a move, and contributed $40,000 between July, 1928 and January of the next year toward keeping the journal running successfully.[58]

At the start of the new year Mahony projected that a quarter of a million dollar investment would make the *North American Review* a paying magazine; he suggested approaching Cyrus Eaton or Clarence Dillon as possible investors. The alternative to raising funds was to sell property, Mahony concluded.[59] Still, the tone of Mahony's correspondence reflected a buoyance of spirit lasting down to the Ides of March, 1929, when he definitely wanted out from under the responsibility of restoring "the fine old periodical back to its well-deserved place of leadership," which had been his "aim and confident hope since it was taken over in the fall of 1926."[60]

Davis offered a counter-proposal establishing Davis as owner, and Mahony as a salaried editor. Under these terms, which Mahony accepted,[61] Davis gave Mahony a three-year note for $111,699 to cover the $50,000 paid Harvey in 1926 plus the $50,000 invested by Mahony since that date, with six percent interest added to the $50,000 contributed by Mahony. The note itself bore six percent interest, and the *North American Review* represented the security for the debt. The agreement further stipulated that Davis would provide operating expenses for nine months, including Mahony's salary of $10,000 per year. Mahony would head up the operation for this time period. At the expiration of nine months, Davis was to take over the *Review* as owner and director of editorial policy. Mahony would remain as editor.

Characteristically, Davis hoped to work out a profit-sharing plan for all employees, provided the magazine became a financial success.[62]

Once again the two friends were caught up in the momentum of a great enterprise together, and the project pressed on with a new mood. Davis vowed to take a renewed interest. Heretofore anything that he "ever said with reference to *North American* was on material and not on Spiritual grounds. "However," he continued, "my interest has now come in the line of Faith and I believe that the Faith in which I entered it and in which you will manage it will be justified by works and crowned with success."[63] These statements fairly breathe the very air of Davis' brand of Calvinism. In other words, for the true believer, uphill struggles diligently overcome result in rewards commensurate with the travail. Mahony, whose enthusiasm had only waned once in the venture, was no less committed. "I shall continue," he pledged to his old friend, "to wholeheartedly seek the success of the oldest monthly in America and covet your counsel not only editorially but in making the property sound and profitable."[64]

The bright future, so anticipated in the spring, dimmed with the hard times that began in the fall, and even though the vital forces of the two capitalists remained strong, funds became short as they approached the 1930's. Although Davis advanced a thousand dollars here and a thousand there, plunging oil prices and resulting losses of profit rendered him unable to meet the three-year note to Mahony when it came due in the spring of 1932, and he had to ask for an extension to the fall of the year.[65]

The periodical itself did not reflect the shaky financial situation and continued to bear the standard of its tradition. "In an era of social, financial and political upset," states a leading authority on American magazines, "the *Review* kept an extraordinarily even keel, swinging far neither to the right nor to the left, interpreting situations and tendencies quietly and interestingly month after month."[66] A subscription to this lively journal was a scant $3.00 a year in 1932. One could renew for only $2.00.

Money, however, was going out faster than it was coming in, and Davis found himself endorsing notes and then extending them even to the landlord.[67] This short letter from Davis to Mahony graphically reveals the hand-to-mouth existence at the lowest ebb of the Great Depression. "I am enclosing a check for $500 on NAR account and am hoping that this will keep things going for a while."[68] And, "If the people to whom we are owing money for rent get uneasy, please refer them to me."[69] Davis had no fear of creditors and simply explained to them that he would eventually pay them, as he always assumed he would. Davis closed out 1933 having endorsed notes totaling over $5,000.[70]

At mid-decade, Walter Mahony brought in a new editor as a fresh effort to make a go of the magazine. An established writer on early American history, John Pell was a great-great-grandson of Edward T. Channing, third editor of the *North American Review*; a member of the family that owned and operated the historic shrine Fort Ticonderoga; and a cash investor in the magazine who accepted for the money he put in, the endorsed notes of Edgar B. Davis.[71] As the ancient journal creaked along in time, those keeping it afloat continued to connect genealogically, historically, and coincidentally. Pell's new associate editor Richard Dana Skinner, who left his position on *Commonweal* as dramatic editor, was a great grandson of Richard Henry Dana, Edward Channing's assistant in 1819.[72] Mahony assumed the duties of president of the organization, John Pell acted as treasurer, and the versatile David Figart formally joined the staff and performed the tasks of secretary in addition to contributing several sound articles on economics.

The new editorial control, so rooted in the history of the *North American Review* symbolized one of the major problems--a great old oak of the publishing world in the winds of change. The general public devoured the modern approach to literature in *The Readers Digest*. Whereas *The Reader's Digest* continued to build economic security through mass circulation, the *North American Review*, not geared to the masses, slipped from leadership because of its traditionally high standards, and the magazine had to be put up for sale.[73]

An obscure publisher, Joseph Hilton Smyth, bought the grand old magazine in September, 1938, at the same time he acquired the venerable *Living Age*. Secretly financed by the Japanese government, Smyth was part of a plan of espionage using respected publications to spread Japanese propaganda. He let the *North American Review* die in 1940 and concentrated on articles in *Living Age*. The FBI brought him to trial in 1942, but he had helped to bury two of the most respected magazines in the United States.[74]

The *North American Review* resumed publication in 1964 under the sponsorship of the University of Northern Iowa with editorial offices at Cedar Falls. The present editor maintains that "since 1815, no magazine in America has had a readership more distinguished or a literary history more rich" and looks forward to the bicentenary of the *Review* in the coming century.[75] Perhaps the present version may last, for it does include articles and fiction reflecting the scatology so common to the flippant and spurious sophistication of today. It may be that the best pages of the current publication are those that reprint articles from the past when Ralph Waldo Emerson, Henry James, Elizabeth Cady Stanton, Woodrow Wilson, and Mark Twain contributed their thoughts.[76] This university-published journal also offers an even greater service than the occasional running of a thoughtful mirror of the past. The University of Northern Iowa provides a complete reprint service for the old series, 1915 to 1940, thereby making available "a remarkable repository, unmatched by that of any other magazine of American thought through nearly a century and a quarter of national life."[77]

Davis had helped make possible a dozen years of this quality publication, but he did not financially support the arts to any notable degree again in his long career, for he once more experienced the empty coffers of the wildcatting days before the Luling oil strike. By the time the *North American Review* folded in 1940, Davis was preoccupied with lawsuits, debts, and dry holes. With no more money to give away, he was seen at times back to the simple pleasures of beholding the wildflowers around Luling, Texas.

Chapter IX
BUT WHEN THE MONEY'S ALL GONE

His complete saga when it is written will reveal a depth of faith totally unfazed by difficulty.

John R. Sandidge

When Magnolia bought out United North and South Oil Company in June of 1926, Davis formed a new corporation, the United North and South *Development* Company, utilizing his old management committee members and taking the theme of exploration and new discovery through wildcatting. Davis held 186,000 of the total 213,776 shares of stock; Kelts C. Baker took 2,833; and Sam Rabon and Charles Rayner acquired 100 shares each. Minor stockholders picked up the remaining 24,000 shares, making the authorized capital of the company $2,500,000. With Davis' large investment there was no bonded indebtedness.[1]

Davis' obsession to discover a deep oil field dominated the early years of the development company, and the organization wildcatted unsuccessfully in the Hondo and Leesville areas from 1926 to 1928 while continuing the drilling of the deep-test Kelly and Tiller wells retained from the United North and South Oil Company in the Luling Field. Here Davis dissipated time, energy, and money futilely chipping away at solid granite far beneath the oil producing horizon in the Edwards lime. Early in 1927, company officials purchased $17,000 worth of new equipment to bore deeper into the near impenetrable formation. At this time logs showed the Kelley well at 6,635 feet, whereas the Tiller bit was spinning at a depth of 5,864 feet.[2] Progress was reduced to making inches instead of feet in between changes of the worn bit, and to the great relief of company executives Davis authorized the abandonment of the sites as dry holes on July 27, 1928, exactly four years after work commenced on building the wooden derricks. The total cost of drilling the Kelly to 7,855 feet and the tiller to 7,503 feet came to one million dollars![3] To this day, one can walk near these locations in the heart of the old Luling Field, and as the wind stirs the needle grass, long obsolete pieces of rusted and broken equipment--fishtail bits, core barrels, and thick cables--peer forth in a mute attempt to speak of the costly drama that unfolded a half century ago when an eccentric wildcatter tried to pierce the unknown.

Ever the cosmopolitan when in the money, Davis moved his main offices to the Milam Building in San Antonio in August, 1928. Legend continued to spin its web around the Davis career in San Antonio. One man whom he dealt with wore oversized hearing aids in each ear connected to wires hanging down to the batteries in his coat pockets. He still could not hear thunder. Davis kept a vacant room in which to discuss secret oil matters in this particular case, but the agitated screams grew so loud as to be overheard anyway. In the meantime, the Luling area continued both to produce oil and to provide discoveries. Major companies and operators finding it hard to argue with success drilled 175 test wells in the Edwards formation between 1922 and 1928, completing 56 producers, a record number for this type of drilling. As geologists studied drill records and mapped surface faults, wildcatter Joseph Bruner of Los Angeles, California, speculated in the Salt Flats, just north of Luling where salt water, seeping to the surface locally, first attracted the attention of oil men to the area. Following the discovery well in May, 1928, additional drilling through October of the same year revealed a smaller but similar fault to the one which trapped the oil for the Luling Field. The Salt Flat Field, though less productive than the discovery field at Luling, increased the geologic knowledge of producing in the Edwards formation and pointed the way to a greater discovery the next summer.[4]

Lease men and oil scouts studied the surface clues in the rough, post-oak country five miles south of the Luling Field in Guadalupe County, where Darst Creek cut its uneven southerly course to join the Guadalupe River. To the practiced eye, the broken lines of the rough terrain suggested exposed fault structures that could retain oil underneath.[5] United North and South officials grabbed up leases in the area in October, 1928, and Humble Oil and Refining Company and the Texas Company leased a large block at the same time with the agreement that the Texas Company would put down the test well, the Dallas Wilson No. 1, which struck oil July 10, 1929, with an initial flow of 1000 barrels a day.[6] William F. Peale, scouting this location from the beginning for United North and South, alertly picked up five leases along the structure tapped by the Texas Company well.[7]

Darst Creek, a field of considerable significance, became one of the largest Edwards strikes and is unique in that some wells produce from two different depths rather than only one level. United North and South purchased three additional Darst Creek leases during the summer of the discovery well, and the company, at the insistence of Davis, began productive drilling operations in November, 1929.[8] The consensus among major and minor companies was that great opportunities were at hand in the new strike.[9] This optimism proved correct and soon United North and South's seventeen producing wells on 180 leased acres produced over 5000 barrels a day. In April, 1930, Davis began selling crude to Louisiana Oil and Refining Company for a substantial income, but this outfit soon wanted to buy more than production: company executives made an offer for the entire property, lock, stock, and barrel. Wildcatting unproved territory was more to Davis' liking, and deep oil, which he still illogically connected in his mind with greater production, preyed on his thoughts; therefore, he chose to sell and the board of directors authorized the contract on May 6, 1930. Louisiana Oil and Gas paid $500,000 down on the $2,250,000 purchase price and agreed to pay the balance out of the profit from the oil extracted.[10]

At the time of this transaction, Davis endorsed personal notes to each member of his management committee: Peale, Mowinckle, Rabon, Baker, and Rayner. These new bonuses of $200,000 each were to come from the $1,750,000 of the balance due for the Darst Creek property. Subsequent events led to financial misunderstandings about the personal pledge of these monetary gifts. In some instances, bitterness led to lawsuits. The root of the problem was that the agreement with Louisiana Oil and Gas Company fell through, ruined by the Depression economy and excessive oil production.[11]

On record as the third Edwards field, Darst Creek also made history as the first oil producing area to be prorated in Southwest Texas. This meant that the Texas Railroad Commission would impose a restraint on the output of this field. Since there was a glut of oil on the market in 1930, the Commission hoped to manipulate the law of supply and demand and effect a rise in the price of crude by lowering the allowable. The Darst Creek proration schedule went into operation on January 1, 1930, immediately reducing the field's capacity by 42 percent, and by August of 1930 the Railroad Commission permitted an allowable daily production of less than 50 percent of potential production.[12]

Since the Louisiana Oil and Gas Company was paying United North and South out of production, proration played havoc with their obligations to Davis' company, especially when the price of oil dropped to ten cents a barrel. The purchasers were unable to fulfill their contract,and Davis took back the property on September 26, 1931. Though not legally required to return the half million dollar down payment, Davis felt morally and ethically bound to repurchase the property, and he refunded the sum through his own sales of oil to Magnolia, for which he sometimes received as little as eight cents a barrel![13]

Characteristically, Davis' attitude was positive, predicting that the company would "make more money out of the property than we could have done had the Louisiana Company fulfilled its contractual obligations."[14] This was the practical Yankee businessman speaking. On the spiritual side, Davis found compensation: "Furthermore, there is always an inside satisfaction in feeling that one has put into practice the economic principle of treating one's neighbor as oneself."[15]

Calvinist Davis went through a brief conversion to pure Christianity in this deal. He could not pull his eye lid and look for green on this one. Calvinism would insist on keeping the half million dollar down payment. Pure, unadulterated Christianity would return the sum, as Davis did, even with the lower prices he was getting for his oil. Here Davis moved from the Old Testament completely into the New Testament following to the letter Jesus' admonition to treat thy neighbor as thyself. Davis' actions here fully illustrate why Christianity is the hardest of the five major religions to follow. There are impractical sides: turning the other cheek; going the extra mile; repaying evil with kindness; but of course Jesus' Kingdom was not of this world. And this is why a corporation is designed to have no soul.

Darst Creek production stabilized the financial health of the United North and South Development Company until the company's dissolution in 1951. Although these properties remained constant, the nucleus of the company, the management committee, began to break apart. Sam Rabon, one of the most practical, thorough-going and knowledgeable oil men in Davis' association, died in August, 1931, and Davis felt his absence keenly. "Men whom I met first on the derrick floor years ago came to pay their last respects to Sam's memory," Davis reflected, for

> he had a well-deserved reputation for just dealing with his fellow men, and his word was as good as his bond. Although he was a master of his profession, there was an absence of egotism and self-assertiveness which made men glad to sit at his feet to learn. He had the Spirit of the pioneer, and reminded me forcibly of the greater character--Sam Houston--for whom he was named.[16]

Even before death claimed the able vice-president and field superintendent, friction between Davis and the other members of the management committee had surfaced on more than one occasion. At the heart of the matter was Davis' insistence on wildcatting.[17] For instance, after the Daisy Bradford No. 3 opened the giant East Texas Field on October 3, 1930, this territory, a history of superlatives in the oil business, was ripe for independents or smaller companies such as the United North and South. The major companies were slow to move in. John Mowinckle advised repeatedly that Davis invest in East Texas. This Davis refused to do. Mowinckle sank some of his own money into the new field with prosperous results.[18]

During the year 1930, John Mowinckle, Kelts Baker, William Peale, and Charles Rayner resigned as directors of the United North and South Development Company, although they retained their stock and their personal notes. Rayner went to work for the Foundation Farm and later took a position with the federal government; Baker and Peale returned to other private business enterprises; and Mowinckle operated as an independent oil man.[19]

Maverick Davis continued steadfastly on his course. With the same stoicism that he accepted the loss of his old associates, he met the Great Depression head on, refusing to overreact to the economic slump. His personal correspondence during the Great Depression reflects the same eternal optimism of his letter-writing during the boom years, and he would close a letter discussing the most gloomy economic losses with a comment on a beautiful sunset or an excellent hand dealt him in a recent bridge game. His prose contains the subtle humor he delighted in, and the references to some article he found interesting or a good meal served take on as much importance as a million-dollar transaction.[20] As to the gravity of the time, to Davis, the Depression required no more concern than that he gave to a dry hole or an empty theatre: "I see no reason to doubt that the same good God who has guided us so wonderfully in the past has gone out of business and I believe that the where-with-all will be found to keep everything going."[21]

Even in the faltering Depression economy, Davis incredibly still manipulated vague and complex schemes to consolidate a rubber cartel of such a large dimension as to forever stabilize the price of crude rubber. In its simplest form, Davis, with millions from oil, would buy up controlling stock in the leading rubber corporations. Then with personal connections he, David Figart, and Walter Mahony had cultivated over the years, the concern could control rubber world-wide without cut-throat competition.[22]

His correspondence is strangely silent on his true mission in life, as he conceived it, to follow the dictates of the mystical "Voice" calling him to be President of the United States. If, as he constantly reminded intimates, his every action was based on the supposition that the experience was real and that success would come his way because of his very mission, he still would not actively seek the ultimate goal. Instead, he somehow believed that attention brought to him through wildcatting, philanthropy, or Broadway antics would cause his draft for high office. This proved to be unsound logic. Why not turn the *North American Review* into an organ to boom his credentials? Money he flittered away on the play *The Ladder* could have been put into a campaign for 1928; or during the dark days of the 1930's he could have turned some deep oil test funds into a move to express himself as a leader. Instead, he maintained that he would "never lift a finger," that the office would mysteriously drift to him.[23] But when a call came in 1928--though a distant summons to second place on a ticket--he did not actively respond.

The 1928 nomination process illustrates so well Davis' game of playing hard to get. Leading the move to draft Davis as vice-presidential nominee to balance the expected candidacy of Al Smith was Massachusetts journalist William McMasters, winner of the Pulitzer Prize in 1920 for service on the Boston *Post.* On the surface, the McMasters strategy of Davis' appeal appeared sound: a descendant of the *Mayflower* Pilgrims, Davis was a hometown boy made good who had recently remembered Massachusetts through philanthropy; his international business experience in the rubber industry and his national reputation as an oil man would rival *Hoover*'s economic standing as a mining engineer and Secretary of Commerce; *Davis* was popular in Texas, where folks looked up to big-spending wildcatters; and finally, he represented an appeal to two doubtful states, Massachusetts and Texas, where Smith expected some difficulty.[24]

As early as January, 1928, McMasters referred to his talks with "leading Massachusetts Democrats" as a fast-spreading campaign.[25] By May, McMasters, who coordinated the move in Texas with Richard B. Ellis, Davis' company lawyer and a prominent Democrat in Caldwell County, had made substantial ground on the grass roots level in both *Brockton* and Luling. The plan called for Arthur A. Hendrick, a Brockton delegate to the National Convention, to nominate Davis with the second given by Elizabeth Gormly, also from Brockton and an established figure in Massachusetts state politics. Ellis lined up several seconding speeches from Texas delegates. All went well in the four counties where Davis primarily operated, Caldwell, Guadalupe, Gonzales, and Bexar, and even San Antonio mayor Charles M. Chambers, a leading party man in Bexar County, endorsed him strongly.[26]

In June, the Brockton district delegation, McMasters, also a delegate, in the lead, arrived in Houston in fine spirits, and Davis, relenting a little from his aloof role, imported the group to Luling by car and rail for a grand dinner at the House in the Oaks and a tour of his oil fields.[27] Back in Houston, the humidity wrinkled McMasters' pressed suits, and he learned firsthand about the heat of Texas politics where the establishment forces that dictated its policies soon wilted the Davis "boom" for the vice-presidency down to a mere "complimentary" nomination. The real Texas powers at the gathering in Houston, whether the "Harmony Democrats," led by Governor Dan Moody, or the "Constitutional Democrats," commanded by Thomas B. Love, reluctantly accepted Al Smith under the intense pressure of the powerful Democratic city machines and only after casting their vote for Houston financier Jesse Jones. In this climate of bigoted allusions to Smith's religion and reaction for the retention of national prohibition, southern and western Democrats took some comfort in the compromise nomination of Arkansas Senator Joseph T. Robinson, a true Southern "dry," for vice-president.[28]

An adopted Texan, Davis retained enough trappings to link him to the Eastern machine that backed Smith and his derby hat and Brooklyn accent; and besides, the oil man had squandered a million dollars on a bad play--an eccentricity not attractive to conservative politics. Finally, Davis refused to act on his own behalf, thereby eliminating any slim chance he may have had to get on the ticket. As the historians Howard and Ralph Wolf point out in their monumental story of the rubber industry:

> He refuses to be interviewed and dislikes being photographed, which may account for the fact that one or the other of the great American political parties have overlooked the best bet in its history by failing to nominate him for the Presidency.[29]

Content to work indirectly for the Presidency, Davis offered his services as a leader in other ways. He hoped to call attention to himself with his remedy for the Great Depression in "The Way Out--and On," the featured article in the October, 1932, issue of the *North American Review.* Davis lists the main cause of the economic condition of the country as vicious competition which brought on the cycle of layoffs and wage reductions. "The most urgent need today in the rehabilitation of business," Davis argued, "is that it should be done at an ample profit, with generous distributions made to the workers, management and shareholders."[30] This "business-for-profit" movement would "perfect capitalism" by making everyone "capitalists."[31] Davis condemned the partisan campaign underway, held up the success of the coalition government in England, and called for cooperation between the parties. "Make relentless war on poverty," he charged, "Make American beautiful,"[32] he advocated, anticipating the slogans of both President Lyndon B. Johnson and Lady Bird Johnson. "Study the science of raising the purchasing power of the public," he urged business and government, "and bring production and distribution into balance."[33]

Davis had practiced what he preached in two separate industries, sharing liberally his profits from rubber production and oil extraction. He more recently exemplified his own advice in an extraordinary move to stop a run on a friend's bank. On December 17, 1931, approximately 300 depositors were jamming the lobby of the Plymouth County Trust Company, a Brockton Bank, when shortly after 1:00 p.m. the cash reserves ran short. Carleton White, a bank officer and long-time friend of Edgar B. Davis, telephoned Davis in San Antonio. Davis owned some stock in the bank but was not an officer; however, he pledged his word that he would guarantee every deposit from his oil fortune. On the basis of this telephone conversation, Brockton Mayor Harold Bent leaped upon a lobby table and shouted the Davis promise. Davis' philanthropy was well-known in his hometown, and soon the crowd melted away, in mute testimony that the Davis name still carried some weight.[34]

This saved the bank and a subsequent wire to the Brockton newspapers clarified the Davis stand somewhat. Davis made the pledge not on his present oil wealth but rather on a future strike which he believed was bound to come.[35] Nevertheless, the bank survived. Davis acted in certainty of its soundness all along--if the run could be prevented.[36] Had the magic not worked many complications threatened ruin to not only the bank but Davis' reputation as well. Davis continued to point to a brighter future, and as he closed out the next year, the very darkest winter of the Depression, he confidently reported to his stockholders that "the motivating force of this Company is Faith in God, Faith in our country--Faith that this depression will be weathered and that America will enjoy a prosperity better than ever in her history--and Faith in the future of the oil industry and of our Company."[37] Faith in Davis required a lot of faith!

Wildcatting in the best of times often reduces to shoestring proportion those who pursue this complicated gamble. Davis followed his favorite pastime of drilling, hoping, believing, and relying on the law of probabilities as well as he could during the economic slump. But with less and less capital he made fewer and fewer locations, and these were all dusters. Between 1926 and 1931, the United North and South drilled twenty-one dry holes, expending three million dollars in this unproductive exploration work. Undaunted, Davis steadily maintained that "the way to success will be by the wildcat route."[38]

In the fall of 1931, Davis determined to concentrate on drilling four different wells on widely held properties in Cass County, Karnes County, Shelby County, and Matagorda County.[39] Efforts on the first three leases brought the company total up to twenty-four dry holes; however, the fourth, the property in Matagorda County that came to be called Buckeye after the nearest town in the area, became the symbol of the elusive dream for which Davis was searching, the ship that was always going to come in. Buckeye often gave some hints of unlimited black gold, but the great wealth remained just out of reach. Instead of the blessing Davis perceived, Buckeye hung a millstone around Davis' neck, ultimately preventing any future success for the United North and South Development Company.

Davis embroiled his company in Buckeye in a fateful manner. While in communication with a prominent Cleveland, Ohio, law firm, one of the attorneys, Henry Kreger, suggested that Davis look into oil possibilities on his mother-in-law's ranch in Texas. Two geologists investigated the location and on the basis of the promising surface structure, recommended drilling. That was more than enough evidence for Davis, who immediately leased the 10,000 acre Laura V. Stoddard Ranch, and on a bright, moonlight night, Davis stumped around the ranch properties and dramatically drew an X in the dirt with his expensive, stylish, oversized shoe for the drill bit to bite into. Thus the fateful location was made.[40]

A month after spudding in Stoddard No. 1, an early "gas showing" at the well sharpened Davis' interest in the lease.[41] As the drill spun deeper, his interest became an obsession; gradually, over the next two decades, this feeling about the possibilities of Buckeye developed into a monomania.

In November, 1931, the drill bit rotated at a depth of 5543 feet and the crew encountered the difficulties common to the technology of the times when man attempted to bore so far into the earth.[42] Problems such as these, however, were the ingredients of eventual success, for Davis believed that nothing worthwhile in life came easy: broken drill stems, snapped cables, costly fishing operations, cave-ins within the hole being drilled, and always the need to go deeper and deeper. Then came the added drama of the replay of the story of the Luling discovery, with only Davis wanting to bore deeper, on the basis of the shaky advice from Hedwig Kniker, paleontologist, who believed that the oil was down there but would prove too costly to recover.[43]

To Davis, there was no question but to probe deeper and "strike the oil which will serve as a lubricant to our endeavors";[44] "I believe we are going to get it in *this* well,"[45] he declared. But he made a personal decision that if Buckeye became dry hole number twenty-five, he would "change our policy on the theory that it was not for us to bring in oil fields but that we should deal in leases after all."[46] In other words, he would quit wildcatting.

Buckeye took on the symbolism of success, and it symbolized challenge in that it became so costly that it simply had to work out. As Davis' personal correspondence shows, it stood for more than a victory in oil exploration as it took on the representation of the financial end of the giant rubber scheme:

> We have not yet completed the work at Buckeye and I believe we are to get something because failure to do so would cripple us for future operations to such an extent that all hope of doing anything constructive in rubber or other things would of necessity be thrown in the discard. I can not believe that I have become, like yourself, something of the magazine of ideas for the development of the business without being the climax--and a grand one.[47]

A month later, he wrote to another friend on the same theme:

> It is the well at Buckeye in Matagorda County upon which my hopes are built of getting back into the rubber atmosphere in an attempt to help in some constructive movement. Like you, rubber is my first love in big business although I think there is more money to be made in oil than in any line of industry which I know.[48]

By February, 1932, all company executives opposed going any deeper than the 7305 foot level. Ernest Brucks, company geologist, categorically disapproved of further drilling, while Hedwig Kniker conceded that the well was "not hopeless."[49] Davis' decision to put down more hole is not unlike the fictional character Captain Ahab and his relentless quest for the white whale, with a crew following disapprovingly into the unknown.

At the time of his decision to bore deeper at Buckeye, indebtedness already pressed in upon him. "Eleventh-hour business,"[50] Davis called it. In addition to the *North American Review* expenses, he could neither pay a $1500 debt due in Massachusetts nor his $2,500 county taxes.[51] A musician whose orchestra had played for *The Ladder* performances was attempting to collect some money he said Davis owed him over and above the $36,397 he had received between 1927 and 1928. The spuriousness of his claim was underscored by his offer to drop his demand for $100 cash.[52] Had this band leader better understood Davis, he could have simply written him telling him he was down on his luck and asked Davis to send him $100.00. The musician would have come closer to getting money in that way. Davis had a touch of gout, which he believed would vanish if he had his tonsils removed.[53] However, he was fifty-nine years of age, and this was decided against. His equanimity among problems, so frustrating to associates and so conveniently ascribed by several of them to insanity, was preserved with his personal belief:

> You were quite right when you say that the pressure on me is terrific and if it were not for my Faith in God I would have thrown up the sponge long ago. However, I believe we will win out handsomely in the Power of that Spirit that guides and directs the affairs of men.[54]

Meanwhile, Stoddard No. 1 developed complications unprecedented in the oil industry, when on February 26, 1932, the bit broke off in the hole, requiring a fishing operation to retrieve the obstructing metal a mile and a half down into the earth. "This is disappointing but we have to get used to disappointments in this business," Davis typically remarked.[55]

Davis avoided pressing matters in Texas for a New York visit from April to mid-June, 1932, and, money matters aside, entertained with at least one dinner party reminiscent of the old 1920's style. He returned to Texas to make the authorization to go deeper at Buckeye than the 7,770 feet. At this point, Davis found a couple of allies, for at least the day and night drillers wanted to continue. They noted actual traces of oil as they read the signs from the well cuttings and cores. On May 15 and again on May 24, gas, mud, and a little oil blasted out briefly 200 feet high from the hole.[56]

In the middle of July, 1932, the drilling crew began a difficult maneuver at 7,829 feet in order to bore to the side of implements which had permanently broken off and lodged in the hole. Penetrating to 7,924 feet on August 30, the crew began operations to complete the well in hopes of tapping an oil sand at that depth. At 3:00 a.m., August 31, they got more than they bargained for when Stoddard No. 1 blew in wild, uncontrollably flowing from 2,500 to 5,000 barrels of high quality oil spewed out under millions of pounds of pressure per cubic feet of gas.[57]

The scene evoked memories of Spindletop thirty years earlier when a lake of oil surrounded the derrick, backed up to the railroad right-of-way on one side and dammed by hastily thrown up earthworks on the other. Men worked in the midst of an enormous fire hazard, requiring only a tiny spark to ignite a conflagration. Laboring under near impossible conditions, men fought for a week to bring the well under control, finally killing the flow by pumping heavy mud into the hole. On September 12, they allowed a controlled flow of 2,000 barrels daily but soon had to reduce this to 600 barrels due to the lack of storage facilities. Davis' company had completed the deepest producer in all South Texas and the Gulf Coast and was only exceeded by the 8,000 foot well on the University of Texas holdings in the Big Lake Field of West Texas. The consensus was that the drill stem had struck dead center in a dome structure.[58]

If Davis, while bringing in this gusher, exhibited a coolness under financial pressures and matters of executive decision, he had in his employ a pusher, drillers, and roughnecks who showed a similar courage on a physical scale which rose to the heights of the unwritten code of indifference to danger in the oil field. Nonchalance toward daily risk was dictated by conditions under which the men worked. As one looks at a photograph of the crew posed before the derrick, he notes that they gaze back at the camera from under felt hats; there was no protective headgear nor steel-toed boots. "Early workers took all this in their stride," explains Mody Boatright, folklorist of the oil industry,

> and thought no more about safety than their employer did. Indeed, the danger they were exposed to was a source of pride. They considered themselves men in a sense that counter-jumpers and pencil-pushers were not. But they knew the necessity for alertness.[59]

David Figart, who himself narrowly missed being killed on the derrick floor in July, made note of the remarkable competence of the men under strain in the conclusion to his history of Stoddard No. 1:

> The drilling of this well required a high degree of both mental and physical courage--besides unusual skill--upon the part of the men. To single out acts of bravery without doing some injustice would be difficult. Men stuck to their posts when in imminent danger; they worked with equipment not designed to carry the stresses placed upon it. When the well blew in out of control and emergency action became necessary, the driller in charge was overheard to say

> to his men: "We may all be killed, but this is what we're paid for, and we've got to do our best." Time after time the almost impossible was accomplished. The devotion of the men to their duty and their sense of loyalty are beyond praise.[60]

Having completed a well, Davis considered the victory won. To penetrate his thought pattern, one only need analyze the syndrome begun with the Luling strike a decade earlier. Davis kept on against the advice of most of his associates and many professionals; he bore up under great difficulties in the best Calvinist tradition. The hand of Providence intervened. When a hurricane roared inland at 100 miles per hour out of the Gulf of Mexico on April 13, 1932, killing 40 people and injuring 200, the United North and South rig was one of the few derricks left standing in a 70-mile path of destruction.[61] Finally, he now had the deepest oil on the Gulf Coast and a greater control of leased acreage than he had held in the Luling Field. As he wrote his closest confidante David Figart in mid-August, all his dreams would come to fruition, not only the giant rubber scheme but also the prophecy of "the Voice" of 1904:

> This may sound crazy to you but I know something of the Power that is back of me. I think--I do not know--that not only will Buckeye come in in time to permit me to meet all my obligations but that it will be of such a size that the whole oil industry will take notice. We will sell all or part to advantage; that it will bring me into National prominence and that there will be a citizens movement (in which I will not lift a finger) for me to run as independent THIS (1932) YEAR.[62]

Davis offered his Buckeye property for sale for twenty million dollars, half in cash and half in oil, before taking a European vacation, leaving many creditors who would have preferred to take his travel money rather than promises of future payment. He returned to Texas before the year was out to find no offers to buy.[63] He was still maintaining the Buckeye lease at great personal sacrifice in 1951, having turned down, much to the consternation of his associates, the largest bid of $1,000,000 from Humble in 1935.[64] The rejection of this offer proved a big mistake.

Stoddard No. 1 remained an extraordinary well, producing 100,000 barrels by the end of its first year, but it proved to be what geologists called a fault-controlled closure; that is, the break in the earth's structure created a limited reservoir rather than the lengthy traps at Luling. Ordinarily, production from such an area will not pay for the drilling costs.[65] Davis hit only one other producer at Buckeye, and this output combined with that of the discovery well amounted to 649,798 barrels by 1938. A dozen more efforts, one to 10,700 feet, ended dry and unproductive,[66] and as the bit went down, the bills shot up.

Not only did Davis, as company president, pile up business-related bills which dogged him but he also incurred personal expenses as varied and extended as his broad extracurricular interests. For instance, he maintained a yearly rental on a large scenic plot of land known as Tiga Ras overlooking his old rubber plantations in Sumatra where he intended to be buried.[67] ("Can you imagine lugging that big carcass half-way around the world!" his brother Oscar commented.)[68] Maintaining the House in the Oaks at Luling and the House on the Sand on Buzzard's Bay, Massachusetts took a further toll on his till. Hotel bills in San Antonio increased his debts. Finally, his offices at 366 Madison Avenue, New York City, were personal, not company, and from here he pumped up his flagging cartel scheme; and he still maintained his interests in the *North American Review.* He was considering parting with his Packard sedan to meet some of these expenses in the summer of 1933.[69]

If he kept up his payments on his burial plot, he did not intend using it too soon, an attitude he underscored by not buying life insurance, much to the concern of his two sisters who depended on his advice and guidance. Davis simply assumed that he would not depart this life until he had completed his "Mission" as outlined by the "Voice" of 1904; that is, until he entered the Oval Office as President of the United States. Just as he would not wear snake boots in the jungles of Sumatra, he would not buy life insurance; to do so would be an affront to his "Faith."

Throughout history, men of limited family have accomplished much simply because they owed little allegiance to those other than themselves. Francis Bacon made reference to the amount of writing done in relation to his barren household. J. Frank Dobie wrote down a million words that found their way into print. But he wrote and his wife typed and revised. With no children they devoted themselves totally to Dobie's remarkable art. Edgar B. Davis enjoyed this advantage. He could wheel (as long as someone else did the driving) and deal with the knowledge that if anyone starved to death it would just be he. Of course in historical context Davis, Dobie, and to some extent Bacon, lived at a time when family came first to the breadwinner; that is, family responsibilities would have definitely drained much time from these conscientious men. Now anyone can avoid family responsibility to devote all time to himself by simply joining the "Me Generation." Successful middle aged men with young wives, younger girlfriends, older ex-spouses, and children and grandchildren from all three females are glibly free to follow their own amusements, leaving the resulting human wreckage to pick up for themselves. But these modern pleasure seekers rarely use the extra time selfishness gives them constructively, often merely finding more hedonism to wile away the hours. Besides, modern man has become too specialized in the work place to have the broad knowledge to do very much. The Davis generation represented versatility. Davis accomplished much in the way of his varied interests. He also had room for more failures.

Incidents such as his narrow brush with death in 1933 always meant to Davis that he would survive to see his destiny fulfilled. In early July, 1933, as Davis' nephew Arthur Lawrence was driving the Davis touring car through San Antonio, he struck a fruit truck, bouncing Davis out the door where his head struck the curb and his shoulder hit the street. Miraculously, according to the doctor, Davis survived the intense blow on the head that required twenty stitches. He was badly bruised overall. No one else was injured.[70] At the turn of the century Davis had received a terrible blow to the head in a train wreck; Davis was known as the only passenger involved who did not sue the railroad.

In the summer Davis retained his habit of wearing the tropical suits of his days in the Far East. "He must be somebody important," remarked an onlooker at the wreck scene, "he's dressed in white!"[71] Davis reveled in this spontaneous evaluation of his social status, but he read into his ordeal a deeper significance. "I believe," Davis declared, "that this all is a part of the great Plan that God has for me and that I have to learn patience through suffering and I wouldn't have this experience out of my life for anything."[72] The traumatic survival of the car wreck heralded other dramatic and complete changes in Davis' life.

Throughout the 1930's Davis gradually abandoned science in wildcatting. He would be guided totally by his "Faith." Heretofore he had clung to some vestiges of his reputation as a systematic rubber grower, the man who had made a success of scientific production. Bit by bit in the oil industry, he would drill against the advice of most learned advisors if he could find just *one* geologist who could concur with him. By the end of the 1930's he was willing to push ahead only on his own intuition. "Why don't you just strike the rock with your staff as Moses did," chided an exasperated David Figart, "and let the oil pour forth?"[73]

Geologist Ernest W. Brucks, who had quit Davis over the deep tests into the granite of the Old Luling Field, was about to depart again in protest against continued exploration at Buckeye. "If I had a million dollars, I wouldn't invest a dollar of it in the North & South," he told a shocked Davis.[74] A month later when Brucks frankly informed Davis that the current effort, the sixth drilling site, at Buckeye would be a disaster, Davis penned the following memo:

> When the history of Buckeye is written, it will be a triumph of Faith over science and I feel that Mr. Bruck's views merely will illustrate that science alone could not successfully work out our problems--or the problems of the nation or the world.[75]

Davis closed out 1933 in the same frame of mind, explaining to Figart, who had recommended acquiring scientific advice from a California expert experienced in other deep production,[76] that Buckeye would "be proved by Faith--not by science. By Faith and the drill stem--not by geology and paleontology."[77]

In two years Davis was flat broke. Deeply in debt and beset by problems he motored from San Antonio to the scene of his old triumph with Rios No. 1, where an audience of 500 Luling citizens gathered to hear him compare the struggles in Buckeye with his success in Luling a dozen years earlier. He predicted that he was destined to control great wealth and hinted at an even greater distribution of his fortune yet to come.[78]

Davis was badly in need of great wealth, for drilling dry holes had thrown the United North and South Development Company nearly one million dollars behind in payments, and on May 28, 1935, creditors petitioned Davis and company into federal bankruptcy court in San Antonio. Davis insisted that whatever the outcome, payment of all bills in full had to be the result.[79]

Court action reorganized the company under Section 77-B of the Federal Bankruptcy Laws. The main problem, to borrow nearly a million dollars, for Davis hoped to pay off his obligations and still keep Darst Creek and Buckeye to protect his stockholders, loomed ahead. Both Davis and the creditors submitted plans, and Federal Judge Robert J. McMillan confirmed and approved Davis' suggestion of action.[80]

Actually, funds which returned indirectly from two acts of philanthropy and friendship when he was prosperous saved the wildcatter. In the first place, the Ohio Goodyear Securities company, organized some time earlier when Davis came financially to the aid of his friend Frank A. Seiberling (this story is told in the next chapter), assumed the claim of the big creditor, $376,000 owed to the Republic Supply Company of Houston. Lien for the Republic Supply loan was the Darst Creek and Buckeye properties, and Ohio Goodyear released this claim as security to the First National Bank of Dallas for a $250,000 loan to United North and South to be repaid at $13,500 monthly from oil production.[81]

The Luling Foundation loaned an additional $250,000 at six percent. After Davis had spoken to the Foundation directors, Jack Shelton concluded, "He's come back before; who's to say he can't do it again. Let's give him the loan!"[82]

Judge McMillan announced in April, 1937, that all creditors had been paid in full, including the attorneys, and that reorganization was complete. This was no small accomplishment in The Great Depression. Creditors had either taken cash or stock in United North and South at $10.00 a share which could be repurchased by the company at $20.00 a share with thirty days notice.[83]

As a further move for economy Davis relocated his main office in Luling. In the new board of directors, of which Davis was chairman, his old friend and associate David Figart served as President. Also a part of this organization was the new treasurer, Tommy Caylor, whom Davis came to admire and rely on for his abilities and hard work.[84] Thus Davis, celebrating his sixty-fourth birthday in February, 1937, anticipated a new beginning at the age that most men are planning for retirement. For Davis, the future meant Buckeye and what he hoped would be another field at nearby Wilson Creek where he was sniffing an oil showing at 9,900 feet.[85]

By extraordinary coincidence, the first Wilson Creek Well repeated the feat of Stoddard No. 1 at Buckeye, for when this well blew in the last of May, it blasted out of the same type of limited reservoir as the Buckeye discovery, this time at 1,500 barrels a day.[86] Although Davis struck dead center both times, he and the company would have fared better had he missed. By being enticed into more costly drilling on the Gulf Coast he poured safe Darst Creek profits down dry holes.

As matters stood in June of 1937, however, Davis in his jubilation, camped both on top and on the bottom of the world. Not only did he own the deepest well in Texas, twenty-two feet short of 10,000 feet, but also in his office in Luling he displayed a bottle of crude from his new producer and invited visitors to "have a million dollar smell."[87]

Twenty-twenty hindsight always outshines foresight, but the mistake Davis made in not seeking the greater wealth at Luling is obvious. Men were making small fortunes in the Luling area at a fraction of the drilling and production costs at Buckeye and Wilson Creek. Putting down a well is always a gamble, but records bear out that the probabilities at Luling were more certain than anywhere else in Texas. The little town remained a locale of semi-prosperity throughout the Depression, as old-timers will testify today, often remarking that "Luling never had a Depression." This hardly overstates the case, and many current residents of Luling left some town where there were no jobs and came to the Luling, Salt Flat, or Darst Creek fields and found work. For example, look at the wildcatting Griffin family of Brownwood, Texas, who lost two drilling rigs, two trucks, a car, their life savings, and their home when the Brownwood banks collapsed over a weekend. All males in the family found employment with Grayburg Oil Company in Luling. The father, William Charles Griffin, hired on as a pumper. His nephew Harry McDow handled field superintendent duties. All sons garnered jobs. Noble bossed the bull gang; Johnny ran a pulling machine; and Morris performed roustabout chores. Son-in-law Raymond Scott kept produced oil flowing into storage tanks. The family built a home on Grayburg property where the fault line peaked at the high bank coming out of the San Marcos River. And they spent their money in Luling, as did a host of other oil related workers. Numerous paychecks, small though they were, kept the Luling merchants going.

Apparently Davis ignored the flurry of success in the three separate discoveries at Luling. Bitten by the deep oil bug in particular and wildcatting in general, he continued to hammer away at Buckeye and Wilson Creek. By the end of the year, his one Wilson Creek well had produced 19,326 barrels; he had no other discoveries.[88] However, he did produce oil, and when World War II and the end of proration brought higher crude prices, other opportunities opened up for the aging wildcatter, who still counted on the decade of the 1940's to realize his mission. Faithful to his passive political quest, he remained confident that God would do the rest.

Chapter X
FAITHFUL TO THE QUEST - DEDICATED TO THE DREAM

How long it will take Edgar to bob up with another fortune now remains to be seen.

Howard and Ralph Wolf

Governments have a passion for seeking funds for perpetuation, and the bureaucrats who scurry after revenue for tax offices often become overzealous, but the length of time during which officials of the state of Massachusetts dogged Davis for a portion of his income may set a record. From the time he acquired his 1926 oil fortune, Davis fought a running battle with the income-tax agency of the state of his birth, losing only after his death. When Magnolia Petroleum Company paid Davis $6,050,000 in 1926 as the down payment on his holdings in the Luling Field, he arranged to settle his federal income tax of $761,230, representing twelve and one half per cent of capital gain, in quarterly installments throughout the year 1927.[1] Massachusetts levied a six per cent dividends tax on the same sum which the federal government taxed. Davis maintained that only the three per cent Massachusetts tax on capital gains could apply, and he negotiated into the fall of 1926 with state tax authorities in hope of working out a compromise. Unable to effect a mutual agreement, Davis used an unusual provision in Massachusetts tax laws whereby he would pay the state no tax whatsoever. According to Massachusetts statutes, a citizen who was not a resident on January 1 of any given year did not owe taxes for the preceding year.[2]

Davis, therefore, in December of 1926, announced that he was changing his residence from Massachusetts to Texas and that he would make Luling his home.[3] His prepared statement explains his moral position in the case:

> I realize the necessity of taxation if government is to endure and desire at all times to pay my just share. I consider however, that the Massachusetts tax on incomes which, incidentally, is about double the tax imposed in similar cases by the great commercial state of New York, is unjust to me. The laws in Massachusetts evidently are designed to meet conditions under which a citizen invests profits made within the state in income producing enterprises outside the jurisdiction of Massachusetts. In my case practically all the wealth which Massachusetts would tax has been made outside the jurisdiction of the state.[4]

Massachusetts tax gatherers, realizing that Davis was within the letter of the law, filed suit against him, alleging that he had not really changed residence, was still a citizen of Massachusetts, and therefore subject to the taxation laws. Realizing that they were up against a determined man who would clearly go through with the court trial, Massachusetts tax attorneys, before matters got into the actual trial state, offered a compromise in 1928 of settling for the three per cent capital gains tax, which Davis had maintained was just and fair. But Davis' fighting blood was up, and he was in no mood to settle for the lesser amount he had formerly been willing to pay.[5] Attorneys for the Massachusetts tax office then secured a change of venue from Plymouth County, where the citizens of Brockton knew Davis well, to Suffolk County, where the case was tried in the Boston court of Judge Webster Thayer.[6] This was the same judge who presided in the trial of Sacco and Vanzetti. Also, by coincidence, Webster Thayer's son Hamilton Thayer was a member of the 1925 graduating class of Dartmouth with Edgar Davis' nephew Lincoln Davis.

Massachusetts undertook some investigatory work in Texas. When a San Antonio lawyer retained by the state snooped for evidence in Luling that Davis was not a citizen of Texas, one resident, who punctuated his statement by sharpening his knife on his boot, told the questioner that anyone who said that Davis was not a citizen of Luling was a liar. Other inquiries produced less forceful but no less supportive replies on Davis' status as a resident of Texas.[7]

Without substantial proof to present from Texas, the Massachusetts trial lawyers based their entire case on their allegation that Davis' mode of living had not changed and therefore he was still a citizen of the state of his birth. He still owned the Brockton home where his sisters lived; he maintained the House on the Sand at Buzzards Bay, and he made the same number of trips into Massachusetts as he always had. The prosecution put this question to the jury: "Did the defendant, Edgar B. Davis, change his domicile from Brockton, Massachusetts, to Luling, Texas, in fact?"[8]

Davis' lawyers showed that he owned a home in Luling. Davis noised it around to the Brockton mayor and other friends that he was moving to Texas in December, 1926. These men testified to these conversations. Davis testified under oath that he had changed his residence to Texas. The prosecution introduced no evidence to refute these sworn statements. The Boston jury found against Davis on April 15, 1930, and returned a verdict for Massachusetts in the sum of $439,538, which was six per cent of Davis' 1926 income plus interest since the original tax bill had been presented.[9]

Davis' lawyers appealed to the Massachusetts Supreme Judicial Court, arguing the case on September 13, 1933. The higher tribunal upheld the jury trial, ruling on September 25, 1933, that Davis owed $530,375. This ruling also upheld the increase by accrued interest.[10]

Davis steadfastly refused to pay either the entire judgment or even an out-of-court compromise settlement. "When I said I was a citizen of Texas in 1926, I either lied or didn't," he indignantly stated. "If I had lied, then I owe the entire amount. But I didn't lie, and I don't owe them a cent."[11] The state of Massachusetts had every intention of collecting, and officials attempted to attach the funds Davis had established for the Pilgrim Foundation. In this case the courts ruled that this money did not in any way belong to the oil man and could not be touched.[12]

As usual, Davis found a silver lining in the cloud that hung over him in the tax judgment. In 1933 he decided to issue new stock at $20.00 a share in the United North and South Development Company. He usually grabbed a ready market in Massachusetts where old friends had profited seven times their original investment in Davis' former oil company. The Securities Division of the State of Massachusetts declined him permission to do business, stating that the new stock issue did not conform to their laws. Through negotiation they later agreed to allow the sale providing that the United North and South pay a geologist named by state authorities to evaluate the company properties. Massachusetts selected Dr. Irving Perrine, a former professor of geology at the University of Oklahoma who had become an independent consulting geologist in Oklahoma City.[13] Perrine produced a glowing report for all United North and South holdings, but the geologist's comment on Buckeye stirred Davis' feeling the most:

> I am so absolutely convinced of the wonderful future of this field which is virtually leased entirely by the United North and South Development Company, that I recommend their stock at the price quoted as one offering an opportunity for sound investment seldom equaled even in these days of depressed values. It can scarcely be classified as a speculative stock in view of the recent developments of its properties.[14]

Perrine, in a personal letter, assured Davis that "engineering difficulties alone represent the only serious obstacle to your demonstrating to the Oil World the existence of a Major oil pool of tremendous size. The oil is there."[15]

So Davis marketed his stock in Massachusetts and Texas raising a hefty $200,000 in a harsh Depression year; moreover, Davis held a prominent geologist's scientific estimation to back his own claim to the immense wealth on the Gulf Coast: "I Believe God would not have allowed Perrine--when I was trying to live a life of Faith in God--to report his opinion that there was 400,000,000 barrels of oil at Buckeye if it were not true.[16]

While Davis raised capital in the state of his birth, authorities there were still attempting to recover over one-half million dollars from the wildcatter. Unsuccessful with a compromise offer in which Massachusetts tax authorities were willing to reduce substantially their claim, lawyers for the New England state began in 1937 the costly battle to seek judgment in the Texas courts.[17]

During this time frame an exchange of letters between David Figart and Edgar B. Davis sets forth the Davis stand as it solidified over the years. Figart took a practical approach in his candid inquiry:

> For my own part I think that since taxes are levied to support government and the fact that you lived in Massachusetts practically all of 1926 would justify your paying a tax for that year no matter what

> you did in the way of protest against unjust taxation. Of course Massachusetts legislators must have known what they were doing when they passed the law then on the statute books but taking advantage of this law savors somewhat of the type of cleverness which is distasteful to you and everyone else.
>
> Consequently, I think we should adopt Baker's policy without delay and settle this dispute on the best terms possible...[18]

Davis remained unmoved from his stand on principle, and his reply is worth quoting as a revelation of the Davis character:

> This acknowledges with thanks your confidential letter of October 13th. I always want my associates to be free to make any criticism or suggestions which their conception of duty or their friendship for me inclines them to make. I appreciate your frankness and realize that the Massachusetts and Seiberling suits have been a cause of great annoyance to you and have interfered with your work.
>
> In the case of the Massachusetts suit, I had felt for nearly a year that I ought to be a citizen of Texas but our family roots were pretty deep in Massachusetts and my friends there were so fine that I could not make up my mind until the end of the year that I should be a citizen of Texas. I was willing at all time to follow the Light in this regard as God gave me to see the Light, Believing that I had a certain Destiny to fulfill and was not sure whether that best could be done as a citizen of Texas or Massachusetts. Then when the tax situation arose and Massachusetts decided upon a tax ratio which was twice as much as the Federal tax, I felt that the issue had been decided for me.
>
> The fact that this decision came at the end of the year might appear to you to be taking advantage of the law which permitted the change but I had spent very little time in Massachusetts that year although actually a citizen until the end of the year.

I had paid Massachusetts in taxes more money than I had taken out of Massachusetts when I left the shoe business to bet my wad on the rubber game so that Massachusetts was in the black as far as I was concerned. Moreover, I followed up this decision with a gift of a million dollars to the Pilgrim Foundation for the benefit of the poor and suffering in the city in which I was born. I also invested in the vicinity something like three-quarters of a million dollars in an endeavor to work out a plan of cooperation between the shoe manufacturers and the workers. That the latter was unsuccessful in no sense means failure of the Idea for I am Sure that when the Time comes, the Spirit of sincerity behind that investment will prove to be like the bread which returns after many days for I have promised myself that when financially able to do so, to endeavor again to work out a cooperative plan with labor.

Does that look as though I intended to take advantage of Massachusetts? Isn't it a case of the Spirit transcending the law in the attitude toward Massachusetts as well as in the amount of money which I felt Led of the Spirit to give rather than have the law take away money made in Texas? Wasn't this greed on the part of the State of Massachusetts to try to take advantage of my loyalty to the State of my birth and my family and friends that she tried to take from Texas, money to the making of which she had made no direct contribution?

Then came the trial and I swore on the Bible that I was a citizen of Texas--no one ever has been able to suggest that I could have done anything more than I did do to prove it without exhibiting disloyalty to everyone--but the jury did not believe me and the Supreme Court supported the jury, saying that it was for the jury to determine whether or not a witness was telling the truth. (Afterward, one of the jurors remarked to a lawyer from Brockton, who asked him, "However could you have decided that case against Davis?" "Oh we just thought he was a rich man and

> could pay.") Cannot you see that in doing this they have attacked the Integrity of my mind--Something so much bigger than I that to yield would be to haul down the flag of Faith?"[19]

On June 23, 1937, the Massachusetts tax men sued Davis in District Court in Bexar County for the state income tax judgment and a garnishment of Davis' 186,751 shares of stock in the United North and South Development Company. Davis retaliated with a counter suit charging harassment by wrongful garnishment, for while his large block of stock and therefore his company became tied up in the courts Davis lost some leases he needed to renew and could not commence a new well scheduled to drill. On October 30, 1939, Massachusetts secured its judgment, now swelled to $725,000, but Davis won $1,550,000 in his cross-action for damages for wrongful garnishment. Now Massachusetts owed him money, and the two combatants worked their way up to the highest tribunal in Texas, where former Governor Dan Moody argued Davis' case. In February, 1942, a few days after Davis' sixty-ninth birthday, the Supreme Court of Texas upheld the Massachusetts income tax judgment but overruled the Davis damage award, concluding that Massachusetts officials could neither have foreseen nor planned any injury to the United North and South Development Company by their suit against Davis' personal stock. Later on in the year the United States Supreme Court refused to hear the case.[20]

This ended the court battles during Davis' lifetime. Apparently Massachusetts officials determined to wait and file their claim on the estate after Davis' death. This they did, and Massachusetts represented the only claimant that refused to scale down its demand for the posthumous court settlement.[21] Collection took time, but Massachusetts tax gatherers proved that Benjamin Franklin was correct in his statement about the inevitability of mortality and pecuniary burdens imposed by governments; and, in the Davis case, the events occurred in the order in which the sage of Philadelphia set them down.

Davis did have the satisfaction of not personally paying and in not doing so continuing to be secure in his own mind that he was right. He kept only a few treasured items in his safety deposit box in the Chase Manhattan Bank in New York. Among these was a letter he received only three months before his death from a partner in a law firm of distinction in San Antonio. "There is no doubt," wrote Wilber L.

Matthews, who knew something of the original trial, "that the Massachusetts decision in this case was a most shameful miscarriage of justice."[22] The personal cost for Davis' long stand on principle was living "for almost twenty years in a tangled world of bankruptcy actions, referees, special masters, foreclosures, garnishee trouble, writs, contentious lawyers, and so on--enough to wholly disrupt the mental equilibrium of an ordinary man."[23]

Many of Davis' associates did not consider him an ordinary man by any standard, but his style of living by the end of the 1930's had changed drastically from the days of the big income and was no longer extraordinary. A 1938 hurricane leveled his Massachusetts House on the Sand where he displayed his art works and collectors' items from the Far East. He put up his House in the Oaks for security on a loan he could not repay and lost it, turning the property over to the San Antonio creditor with the cheerful care of one loaning his home to a friend for the weekend. Davis got the grounds in order and warned the new owner to keep the moss out of the massive, 300-year-old oaks. He spent the last decade of his life in a modest, two-bedroom, one-bath, frame house on Pecan Street in Luling.[24] His manner of comporting himself never changed, and his conduct continued to reveal the same dominant personality that was now and again supported by millions.

If Massachusetts beat him badly in the courts of two states, Davis triumphed in other million-dollar litigations, though his victories dragged out just as interminably. His perpetual intrigue to create the rubber cartel landed the schemer again in the law courts. Much of this story ties to the rising and falling fortune of Frank A. Seiberling, the man known as the Little Napoleon of the Tire Industry.

Frank Seiberling had begun Goodyear Tire and Rubber Company of Akron, Ohio, in 1898 with less than $50,000 investment, mostly borrowed. Showing excellent business acumen, he built a tire business that increased the original stock value tenfold in a quarter of a century while paying high yearly dividends to stockholders during the same years.[25]

While Davis was with the United States Rubber Company, he became so impressed with Seiberling and his company that Davis arranged a conference in 1916 between Seiberling and U. S. Rubber executives on the subject of a merger on these large concerns.[26] Though unsuccessful, this discussion marked an early step toward the concept of creating a rubber cartel that would monopolize much of Davis' energy for the rest of his life. As Davis continued to analyze the progress of Goodyear Tire and Rubber Company he came to believe that Seiberling epitomized one of the greatest manufacturing geniuses in the industry, and although Davis and Seiberling met again only a few times in the next decade, Davis so admired him that in 1926 he presented a gift of $10,000 to Seiberling, who at that time was suffering a reversal of fortune.[27]

The post-war depression of 1920 and 1921, the root of Seiberling's problems, saw two bad years of warehouses full of tires but little market for them and large supplies of crude rubber with no immediate manufacturing needs. The high yearly dividends paid to stockholders left insufficient cash reserves to weather the slump, and a personal debt of over three million dollars which Seiberling owed to his own company further aggravated the situation. Seiberling had always sought finances in Ohio, but when his efforts to borrow funds were unsuccessful locally, he appealed for the first time in his business career to Wall Street for financing. Clarence Dillon, of Dillon, Read, and Company, to save Seiberling from a bankruptcy that would affect the whole industry, agreed to refinance Goodyear Tire and Rubber but insisted on a reorganization of the company without Seiberling as an executive.[28]

Seiberling departed, but the Little Napoleon was not finished. At sixty-one, Frank A. Seiberling launched a new and independent venture, Seiberling Tire Company, into the same successful climb that Goodyear Tire and Rubber Company had experienced, remarkably driving the company that bore his name into the tenth largest rubber company in the nation by 1925.[29]

Edgar B. Davis played an important role in the Seiberling comeback. When Seiberling left Goodyear in 1921, he owned 110,000 shares of stock. These he placed in a holding company, Prudential Securities Company, along with his other assets and property. Since Seiberling owed Goodyear money, he placed 2,500 shares of the Prudential Securities Company in the hands of the new directors of Goodyear as collateral on his debt.[30] In 1926 a group of Goodyear stockholders filed a suit charging mismanagement against the new directors of affairs of the company. These executives, believing that Seiberling might be the instigator of their legal problems, refused to renew at the end of 1926 the notes they held on the Prudential Securities company.[31] His back to the wall, Seiberling approached Davis for financial assistance. There was a vague understanding that the agreement entered upon between Davis and Seiberling would lead eventually to the creation of the giant rubber concern which Davis had long visualized. Essential to Davis' plan would be keeping Seiberling active in the rubber industry. In this deal, Davis took on a financial burden requiring extensive risk to the wildcatter. On January 28, 1927, Davis assumed the indebtedness of the Seiberling Prudential assets, plunked down a half-million in cash and underwrote the rest of the Seiberling debt of $5,500,000.[32]

For this kind of note endorsement, Davis pledged all of his oil interests, motivated into this unsound investment by his obsession with the rubber cartel. Davis' own explanation for his action, made to a prominent New York banker in 1932, reveals the remarkable extent to which he believed in his fantastic project to combine separate firms to maintain prices:

> I entered into the Seiberling situation as the servant of what to me then was–and still is--a great idea. The objective was to emancipate the American industries dependent upon rubber--because motor cars run on rubber tires and burn gasoline, not only the rubber manufacturing business but the motor car and to a great extent the oil industry and a part of the steel industry all are dependent upon crude rubber--from the foreign control which had cost the American public hundreds of millions of dollars and had caused the rubber companies in particular the enormous inventory losses which have been one of the most important factors in making the industry as a whole unprofitable. It was a part of the Idea to achieve this result by a plan of International cooperation between the American manufacturers and the foreign planters which would be fair and to the best interests of all concerned.
>
> I have worked on this Idea with unabated enthusiasm for over seventeen years and this world-wide economic situation which has arisen foreshadows an opportunity which makes me more confident than ever of ultimate success.
>
> I felt I was furthering this Idea when I went to the assistance of Mr. Seiberling and the banks in the Seiberling debenture matter and while I deeply would

> regret to see steps taken which would cause a loss to the banks and the Seiberling Company, yet I would much rather see the equity in the United States Rubber shares wiped out than to be unfaithful to this Ideal.[33]

The Prudential indebtedness Davis had underwritten came due in December, 1927. Here Davis passed up a chance for a handsome profit with the Goodyear Tire and Rubber stock which had risen since Davis came into the picture. Not about to relinquish voting power with Goodyear Tire and Rubber Company, where his old friend Walter B. Mahony sat on the board of directors, Davis hoped to return Seiberling to presidential status. Davis and Seiberling formed at this time the holding firm Ohio Goodyear Securities Company to preserve the Goodyear Tire and Rubber stock intact. For this refinancing and rearranging they decided to borrow funds to pay off the Prudential obligations. They obtained a little money from Ohio banks, but the balance came from a remarkable Cleveland business man, Cyrus Eaton, who bought into the Ohio Goodyear Securities Company at a bargain price by verbally agreeing to support Davis' cartel scheme.[34]

Money from Eaton plus that from the banks provided the funds for Seiberling to liquidate his three million dollar debt which had forced him in 1921 from the company he had founded. Davis' indispensable role in these complicated maneuvers carved another niche for the wildcatter in the folklore of business history. In the stereotyped harsh world of dog-eat-dog capitalism, an entrepreneur, with no thought of personal gain, had come to the aid of a fellow businessman. Though not accurate, the legend as it is usually told makes a fascinating story and is best preserved in its original wording:

> On the last day of 1927 a dramatic sequel was staged in a room of the Cleveland Trust Company at Cleveland. Had there been a peeping janitor he would have been convinced that one of the heaviest poker games in history was in progress in those chaste premises. In the dealer's spot sat a short, square, moustached fellow counting out the money to be raked in by those gathered about the table in showdown formation. It was, however, no more than 67-year-old F. A. Seiberling paying off his

> obligations—and in cash. When it came the turn of Edgar Davis to collect, there was a protest. Seiberling was trying to shove interest on him. Protested Edgar in surprise real or simulated, "That was no business proposition; it was just a friendly loan." Nor could he be prevailed upon to accept the six percent.[35]

That Davis' aid was unselfish is unquestioned. That he had no ulterior motive is incorrect. While Seiberling settled his debts, Davis had incurred heavy responsibility, and he always assumed that the underwriting of Seiberling's affairs gave him (Davis) control of the collateral.

If Davis involved himself with a "wheeler-dealer" on a large scale in Frank A. Seiberling, he briefly teamed up with the grand man of mergers in his abridged connection with Cyrus Eaton. Although born in Nova Scotia, Eaton had come into business prominence in Cleveland, Ohio, where he had the good fortune to be associated with John D. Rockefeller as his secretary in 1900. Rockefeller gave Eaton his start in the business world by advancing him in the company to the management ranks, but in 1917 Eaton launched out on his own, buying his first power plant on borrowed money, and by building up a chain of utility franchises in the Midwest Eaton made his first fortune. In 1925 he began to buy into the steel, rubber, and paint industries, quickly showing an ability to aggregate his holdings into controlling interest. By 1930, he was powerful enough to resemble one of the last tycoons of the Robber Baron Era, for his personal power was magnified through holding companies controlled by him with large investments in most major United States industries.[36]

In Ohio Goodyear Securities, the holding company for the Davis-Seiberling interest, the most important asset was Seiberling's block of stock in his original Goodyear Tire and Rubber Company. Seiberling was the largest single owner of stock in this company . When Eaton bought into the Davis-Seiberling holding company in 1928, Davis and Eaton formed Goodyear Shares, Inc., to hold the 285,000 shares of Goodyear Tire and Rubber Stock now jointly controlled by the wildcatter and the Cleveland tycoon.[37]

When the names Seiberling, Eaton, and Davis were publicly associated, the press in New York City and Cleveland immediately began to speculate that a merger of Goodyear Tire and Rubber Company, United States Rubber Company, and Seiberling Rubber

Company was in the works. Spokesmen for the firms denied the reports, but this type merger was in fact essentially what Davis had in mind in a first step to lay the groundwork for his cartel to lessen the ruinous competition among the rubber concerns.[38]

Though the firms involved denied the merger rumors, during the year 1928 Davis came as close as he ever came to effecting his big scheme. Largely because of Davis' efforts, representatives of these three top rubber companies seriously talked about a merger. At this time other men prominent in world affairs and the rubber industry showed interest in creating a giant combination of corporations. Internationally minded Newton D. Baker, who owned Goodyear Tire and Rubber Stock, endorsed the plan. Irenee Dupont, the family representative of the Dupont interests which later bought control of United States Rubber Company, lent his support. In fact, Clarence Dillon engaged a firm to outline a plan which could lead to the consolidation. The consensus was that so large a trust would be supported by the government because the stabilizing influence would be in the public interest.[39]

For two reasons the talk and planning did not materialize into a merger. In the first place, in the Davis scheme there was room for only one leader--Davis. To such a spectacular figure as Eaton, the leader would be he. The clash of the two dominating personalities was inevitable, although cordiality prevailed in the early stages. "I shall look forward," Eaton wrote Walter Mahony, who played a leading role in the complicated financial arrangements with Eaton and the bankers in the transactions guaranteeing Seiberling's loans, "to seeing much of you as we work together with Mr. Davis in developing plans to make the rubber industry a truly great one."[40] Davis was concerned early about his position in relation to Eaton, whose vast holdings in United States Rubber Company, Firestone, and Goodrich dwarfed Davis' control of only a large block of Goodyear Tire and Rubber Company.[41] Gradually, Davis came to believe that Eaton was taking too much independent action. "He was trying to push me off the driver's seat," Davis concluded.[42]

The second reason for a collapse of Davis' plans was the chain of events at the end of the year 1929. The great Depression ended the optimism Davis had found in discussing the international cooperation in the rubber industry throughout the bright planning stages of 1928. Davis had entertained such high hopes for carrying out his scheme as he went into 1929 that he arranged a publicity trip to London. Here, he, Mahony, and Figart would attempt to convince the

British rubber growers that the Americans had the extensive support of United States capitalists required to amalgamate the entire industry, including those businesses which only represented plantations. Davis gave a luncheon on October 3, 1929, at the Savoy Hotel for officials of the British Rubber Growers Association and for representatives of British firms that dealt in crude rubber. Here he spoke at length of his international rubber plans. There was some friendly interest but mainly the reception was cold. The prevailing mood was the Americans were attempting to subvert British interests to the advantage of the United States. Also, the sheer size of such adventure appeared an unwieldy scheme rather than the streamlined operation that Davis described.[43]

The men returned to the United States to find the stock market a shambles and the mood of cooperation founded the previous year gone with the panic. Men became locked in personal struggles just to prevent greater and greater losses. Only Davis kept his cartel dream alive through the Depression decade. In the year 1930 even Cyrus Eaton tottered economically toward the decline from the peak of his powerful first 100 million dollar fortune.[44]

Preoccupied with other interests in utilities and steel in addition to his wide-ranging control in the rubber industry, Eaton began to give Davis the impression that he was not as interested in the merger scheme as he had previously been, and if he still had concern for the project he would make the major decisions. Davis was apprehensive that Eaton was trying to subordinate the very author of the idea to a minor position.[45] By February, 1930, the friction between Eaton and Davis warmed even though Eaton maintained that relations had not reached the breaking point.[46]

In the area of utilities and steel, cooperation was the last thing on Eaton's mind. Rather, he was locked in a life-or-death conflict to preserve his incredible diversification. Eaton's enlargement of his utilities empire over the years had begun to encroach upon the king of the Chicago area utilities, Samuel Insull, and the Illinois businessman resented a man of Eaton's caliber buying up large blocks of shares in his companies. Insull began to repurchase his own stock, and as he tried to out-buy Eaton, Insull stocks soared to incredible heights. In 1930 Eaton threw his Insull stocks on the market at pre-Depression prices. Insull bought these at high profits to Eaton. This desperate move forced Samuel Insull into bankruptcy and retirement, whereas Eaton took enormous profits.[47]

Eaton used these gains in his monumental steel fight, which dwarfed his utilities battle. Having built up great control in Republic Steel, Eaton planned to promote mergers with Republic until the resulting corporation rivaled United States Steel itself. His first step was to be a combination of Youngstown Sheet and Tube with Republic. On March 7, 1930, Eaton learned that Bethlehem Steel had already proposed a merger with Youngstown Sheet and Tube. Eaton began to acquire enough shares in Youngstown to prevent a merger. Unable to accomplish his ends by this method, Eaton began a costly court battle charging that the Bethelehem-Youngstown merger was illegal on the basis that a fraud was being perpetrated on the Youngstown stockholders by Wall Street financiers. In other words, the merger between Bethlehem and Youngstown would benefit the former's stockholders more than the latter's. Eaton won his case and prevented the combination, but the publicity of the trial brought to light unfavorable information about the way Eaton himself used his own stockholders' money in his varied and complicated operations. Consequently, Eaton's great victory in the steel battle was followed by numerous lawsuits against him by his own stockholders, and although Eaton was not completely ruined financially, he did lose much of his immense power through the bitter court fights and the general effects of the Great Depression.[48]

Edgar B. Davis took the opportunity of Cyrus Eaton's distress to cut his ties with him. The bone of contention between the two men was incorporated in Goodyear Shares, Inc., the holding company formed to contain the 285,000 shares of Goodyear Tire and Rubber Company jointly controlled by Eaton and Davis. The latter's portion amounted to 77,548 shares. Believing Eaton, who was up to his neck in litigation, would be willing to part company with a troublesome partner, Davis asked that his shares be returned to Ohio Goodyear Securities Company. Eaton refused. Davis informed him that his attorneys were preparing a lawsuit to retrieve the stock; Davis was not bluffing, and the Cleveland firm of Thompson, Hine, and Flory worked up a brief for Davis, billing him $7,500 for the service. Apparently the threatened legal action resulted in Eaton's decision to divide the shares held by Goodyear Shares, Inc.[49] However, Eaton offered a compromise: Eaton would trade Goodyear Tire and Rubber stock for United States Rubber Company stock; this would keep Eaton's hold on the large block of Goodyear Tire and Rubber stock intact. The settlement, which Davis agreed to, gave the wildcatter 59,431 shares of U.S. Rubber Company stock. Davis was quite content, for he was familiar with the company policy, and he believed the large plantation holdings, which he had developed himself, to be more in line with the international plans.[50]

Though Davis was content with the results and Eaton, who had enough problems of his own, was pleased to be free from Davis, whom he had come to regard as visionary and impractical, Frank Seiberling was disturbed. The Goodyear Tire and Rubber stock had originally been Seiberling's before Davis got control by coming to his aid in 1926-1927. Seiberling was naturally partial to Goodyear, for he had built this company, and even though Davis had gained possession by rescuing him financially, he was not certain that the stock was Davis' to trade. Davis had no qualms here, for he had taken up Seiberling's indebtedness and foregone several opportunities to sell the Goodyear stock at an enormous profit. He had not sold to preserve control for work toward his cartel scheme.[51]

Even though upset by Davis' action, Seiberling was not in a position to protest too strongly. He had gotten into financial difficulty again as a result of the Depression and had to have Davis come to his aid once more.[52] Seiberling Rubber Company owed several banks $3,000,000, and these notes which Frank Seiberling could not meet were due. For the second time Davis came to Seiberling's aid, and in this instance Davis had to pledge his share in the restored Ohio Goodyear Securities Company, the holding company which now contained the U.S. Rubber stock traded from Eaton. This created a new Seiberling debt, but Seiberling Rubber Company was in the clear. The personal financial standing of Seiberling himself was also improved, for originally, when Seiberling had conveyed his rubber corporation stock to the holding company, he had also included in this transfer his ownership in Akron realty. Now Davis returned to Seiberling all personal property such as real estate held by Ohio Goodyear Securities Company. This left the holding company with only the U.S. Rubber stock plus any cash dividends which had accumulated.[53]

In all these refinancing transactions, Walter B. Mahony, who had moved from the Goodyear Tire and Rubber Company board of directors to the United States Rubber Company board to keep an eye on Edgar B. Davis' interests, was an indispensable link with the bankers who provided the funds. The friendship, though strained off and on by misunderstandings such as those associated with *North American Review* affairs, was as strong as ever.[54]

The breach between Davis and Eaton finalized. The two men could not get along, and at the time of the formal break they were not on speaking terms. On the other hand, the relationship that came apart between Davis and Seiberling unraveled slowly over several years, and they at least remained in an amicable state in spite of litigation. The ambiguous problem between them fluctuated between the complicated and the clear cut: Davis maintained that he owned the U.S. Rubber stock held by Ohio Goodyear Securities Company, whereas Seiberling insisted that the shares were his. Davis had begun to suspect that Seiberling's interest in the Davis international scheme to free American industry from the violent fluctuations in crude rubber prices would rise and fall with the solvency and insolvency of Seiberling's personal and company fortunes. In July, 1936, Seiberling settled the long outstanding suits against him by the Goodyear Tire and Rubber Company. This was the litigation that had originally brought Davis into Seiberling's affairs ten years earlier. In September, 1936, Seiberling suggested that Davis return the holdings in Ohio Goodyear Securities Company to him.[55] The old Yankee trader and wildcatter had no intention of *giving* anything away in a *business* arrangement, but he remained charitable to Frank Seiberling. Davis wrote Walter Mahony:

I think we should not blame F.A. for his attitude, for a drowning man naturally will catch a straw; and he found not a straw in my Idealism, but a life-boat financially. But from now on out I am not going to rely on him to fight for our big merger, but I shall take the leadership in putting it through if necessary and then give him the position to which his experience, ability, and standing in the industry entitles him.[56]

Getting nowhere with Davis, Seiberling filed suit in July, 1937, against Ohio Goodyear Securities Company and against Davis personally, claiming the holdings. The suit alleged that Davis had been a trustee and had never really owned the assets of Ohio Goodyear Securities Company. An important question raised by Seiberling was that Davis had always insisted that any profit from Ohio Goodyear Securities Company could go to Seiberling. If Seiberling was to get the profits, then did he not own the principal?[57]

Davis used again the services of Thompson, Hine, and Flory, and he meant to hold on to what he considered his property. Davis saw the situation thus: when he put up the funds to rescue Seiberling in January of 1927, he purchased the assets in Ohio Goodyear Securities Company outright to be used to promote his cartel. He had also repeatedly chosen not to make large profits as Goodyear Tire and Rubber stock increased in market value. Finally, when he had traded this stock for shares in U.S. Rubber Company, he had saved the day, for Goodyear Tire and Rubber had suffered severe financial reverses in the Great Depression, whereas United States Rubber weathered the storm with profits from their plantation holdings.[58] Moreover, Davis had already used the Ohio Goodyear Securities Company personally to play a key role in reorganizing the United North and South Development Company during bankruptcy proceedings.

In a clever move, lawyers Amos B. Thompson and Charles P. Hine persuaded Seiberling's attorneys to drop Davis from their suit and bring action only against Ohio Goodyear Securities Company. The concession Thompson and Hine made in the bargain is not clear, but possibly the Seiberling representatives believed that they gained a victory in the move since most of the directors of Ohio Goodyear Securities Company were prominent Cleveland businessmen. They must have reasoned that the company's connection with local Ohio figures made it appear closer to Seiberling than to Davis, the outsider. Thompson and Hine correctly reasoned that with Davis out of the way, his idealism, sincere as it was, could not complicate the cold, hard facts needed in a court of law.[59]

Though Davis was released from the suit itself, he was present off and on during the trial, and the *Time* magazine reporter covering the proceedings has left an interesting journalistic impression of two capitalists who first developed their business skills in the last decade of the nineteenth century:

> Across the trial table in Cleveland's Common Pleas Court last week two aging tycoons, once inseparable friends, faced off each other in bitter litigation. Plaintiff was tiny (5 ft. 3) Frank A Seiberling, board chairman of Seiberling Rubber Co., keen and dapper despite his 80 years. On the other side was mystic, eccentric, 275-lb. Edgar B. Davis, 66, oil & rubber man, who has made and spent four fortunes, given away some $6,000,000 to charity and friends because he believed his money "came from the good God himself."[60]

This reporter was inaccurate about the friendship. The two men met and spoke at least on a social level after the trial was over. The journalist was correct in his estimation of Davis' cartel scheme, and the flippant concluding sentences, so typical of the stylized journalism of *Time*, connotes a mood of romantic finality: "Last week the ex-friends were in court over Ohio Goodyear assets. At recess they sometimes passed the time of day, but that was all. The friendship was as dead as the dream."[61]

Davis provided some comic relief midway though the trial, although it was of a serious nature. Davis raised some money with a loan based on the assets that were subject to the question of ownership in the trial. He then planned a vacation in Massachusetts. Thompson, believing that such expenses could be better put to use retiring his unpaid $7,500 bill dating from the prepared suit against Eaton which never came to court, threatened to quit the case and allow Hine to finish without him. Thompson proposed to stay on only if Davis agreed to settle all bills the moment the trial concluded. Although only a negative outcome could result from Thompson's dropping out at a crucial moment, Davis refused the terms. As usual, Davis did as he pleased, took his vacation, and left Figart to settle with Thompson. Figart had no choice but to agree to Thompson's demands.[62]

The court of Judge Frank Lausche found for Ohio Goodyear against Seiberling, ruling January 23, 1941, that Seiberling's claim that the holding company was simply a trust held by Davis was inconsistent with Seiberling's pronouncements for ten years while suits were pending against him that Edgar Davis was sole owner of the assets. The appeals court upheld this ruling.[63] So Davis triumphed at last, but in settling with the lawyers and other creditors that had piled up over the years, Ohio Goodyear Securities was reduced to roughly 10,000 shares of U.S. Rubber Company stock and several thousand dollars in cash held by Chase National Bank in New York City.[64]

Davis ended his connection with Ohio Goodyear Securities company by giving most of it away. In 1947 and 1948 he distributed his remaining shares to employees, friends, and associates in blocks of ten, twenty, and fifty shares. United States Rubber stocks were down and by ratio the shares of Ohio Goodyear were worth relatively little. The letter accompanying all gifts predicted that the shares would return wealth to the recipient some day. Suddenly U.S. Rubber stock rose swiftly as did Ohio Goodyear. Most new owners unloaded their stocks on the market quickly and received the monetary blessing Davis had predicted.[65]

But if you make enough predictions, the odds are in your favor that at least some of them will come true. Conversely some forecasts will not develop. Davis was right about the rubber stocks going up in price but dead wrong about Buckeye. And burning his candle at both ends between Buckeye dry holes and rubber cartel dreams gave neither a lovely light nor much success. The elusive dream of the cartel wasted enough time, money, and energy for several lifetimes. Only Davis really believed wholeheartedly in his idea; like many another promoter before and after him, Davis had convinced himself with his own arguments geared to persuade others. He had made his sales pitch so many times that it had become a part of his very being. Neither Cyrus Eaton nor Frank Seiberling saw the cartel as a primary goal. Walter B. Mahony and David Figart joined in to the promotional aspects through their close personal ties to Davis. Davis himself seemed unable to see or unwilling to grasp the truth that cartels, first organized in Germany in the 1860s, represented an old idea that had never worked, that international trade agreements to sustain prices in the face of world-wide overproduction were generally unsuccessful. The key to the Davis philosophy, though, was to be right when everyone else was wrong; but when he was correct about the rubber stocks going up in price no one who got the free shares was complaining. Instead they were cashing in, and the Davis legend lived on.

Chapter XI
THE TRUE BELIEVER

What matters is not the idea a man holds, but the depth at which he holds it.

Ezra Pound

When Davis won his victory in the Ohio Goodyear affair, he was in no physical or mental condition to enjoy his triumph. He suffered a prolonged illness from 1941 to 1943, probably the result of a poor diet. In his bachelor life style, Davis developed poor eating habits, and this deficiency told heavily on him as he approached his seventieth year. For the first time in his adult life he weighed less than 200 pounds. Most of his maturity had been spent at over 300 pounds. Symptoms in his illness included physical and mental infirmity with loss of memory. Finally his local doctor sent Davis to a specialist at Galveston who restored him to health by confining him to a hospital on a balanced diet. By October, 1942, Davis was back to 200 pounds, had returned to work, and his memory was restored.[1]

With renewed health, his thoughts returned to Buckeye, and he began drilling another well in January, 1942, against the advice of everyone in his organization. Davis styled this one his "Faith" well,[2] an attempt that produced temporarily from 9300 feet, then abruptly ceased, a complete failure.[3]

Now Davis finally began to drill the Luling area again, where success after success came in for major companies and independent operators. For the purpose of this new drilling campaign, Davis brought Ken Blackmar, a geologist trained at the University of Oklahoma, into the organization. Blackmar had brought in several fine wells at Luling working as an independent operator. Ironically, Davis, the discoverer of the Luling Field, missed pay dirt in the area he had pioneered. United North and South drilled three dry holes to only one producer between May of 1943 and August of 1944. Davis also could not resist boring one more hole at Buckeye in the spring of 1944. Although this location proved dry, Davis still remained optimistic about eventually making big strike on the Gulf Coast, but he suspended drilling operations there for a time.[4]

A curiosity and phenomena, the Luling Field -- and the connected and related fields, Salt Flat, Bruner, Darst Creek -- have held up remarkably as producers over a great number of years. Rios No. 1, Davis' discovery well of the summer of 1922, still produces two and one half barrels of oil a day sixty years after its historic beginning as the first well in the Luling Field. Magnolia Petroleum Company, later Mobil Oil Corporation, took millions out of that property, literally millions of dollars in profit and thousands of barrels of oil. What other oil reservoirs await in secret hiding places down there below Luling? What of the logs of the two deep test wells put down by Davis? Rumored to be very valuable, they are highly sought after. There were some showings of oil from time to time at strange levels and at much lower depths. Those who possess copies of the logs say they don't have them and those who have never seen them seek in vain for a look at them. What if Davis was right about the deep oil? In the 1960s Magnolia completed a 6000 foot producer in the Luling Field. Old timers entertain some fascinating theories about why the Luling oil has not all been recovered, maintaining that oil continues to seep into the Luling area through formations far underground, possibly even from lower levels. Professionals who scoff at these myths are unable to explain how grizzled, old-time wildcatters could predict the increase and decrease of production in the Luling Field as related to the high and low tides at Galveston or the pull of the moon as recorded in the *Farmer's Almanac.* It is still worthwhile to drill new sites at Luling and some pretty good flowing wells bubble and gush up at times even though most have to be put on the pump upon completion.

Then there are new ways to recover oil that Davis never heard of. In the early days of the oil industry, reckless characters known as shooters set off nitroglycerin at the bottom of the hole, sometimes breaking up formations to bring in a well. These same charges could often seal off a promising show of oil, ruining any possibilities of oil recovery at the site. Using nitroglycerin flirted with danger at all points and spectacular explosions at the wrong place wiped out people and property regularly before the process of acidization made blasting with the temperamental explosive liquid obsolete.

Putting acid into a well at Luling at times dissolved the Edwards lime, opened up the formation, and increased the flow of oil. Noble Griffin and Harry McDow acidized the first well in the Luling Field in the 1930s for the Grayburg Oil Company. In time oil operators returned to the device of setting off small charges of dynamite scientifically at various levels of a prospective well with amazing results. Even old drill sites spoiled by early nitroglycerin detonations could be redrilled, reshot, and redeamed for profit. Separate companies specializing in either acidizing or fracturing with explosives developed to serve the oil industry.

Then there was that patch of rich oil property bordered by the Luling Field and Salt Flat Field that had never felt a drill bit, the Luling City Limits. Shortly after Davis discovered oil in 1922, the Luling City Fathers wisely passed an ordinance prohibiting drilling within the city limits. Surprisingly, this sound policy lasted for forty years until greed did its worst in the early 1960s when oil operators and promoters promised town citizens much more than they ever delivered in oil royalties. The city council bowed to the pressure and opened the town to the drilling rigs. The operators made money, of course, but most home owners lost out. No matter how much the royalty is, breaking it up between twelve to twenty-four families on a city block whittles down the pay check considerably. Then who pays for the smell, unsightly equipment, and inconvenience? Decorating the pumping units with cleverly designed animals that move ingeniously with the pump jack has given Luling a further claim to fame in the Lone Star state but at a heavy cost.

There was a greater loss to all townspeople. Luling had some of the finest drinking water in the nation. The soft mineral liquid gave Luling residents a healthy luxury purely by turning on the tap or faucet. For years an inexhaustible flow from the two water wells in the middle of town served the city. Then the oil wells within the city came. Drilling, fracturing, and otherwise disturbing the delicate formations furnishing city water cracked them and let in the impurities of salt water and oil and sediments to the point that these priceless fountains had to be abandoned. Luling now gets its drinking water from the San Marcos River after the great expense of pumping and purifying. This story is a grim reminder of the shortsightedness of making policy changes exclusively on the basis of economic reasons.

Modern technology has also brought blessings to Luling. Although the natives did not notice it, Luling smelled to high heaven.

When a citizen left home and introduced himself as being from the little oil city, he was usually greeted with the shock of being told he came from a place with the most disagreeable odors the non-resident had ever inhaled as he traveled. "How do you stand to live there!" people exclaimed. Escaping gas caused the effluvium which shrouded the town. Flaring some wells by constantly burning the sour gas on the end of an escape pipe fitted for that purpose got rid of the worst vapors, but plenty of gas still seeped out into the atmosphere to smell up the town permanently.

Phillips Petroleum Company solved this problem in the 1960s first by finding a way to contain the gas. More importantly, Phillips developed a technique to refine the miasma into a useful by-product, and Luling is a far healthier place to dwell. Only one group misses the old flares burning twenty-four hours a day. Herds of cows used to gather around the fires in winter and pass a comfortable night during the worst of northers. Such is progress.

For the last decade of the twentieth century, new technology promises new oil production for Luling. Mobil Oil, once Magnolia Petroleum Company, has sold its Luling properties acquired from Davis to Meridian Oil Company. Meridian, a much smaller operation than Mobil, is making money at Luling with less overhead, particularly in having fewer employees. Not only is Meridian extracting oil from the old wells but the company is also utilizing the very latest technique in the oil world, horizontal drilling. That is correct, American technology has really developed a device that can drill sideways at right angles from the bottom of the hole. In this way, drillers can bore directly into the formation to get the oil that would eventually seep into the vertical hole. Recovery is quicker, of course, but will this modern development finally mean the end of the oil at Luling? Conservation laws require that wells be spaced to prevent the exploitation and ruining of a field as was done at Spindletop early in this century. With holes running at right angles, are the wells really spaced any more? If Luling does not dry up this time the theory that oil continues to seep in may be proved correct. The Luling Field may be an endless reservoir.

Luling, in a mild economic slump at present, now awaits its third boom. The first came with Davis and the 1920s. The second occurred with the skyrocketing oil prices in the 1970s when at one time 100 drilling rigs were running within a 100 mile radius of Luling boring away for the profitable black gold which was being found in great quantities in the Austin chalk formation which Davis had proved an oil bearing strata. The farther one moves away from Luling the deeper one has to drill to hit this formation but it produces the same oil. Perhaps the horizontal drilling with a little help from the rising oil prices will provide Luling with its third boom. Wildcatters in particular and oil men in general have to be optimistic to stay in the risky business, and their patience and perseverance may reward them with the next boom which is always just around the corner for any true oil man.

Davis certainly understood both patience and perseverance. At age 70, he took the same newfound interest in world affairs that he did in the oil business, and he again considered another attempt indirectly to complete his "mission" and reach the Presidency. As in the past, this would be accomplished by calling attention to himself with some spectacular achievement. He had unsuccessfully tried the same plan during World War I. This time he would be a success. He would end World War II by promoting his project of strategically bombing German transportation lines at key spots.

Davis' plan for a decisive blow to transportation networks to disorganize the enemy distribution of production was the same proposal he and Figart presented shortly before America's entrance into World War I. Figart's report, "A Statistical Analysis of Aerial Bombardments," came out in its final form a few days before Armistice Day 1918.[5] This study was lying unread when World War II opened in 1939, but Figart began a letter-writing campaign to the British and United States governments calling attention to the bombing strategy he had developed for the first World War.[6] He received courteous replies from the British but no requests for further information. American authorities, however, searched out his investigatory study and sent it to Kelly Field, San Antonio, Texas for analysis. It began a trip through department channels on several bases[7] and finally landed back in Washington where an air force historian, Raymond Fredette, unearthed the surviving battered copy in the 1960s.[8] Fredette, author of a history of the German bombing raids on Britain during World War I, *The Sky on Fire*,[9] believes "A Statistical Analysis of Aerial Bombardments" to have been the original concept of the use of air power to destroy systematically the enemy's transportation lines:

> To return to 1918, it is quite evident that you were the first individual from the American side to tabulate the value of bombing railway lines. In light of your carefully prepared report and follow-up

> letters of September 1939, it is ironical indeed that the Allied air strategy in World War II, as formulated at the Casablanca Conference in January 1943, should have given such a low priority to the bombing of the German transport system. That system was actually given ninth place in a list of ten priority target categories.[10]

If Figart's letter-writing was ignored, Davis' personal approach and verbal presentation of the plan was a repeat story of his 1917-1918 round of talks with anybody who would listen in a frustrated attempt to gain the ear of the commander-in-chief. Though Davis was selling essentially the same plan he had presented in World War I, Davis' physical condition had greatly changed. Instead of being at the prime of life, he was 70 years old and only recently recovered from a severe illness. Even in this condition he showed remarkable alacrity in at least the sheer number of persons he gained interviews with in the busy, war-time capital.[11]

In June of 1943 Davis began his program of enlightening the Allies by presenting the plan to the head secretary of the Chinese Embassy. He fared better at the British Embassy, where Senator W. Lee O'Daniel arranged a pleasant visit with the ambassador himself, Lord Edward Halifax. Senator Tom Connally made it possible for Davis to make a presentation to the seven member Sub-Committee on War and Peace Aims of the United States and Allies.[12] Uppermost in Davis' mind was an audience with Franklin D. Roosevelt, or at least General George Marshall, and Davis was not easily put off, as the front offices learned;[13] but, at his age and state of physical health, he did not seem to grasp that he was being dodged:

> Mr. Potter, the able secretary of Senator O'Daniel, at the suggestion of the Senator, made two appointments for me with General H. H. Arnold, head of the Air Force, neither of which General Arnold was able to keep because he was called into conference with some of the higher-ups. In each case I was on hand at the appointed time.[14]

Probably Davis read the wrong meaning into his getting "top priority" for a seat on a plane from Washington to Houston in July. To

Davis, this treatment that was reserved for the elite in the hectic war years meant that someone was at last listening to him when obviously the special attention to assure him a seat on a plane was simply to remove him from the scene.[15]

Whether Davis and Figart had any influence, directly or indirectly, on the Allies' finally conducting bombing raids precisely as the two men had outlined remains unanswered. Probably by trial and error the commanders who developed the strategy of bombing transportation lines came to belated conclusions about choosing targets for air strikes.[16]

That the directional bombing in the last months of the war conformed to that suggested in "A Statistical Analysis of Aerial Bombardments" is made clear by the United States government survey of the air raids in the European theatre. Germany's excellent transportation network was geared to its rail system, which handled seventy percent of its transport; rivers and canals carried twenty-six percent; and highways took the balance. In spite of these statistics, Allied bombers did not single out rails as a top priority target until September of 1944. By November, 1944, even though the Germans showed the amazing capacity actually to increase productions from factories sustaining both day and night bombing raids, German transportation of supplies was down by twenty-five percent. By March of 1945 the Germans were able to move only twenty-four percent of the goods they had rolled before the September, 1944, Allied bomber concentration on transport. Just as they could not take factory products to the front, neither could they bring raw materials into the plants, and for the first time during the war the German factories were idle, stopped not by the incessant direct raids on them but by the havoc unleashed on the network of rail lines outside the industrialized centers.[17]

Conclusions to the 1945 survey of bombing transportation lines in Germany read very much like Figart's 1918 projections. Figart emphasized the traffic "jams" that could be created:

> Railway experts consulted in the preparation of this report estimated the total delay in the movement of trains from the moment of the attack to the completion of repairs to one track at approximately six hours. This figure does not tell the whole story, because no account is taken of the disorganization of traffic and the congestion of trains

> produced by a delay of this length--particularly under high pressure war conditions--at other points on the line. This alone would constitute a serious problem for the operating force and if the attacks were repeated at frequent intervals would eventually force the diversion of part of the traffic to other lines or the substitution of motor transport so far as was possible.[18]

The 1945 government survey of the 1944-1945 bombing raids revealed events strikingly similar to the Figart predictions:

> It appears that serious effects upon the nation's output developed at a fairly early date following the September and October attacks and resulted in large measure from the decline in marshalling capacity on the railroads with attendant accumulations of trains set aside short of destination. Marshalling capacity declined to perhaps 40 percent of normal by the turn of the year and was eventually reduced to perhaps 20 percent. This condition was greatly aggravated by extensive line cutting and the backlog of trains delayed more than 6 hours reached the 1,700 level in the second week of November. Although the reduction in air activity incident upon bad weather in the late part of November enabled temporary recuperation, the backlog again reached levels of 1,400 to 2,000 trains daily during the month of December. When the 2,000 level was reached, nearly 100,000 cars or some 7 percent of the total car supply were tied up under load throughout the railway system. As the efforts of fighter-bombers grew, the demoralization of the line movement became even more serious than the marked reduction in marshalling capacity. In many areas remaining yard facilities were not worked to capacity because of the severe disruption of line operations resulting from widespread line cuts.[19]

Back in Luling, far removed from bombs and bombers, Davis supported the war effort by the continued production of valuable oil, and here in the midst of his oil properties he settled down to wait for the future events that had become standard with him. That is, Buckeye would still blow in the millions of barrels of oil that lay somewhere beneath the surface of the Gulf Coast; and, he would still become President of the United States; the prophecy of the "Voice" of 1904 would be fulfilled.[20]

He portrayed a unique figure in the environs of Luling. Having been a legend in his own time for so long, as a fading septuagenarian during the last half of the 1940s he gravitated into a misplaced New England lost leaf, a quaint personage known by every citizen, young and old, in a little town of 4,000 which boasted him as its first citizen. On the silver anniversary of his discovery well, August, 1947, he felt deeply touched by the attention given to him by his adopted town. Luling staged a fine parade and Governor Beauford Jester spoke at the dinner. To a crowd assembled in front of Rios No. 1, Davis pledged even more good works with his greater oil strike, still just around the corner.[21]

But Buckeye never did come roaring in as predicted, and Davis, patient and content, carried on in the role he had cut out for himself. He always stood out anywhere, but he lingered on particularly atypical in Luling. For instance, he practiced a courtesy and style marked by years of cultivated living in business and social circles in Texas, New York, Massachusetts, Ohio, England, and the Far East. For years people had deferred to him, to his judgment, his opinion, and this habit endured as is often the case with celebrities. He never lost his ability to recount a fascinating story based on some incident during years of travel throughout a long and exciting life, and his many world experiences gave him a rich storehouse of anecdotes set in locales from Wall Street to interior Sumatra. Never losing his sparkling sense of humor, he would insist good-naturedly that his baldness was not from worrying over money or he would proclaim that he intended to marry and have children at the proper time. Davis typified a fine conversationalist in the old sense of the word; that is, he was a good listener. The coffee breaks he supplied his office force twice a day drew visitors from all over the world who dropped by when in Texas. Regularly the United North and South headquarters boasted the brightest intellectual gatherings in town.[22]

Davis' distinctiveness extended to his mode of travel. Chauffeurs at that time were rare in Texas and were unheard of in Luling and the surrounding towns, with the exception of Fred Trevino, who drove Davis. The ancient and elongated eight-passenger limousine in which he rode belonged to a past era and added to the image of the celebrated character Davis had become.[23] He spent many Sunday afternoons motoring through the long, twisting roads that outlined the fault line through Caldwell and Guadalupe Counties, the pumping units monotonously drawing out the oil that represented the millions of dollars he had brought to the area with his determined wildcatting. As he rode, he dreamed of the greater wealth to come.[24]

He looked back also on the glory that was gone in the days even before the first gusher. A letter to an old dear friend of the U.S. Rubber Company days, steeped in nostalgia, reveals a longing for that time when the doors of the giants of the New York business world always opened to him:

> I always believed, and still Believe, the Good God brought us together, and my mind went back to what an indefatigable worker you were and what a wonderful assistant. Time did not matter if there was work to do, and you must have Believed in my Vision of Progress for you seemed willing to do <u>all the work</u> to allow me to dream. I recall how we put through the Value Sharing plan--not the right thing but a step in the right direction—against the combined opposition of all the Vice Presidents; the switch from the First Bank and Morgan and 6%, to Kuhn Loeb and Sixty Million Dollars at 5%. I remember how, for inaugurating the switch, Colonel Colt first offered me a seat on the Executive Committee, which I declined but agreed to sit with them by invitation when in this country; how the discussions so often about salaries bored me and I would send you a note about something that seemed important and Progressive; how, without having schemed for self advancement but merely by "playing the game" and doing the best I could for the interest of the Company at all times, Mr. Leland first suggested that I take the Presidency, then Colonel Colt also, which I declined, and finally the

> Colonel asked me again saying, "Mr. Davis, you have to be President or find me a President." How old Jacob Schiff must have caught the Spirit which was Urging me on when he said I "reminded" him of J. G. Hill, and Otto Kahn also when he told me "We will give you the same support we gave Harrison" (who had made $150,000,000 in railroads and other things backed by Kuhn Loeb). Then I recall how Irenee DuPont told Walter Mahony and me at Wilmington, "The principle [sic] reason for our going into the United States Rubber situation is the plantations," and how taking the Nineteen Million Dollars out of the Plantation Company led Mortimer Schiff to remark, "The Plantation saved the United States Rubber Company from receivership."
>
> I am told that my name is never mentioned now at U.S.R. Co., but I am writing this to let you know that I never expect to have another assistant more thoroughly dependable and extraordinarily able. Well, enough of Dreaming.[25]

Davis grew concerned about how history would deal with him and left a singular note among his papers for anyone who might write his life story. He believed that an editorial about him in the Brockton *Enterprise* of February 10, 1945, entitled "Edgar B. Davis' Letter," was "a work of the Spirit," and he asked that it be quoted:

> A Business Letter is viewed with suspicion, as a rule, when it deals with other than business affairs. Edgar B. Davis' letter from Luling, Texas, to Brockton district friends who share his unusual philosophy is that exception.
>
> The exception is made because of his proved sincerity. His remarkable business career also sets him apart.
>
> Mr. Davis pumped more than 200,000,000 barrels of oil from deposits some two miles below the crust of Texas, though the best minds in the oil business advised against wasting money on the experiment.

> No-one knows if this success is to be repeated in another area, though he says, "Science now backs up our faith that we have a deep-seated dome in our properties in Matagorda County."
>
> Brockton knows he is honest in his convictions--and that he is one of the most unselfish persons this city has known.[26]

Just as Brockton continued to supports its own hometown boy, Davis maintained a rare sense of community support of his adopted Luling. He harbored a long-held plan to rebuild one section with modern, clean housing. He had already made a start on a limited scale. When the law of eminent domain displaced a group of blacks from their modest homes to make way for a WPA elementary school, Davis financed new, well-built homes for the entire group. This gave him the idea to rebuild the whole area on the north side of Luling known locally as "The Flat" and occupied almost exclusively by blacks. He bankrolled six homes in this area before the grim reaper cut him short.[27]

Luling's only movie theatre, *The Princess*, burned in 1947. The owner ran an outdoor "picture show" temporarily, improvising the charred walls and using the night sky for a roof. On opening night, Davis left his chauffeur double parked, sat through the first five minutes of the feature, and then departed. He sincerely believed that he had helped a fellow capitalist toward a comeback.[28]

Though no longer on a lavish scale Davis continued into these last years the peculiarity of his impulsive generosity. The tips he left in the small Luling cafes would double the amount of the bill. He kept a pocket full of nickels for trick-or-treaters rather than dispensing candy on Halloween night. The twenty-dollar gold pieces he had for years given to employees' children on their birthdays would have taxed his limited funds even had they still been available; but Davis continued to delight the children's birthdays with silver dollars, one for each year of age. Lorraine Crockett, Inez Griffin, and Catherine Davis, three of his secretaries, kept the yearly records, gathering silver dollars which Davis insisted they shine before delivery. Davis made these remembrances appear more important than a costly dry hole or a new well that promised him a profit. Occasionally, Davis delivered these gifts himself, delighting the youngster with a small speech and a tip of the hat.[29]

So Davis kept his company going, for he had not lost the innate instinct to gain from the employment of his capital in a wildcat well, and his Darst Creek property continued its rich production. The rub in this progress was the insistence that new profits should go to the development of Buckeye: "As I see it, our job is not to pay small dividends like savings banks and ordinary investments, but to try to Multiply the investment of the Shareholders on the Principle enunciated in the parable of the sower."[30]

Ironically, his returned interest in the Luling area uncovered a new discovery which profited not him but rather the Magnolia Petroleum Company. In his 1926 sale of the Luling Field to Magnolia, Davis, in a contract unique in oil field history, reserved all mineral rights below 3,000 feet. In 1946 Davis persuaded Magnolia to share in the cost of the drilling of a deep test on the northeast end of their field. For the joint expenditure, Davis would get any deep production, whereas Magnolia would gain scientific knowledge. Drillers stopped just short of 5,000 feet, and there was definitely no oil in the deeper strata; but the drill stem passed through a new fault line in the shallow Edwards formation which previously lay undiscovered, and Magnolia subsequently made forty-two new wells in this segment.[31]

While Magnolia was benefiting from the 1946 test well in the Luling Field, Davis wildcatted three more dry holes in Guadalupe, Robertson, and Leon Counties. These dusters did not prevent him from reporting to stockholders that with the rise of oil prices to $1.84 a barrel and a new allowable he could still look forward to profits.[32]

Company reports in the spring of 1948 reveal a widespread drilling campaign running from the Gulf Coast through Luling and on to Coleman County, high on the Edwards Plateau. To offset the news that none of these efforts had brought in more than small producers was the increase of the price of crude oil to $2.54 a barrel.[33] Much of the success of the United North and South during this stage resulted from the energetic leadership of Tommy Caylor, treasurer and vice-president of the company. Caylor had a business sense for paper work in the office combined with an ability to oversee the mechanical work in the field, and Davis trusted him and counted on him in both of these areas of his enterprise.[34] Caylor's loyalty to and concern for Davis matched those same solid qualities David Figart provided over so many years.

As the sands of time ran towards the mid-century mark, Davis' unbridled optimism prevailed, and his attitude gave no indication that he realized that time was running out. He even had a prominent San

Antonio Jewish doctor perform the religious rite of circumcision on him in this advanced age, announcing to close friends that he had become a True Son of Abraham. As Davis carried his company into the second half of the twentieth century, he really started to hit sought-after oil, making good, shallow, profitable wells in several of the seventeen counties where the company owned leases, and after expending millions of dollars over twenty years at Buckeye, Davis finally agreed to work out an option with Phillips Petroleum Company for exploration at Buckeye with Phillips bearing the expense in exchange for a percentage of the profits paid to the United North and South Development Company. Davis closed his last report to his shareholders with his usual "Faith" in "Success" in the "Future": "I am entering my thirty-second year of wildcatting, which I believe to be one of the toughest businesses in the world, but it is one in which Success means a large financial gain, not only for ourselves but to almost everyone within a broad radius."[35]

Having spent over three decades wildcatting, Davis was nearing the fifth decade of waiting for the prophecy of the"Voice" of 1904 to be fulfilled. "It was forty-five years ago today," he wrote Walter Mahony shortly before mid-century, "that I was led to Believe that God had a Mission for me in life and I still Believe that Mission is to be achieved."[36]

Did Davis accomplish anything? This is the important question to answer in evaluating the man. Obviously he brought to completion several success stories in the business world; and, his achievements are notable. The flaw on his record lies in his eccentricities which, when viewed in light of the larger canvas of history, take away from the solid work.

As a Horatio Alger story, Davis fits the mold of the self-made man nicely in his climb in New England commerce to his first million dollars in the shoe business. In addition to his reinforcement of the myth that anyone could achieve success in the United States through ambition, dedication, and the initiative to seize the unexpected opportunities that fall in one's lap, Davis' career is an embodiment of and a tribute to the Puritan work ethic. But it was in the rubber industry that he brought his entrepreneurial skills to their perfection. Top management policy flowed through the Sumatra plantations from planning stage to finished product so smoothly as to be a textbook model of efficiency. The concept of profit sharing Davis championed further enhances his place in history, for the record is clear that Davis pioneered this cause in American business, that he strove to make workers capitalists with a stake in the very enterprise that paid them their wages, and that he understood fully what such a partnership between labor and management could mean in both loyalty to the company and production output of the firm. Moreover, Davis set a personal example by liberally spreading around his own capital gains. Ideas do not die, though the people who generate them do, and variations of Davis' concept of value sharing have found favor throughout the successful modern business world.

In the oil industry, Davis brought the risk factor of the entrepreneur to the same level he pushed management skills in rubber production. By definition, the entrepreneur must assume the risks of business enterprises, but Davis reveled in taking chances and when his first wildcatting experience brought him fantastic net gain he kept on gambling on oil, suffering repeated net losses. In the meantime he made it possible for a host of other people in a wide range of positions in life to profit one way or another from oil. As a wildcatter, Davis will always hold a place in the folklore of the oil industry. It is intriguing that Mody Boatright, the authority on oil field lore, discovered that the old, pioneering, free-wheeling wildcatting period of oil-related history phased out in the 1940s to give way to the scientific story of oil production. This date corresponds perfectly with Davis' decline in the same decade from a man of powerful intellect and ability though somewhat limited by his eccentricities to a figure touched by peculiarities and characteristics of old age.

Long before senility began seeping in, Davis wrapped himself and his associates in the troublesome cartel project that tied him to the futile Buckeye drilling since felt he needed the big bucks to push the bigger scheme. Only an egomaniac could lose himself for years in an antiquated ideal like the cartel in the face of all evidence to the contrary that the giant undertaking would fail in the end. He did entertain the fantastic notion that success in this enterprise would indirectly put him in the Presidency of the United States, and even within this thought pattern he retained the redeeming quality of generosity for mankind in his sincere belief that the cartel would serve the best interests of the world. In fairness to Davis, it must be admitted that failure looks more evident from hindsight, that Davis was not alone in his belief that international cooperation was necessary to the essential rubber industry, and that some sort of cartel was at least a bare possibility to ensure supplies of this indispensable product to keep the business world turning.

Courage to keep on was Davis' strong suit and the same indomitable character that brought him success led him into failed enterprises. But mastery in three separate businesses from shoes to rubber to oil is no small attainment. So in spite of all his limitations Davis accomplished plenty in his life, did much good, and enriched the lives of many people.

When coming out of his home on October 7, 1951, he took a bad fall and sustained a concussion, severe bruises, and other injuries from which he never recovered. He died October 14 in a Galveston hospital. Burial services took place in Luling on October 17 on the former grounds of his House in the Oaks simultaneously with as memorial service in Brockton. Schools closed and flags flew at half mast in Luling, and the Texas Lutheran College Choir sang one of the wildcatter's compositions, the anthem "Brotherhood of Man." Every white and black minister of Luling's churches took part in the eulogy.[37]

Davis died intestate, and his estate quickly vanished under the demands of creditors and laws of probate. La Gloria Oil Company bought out United North and South Development Company by purchasing Davis' eighty percent block of stock and by acquiring the balance of the remaining shares over the next few years. Tommy Caylor and Davis' nephews John and Lincoln Davis acted as administrators of the estate. Since Massachusetts tax officials refused to scale down their demands,[38] the remaining creditors, including the holders of the bonus notes of the long ago sale of Darst Creek, reasoned that by reducing their claims, at least a settlement could be made. The alternative was a long delay in court.[39]

Massachusetts, claiming further interest increases, billed the estate for $1,373,400. Holders of the bonus notes took another $885,000. Another $100,000 went to creditors in various businesses to which bills were owed. Legal fees balanced out the estate, and both Davis and his last dime were gone.[40]

Since Davis achieved legendary status in his own time, myth rather than truth about him more easily found its way into print after his passing, for fantastic characters make good copy in numerous publications, and his story has continued to attract interest to the present day. The Davis image developed over the years generally is the repetition of half-truths and exaggerations by free-lance journalists emphasizing the eccentricities at the expense of history.[41] Just how strongly the myth gained credence over the truth is illustrated by the account of Davis written in the supplement to the *Handbook of Texas*, published in 1976. Although the *Handbook* stands as a monument to scholarship, the entry on Edgar B. Davis, obviously based on newspaper and magazine articles, is marred by numerous errors. For instance, the sketch lists Buckeye as an oil field discovered near Luling which Davis sold before giving the proceeds away.[42]

A better example of repetition of the legend at the expense of the facts appears in James Presley's *A Saga of Wealth: The Rise of the Texas Oilmen*, published by G. P. Putnam's Sons in 1978. The five pages devoted to Davis are paraphrased from a 1949 article in the *New Yorker*, and while adding nothing new to the Davis story Presley does in turn keep the myth alive.[43]

The truth is that Davis was much more than an eccentric millionaire; rather he was a host of complex characteristics, some of which are difficult to fathom. Some sides to his nature he refused to share with anyone.

In 1934 Davis attended a masked ball in Bay City, Texas, near Buckeye. He had no costume but friends persuaded him to join them anyway. At the stroke of midnight the host called on each guest to make a statement about his impersonation. When the spotlight fell on Davis, he rose to the occasion. "I am but a poor wildcatter," he intoned, "masquerading as a gentleman."[44] For years in joking shipboard conversations, Davis used the phrase "disguised as a gentleman" to follow "a poor shoeman" or "a poor rubber planter," and believed that Providence put *masquerading* in his mouth since the other word had a less wholesome connotation.[45] Possibly so. But from the mind of a first-rate promoter the wholesome term could just as easily slip reflexively out of the subconscious.

Davis appeared the perfect gentleman outwardly, but companions rarely knew exactly which character lay behind the excellent manners: the pious, mystical Yankee or the sharp Yankee trader. "To whom am I speaking?" one of his oldest friends frequently inquired. "The Yankee or the mystic?"[46] Davis did not always tip his hand even to his closest comrades. For over half a century in business arrangements around the world in shoe sales, to rubber manufacturing and oil production his conduct remained scrupulously honest, highly principled, and conscientiously ethical. At the same time, Davis drove as hard and shrewd and calculating a bargain as possible in his profit-seeking. He epitomized the very spirit of capitalism in his enterprises for private gain.

Davis' unusual way of sharing his riches highlights another dimension to the man. Apparently, amassing a fortune was not the goal to Edgar Davis but a means to a variety of beneficial objectives. Without knowing the whole story, many have evaluated Davis as little more than a wealthy eccentric. He was much more, of course. Davis was an entrepreneur of the first order who was a capitalistic success in spite of his peculiarities, not because of them.

Monuments live after him through his philanthropy: the Luling Foundation, the Pilgrim Foundation, and the Brockton pools. More meaningful than these broad gestures were the personal gifts to hundreds of individuals over four decades. After Davis sold out in 1926, he gave each one of the contractors that drilled the exploratory wells a check for five thousand dollars. This proved a timely windfall to one of the oil men temporarily down on his luck.[47]

Davis' unusual conduct was especially lucrative for his associates until 1926. That his method of running his business and his affairs did not profit so well after that date does not indicate an inconsistency in Davis but rather a stronger dedication to the deep oil strike he believed would bring him national attention and the nomination for the Presidency. He really did believe in the "Voice," and his "Mission," and he never wavered in this "Faith."

This imperturbable egocentrism was maddening to friends, relatives, associates, and, at times, creditors, for nearly fifty years. He was pronounced stubborn, eccentric, foolish, and insane, but once one accepts Davis' sincere belief in the verity of mystical experience, Davis is more easily understood. The "Voice" led him to assume the correctness of his every action, but Buckeye became the ultimate test of the fallibility of his judgment, becoming the luxury neither he nor his company could afford.

The marble slab marking his grave bears the single inscription:

EDGAR B. DAVIS

A MAN OF FAITH

In the sense that this unusual figure had diligently maintained devotion to a personal prophecy through so many changes of fortune, it is a fitting epitaph.

Endnotes

Chapter I

Unless otherwise noted, all references to Edgar B. Davis' letters, memos, reports, etc. are located in the Archives at Texas A&M University, College Station, Texas.

1. Lincoln K. Davis to Riley Froh, May 13, 1968.
2. Edgar B. Davis to Howard E. Coffin, December 31, 1917.
3. Lincoln K. Davis to Riley Froh, May 13, 1968.
4. Edgar B. Davis to Howard E. Coffin, December 31, 1917.
5. *Ibid.*
6. *Ibid.*
7. Lincoln K. Davis to Riley Froh, May 13, 1968.
8. Edgar B. Davis notation, Poems and Quotations File.
9. Lincoln K. Davis to Riley Froh, May 13, 1968.
10. Allen Nevins, *The Emergence of Modern America* (New York: The MacMillan Company, 1927), p. 44.
11. Lincoln K. Davis to Riley Froh, May 13, 1968.
12. "Local Press Comment," *Walk-Over Shoe Prints*, No. 75, March-April, 1922, p. 4.
13. Lincoln K. Davis, Biographical Sketch of Edgar B. Davis, Typescript.
14. Interview with Inez K. Griffin, Luling, Texas, June 7, 1967.
15. Nevins, *The Emergence of Modern America*, pp. 291-294.
16. *Ibid.*, p. 295
17. *Ibid.*, p. 301.
18. Lincoln K. Davis, Biographical Sketch.
19. Howard Wolf and Ralph Wolf, *Rubber, A Story of Glory and Greed* (New York: Covici-Friede Publishers), pp. 156-160.
20. Karl Schriftgiesser, "The Man Who Gave Brockton a Million," Boston Evening *Transcript*, February 9, 1927.
21. Edgar B. Davis, Personal memorandum on speech, May 26, 1948.
22. David M. Figart to Riley Froh, June 16, 1967.
23. Edgar B. Davis, Personal memorandum on speech, May 26, 1948.

24. Poems and Quotation File.
25. Edgar B. Davis to David M. Figart, May 16, 1918.
26. Edgar B. Davis, Address to the graduates of the Brockton Evening High School, March 27, 1928.
27. Lincoln K. Davis, Biographical Sketch.
28. David M. Figart to Riley Froh, June 23, 1967.
29. Lincoln K. Davis, Biographical Sketch.
30. Lincoln K. Davis to Riley Froh, July 15, 1967.
31. Mrs. Fred A. Chilton to Catherine Davis, September 19, 1953.
32. Lincoln K. Davis to Riley Froh, May 13, 1968.
33. "Local Press Comment," *Walk-Over Shoe Prints*, No. 75, March-April, 1922, p. 4.
34. Brockton *Enterprise*, Undated clipping, Davis Papers.
35. Lincoln K. Davis, Biographical Sketch.
36. Interview with Inez K. Griffin, Luling, Texas, June 7, 1967.
37. Edgar B. Davis, The Romance of Rubber, address to the Rotary Club of San Antonio, Texas, October 14, 1941.
38. Lincoln K. Davis, Biographical Sketch.
39. Edgar B. Davis, The Romance of Rubber.
40. Lincoln K. Davis, Biographical Sketch.
41. Edgar B. Davis, "A Campello Boy Goes Abroad," address in Memorial Hall, Brockton, November 17, 1926, clipping, Davis Papers.
42. *Ibid.*
43. David M. Figart to Riley Froh, July 19, 1967.
44. *Ibid.*
45. David M. Figart to Riley Froh, July 9, 1967.
46. Lincoln K. Davis to Riley Froh, May 31, 1967.
47. *Ibid.*
48. Lincoln K. Davis to Riley Froh, May 31, 1967.
49. David M. Figart to Riley Froh, July 9, 1967.
50. Interview with Inez K. Griffin, Luling, Texas, June 7, 1967.
51. David M. Figart, Notes made by D.M.F. from his diaries, April and May, 1915.
52. David M. Figart to Riley Froh, June 23, 1967.
53. *Ibid.*
54. Interview with Lorraine E. Crockett, Luling, Texas, June 28, 1967.
55. Poems and Quotations File, Davis Papers.
56. David M. Figart to Riley Froh, July 15, 1967.

57. David M. Figart, Recollections of Edgar B. Davis, typescript.
58. *Ibid.*
59. David M. Figart to Riley Froh, July 16, 1967.
60. Interview with Inez Griffin, Luling Texas, June 7, 1967.
61. David M. Figart to Riley Froh, July 15, 1967.
62. *Ibid.*
63. Murdock Pemberton, "Walking Under the Ladder," *Esquire*, XI (February, 1939), 82.
64. David M. Figart to Catherine Davis, July 18, 1953.
65. Pemberton, "Walking Under the Ladder," p. 82.
66. Edgar B. Davis, Personal memorandum on speech, May 26, 1948.
67. Edgar B. Davis, Confidential Memorandum, 1949.
68. Statement written and signed by Anne M. Lawrence, June 30, 1933. Anne Lawrence was the wife of Davis' nephew.
69. David M. Figart to Catherine Davis, July 18, 1953.
70. *Ibid.* See also Edgar B. Davis to W. E. Nesbit, August 30, 1932.
71. Edgar B. Davis, Confidential Memorandum, 1949.
72. David M. Figart to Catherine Davis, July 18, 1953.
73. Edgar B. Davis to Kate Nugent, July 31, 1936.
74. David M. Figart to Catherine Davis, July 18, 1953.
75. *Ibid.*
76. Stanley Walker, "Where Are They Now? Mr. Davis and His Millions," *New Yorker*, XXV (November 26, 1949), 37.
77. Edgar B. Davis, Confidential Memorandum, 1949.

Chapter II

1. Wolf and Wolf, *Rubber, A Story of Glory and Greed*, pp. 161-162.
2. *Ibid*, p. 168.
3. *Ibid.*
4. *Ibid*, p. 173.
5. *Ibid*, pp. 173-174.
6. David M. Figart to Riley Froh, August 3, 1967.
7. Edgar B. David, Confidential Memorandum, 1949.
8. *Ibid.*
9. Edgar B. Davis, The Romance of Rubber.

10. Edgar B. Davis, Confidential Memorandum, 1949.
11. Edgar B. Davis to Colonel Samuel P. Colt, March 11, 1918.
12. Edgar B. Davis to John J. Watson, March 1, 1910.
13. Edgar B. Davis, Confidential Memorandum, 1949.
14. Interview with Inez K. Griffin, Luling, Texas, July 3, 1967.
15. Wolf and Wolf, *Rubber, A Story of Glory and Greed*, pp. 240-241.
16. Edgar B. Davis, Confidential Memorandum, 1949.
17. *Ibid.*
18. *Ibid.*
19. Bruce Barton, "Do You Believe in Luck? I Do," *The American Magazine*, April, 1928, p. 160.
20. Edgar B. Davis, Confidential Memorandum, 1949.
21. *Ibid.*
22. Interview with Lorraine E. Crockett, July 3, 1967. Also, interview with Inez K. Griffin, Luling, Texas, July 3, 1967.
23. Edgar B. Davis, The Romance of Rubber.
24. David M. Figart to Riley Froh, June 23, 1967.
25. Edgar B. Davis, The Romance of Rubber.
26. Brockton *Enterprise*, June 16, 1934.
27. Edgar B. Davis, The Romance of Rubber.
28. *Ibid.*
29. Edgar B. Davis, Confidential Memorandum, 1949.
30. Catherine Davis, Davis and the Plantations.
31. *Ibid.* Also see Murdock Pemberton, "Walking Under the Ladder," p. 82.
32. Edgar B. Davis to David M. Figart, February 23, 1923.
33. *Ibid.*
34. *Ibid.*
35. David M. Figart to Riley Froh, June 23, 1967.
36. *Ibid.*
37. Wolf and Wolf, *Rubber, A Story of Glory and Greed*, p. 243.
38. *Ibid.*, p. 242.
39. *Ibid.*
40. Wolf and Wolf, *Rubber, A Story of Glory and Greed*, p. 242.

Chapter III

1. Wolf and Wolf, *Rubber, A Story of Glory and Greed,* p. 151.
2. "U.S. Rubber," *Fortune,* February, 1934, p. 57.
3. Edgar B. Davis to John J. Watson, March 1, 1910.
4. *Ibid.*
5. *Ibid.*
6. *Ibid.*
7. Edgar B. Davis to Florence Bicknell, August 12, 1949.
8. "U. S. Rubber," *Fortune,* February, 1934, p. 60.
9. Catherine Davis, Davis and the Plantations.
10. "U. S. Rubber," *Fortune,* February, 1934, p. 60.
11. Wolf and Wolf, *Rubber, A Story of Glory and Greed,* p. 241.
12. *Ibid.*
13. Edgar B. Davis, Confidential Memorandum, 1949.
14. Wolf and Wolf, *Rubber, A Story of Glory and Greed,* p. 243.
15. Edgar B. Davis, Confidential Memorandum, 1949.
16. Catherine Davis, Davis and the Plantations.
17. Wolf and Wolf, *Rubber, A Story of Glory and Greed,* p. 241.
18. Lincoln K. Davis to Riley Froh, August 6, 1967.
19. Lincoln K. Davis to Riley Froh, July 25, 1967.
20. David M. Figart to Riley Froh, July 9, 1967.
21. *Ibid.*
22. David M. Figart to Lincoln K. Davis, July 20, 1967.
23. David M. Figart to Lincoln K. Davis, July 28, 1967.
24. David M. Figart, Recollections of Edgar B. Davis, 1933.
25. David M. Figart to Catherine Davis, July 18, 1953.
26. Lincoln K. Davis to Riley Froh, July 25, 1967.
27. David M. Figart, Recollections of Edgar B. Davis, 1933.
28. David M. Figart to Catherine Davis, July 18, 1953.
29. David M. Figart, Recollections of Edgar B. Davis, 1933.
30. *Ibid.*
31. David M. Figart to Lincoln K. Davis, July 28, 1967.
32. David M. Figart to Riley Froh, June 16, 1967.
33. David M. Figart to Catherine Davis, July 18, 1953.
34. Catherine Davis, Davis and the Plantations.
35. *Ibid.*
36. *Ibid.*
37. *Ibid.*

38. Thomas L. Caylor to Riley Froh, July 20, 1967.
39. Interview with Lorraine E. Crockett, Luling, Texas, July 3, 1967.
40. Lincoln K. Davis to Riley Froh, August 6, 1967.
41. Catherine Davis, Davis and the Plantations.
42. David M. Figart to Riley Froh, June 16, 1967.
43. Edgar B. Davis to Sanford K. Gurney, July 11, 1934.
44. David M. Figart to Riley Froh, June 16, 1967.
45. Edgar B. Davis, Confidential Memorandum, 1949.
46. Pemberton, "Walking Under the Ladder," p. 82.
47. David M. Figart to Riley Froh, July 9, 1967.
48. Edgar B. Davis, Confidential Memorandum, 1949.
49. Pemberton, "Walking Under the Ladder," p. 82.
50. Edgar B. Davis to Florence Bicknell, December 8, 1948.
51. Walker, "Where Are They Now? Mr. Davis and His Millions," p. 37.
52. Lincoln K. Davis to Riley Froh, August 6, 1967.
53. David M. Figart to Catherine Davis, July 8, 1953.
54. Lincoln K. Davis to Riley Froh, August 6, 1967.
55. Lincoln K. Davis to Riley Froh, July 25, 1967.
56. Poems and Quotation File, Davis Papers.
57. Lincoln K. Davis to Riley Froh, July 25, 1967.
58. Lincoln K. Davis to David M. Figart, July 16, 1967.
59. David M. Figart to Riley Froh, July 15, 1967.
60. David M. Figart to Riley Froh, June 23, 1967.
61. *Ibid.*
62. Catherine Davis, Davis and the Plantations.
63. *Ibid.*
64. *Ibid.*
65. David M. Figart to Riley Froh, June 23, 1967.
66. Edgar B. Davis, Confidential Memorandum, 1949.
67. Edgar B. Davis to John Warren Bicknell, December 8, 1948.
68. Pemberton, "Walking Under the Ladder," p. 82.
69. Edgar B. Davis, Confidential Memorandum, 1949.
70. Lincoln K. Davis, Biographical Sketch.
71. *R.G.A. Bulletin*, August, 1926, clipping, Poems and Quotations File.
72. Donald Wilhelm, "The Story of Rubber," printed by U.S. Rubber, clipping, Poems and Quotations File.
73. Edgar B. Davis to John Warren Bicknell, December 8, 1948.
74. Pemberton, "Walking Under the Ladder," p. 82.

75. E. S. Underhill, "America's Part in the Production of Crude Rubber," *Motor Travel*, June, 1927, p. 6, clipping, Davis Papers.
76. Edgar B. Davis, Confidential Memorandum, 1949.
77. Edgar B. Davis, The Romance of Rubber.
78. *Ibid.*
79. Edgar B. Davis to David M. Figart, October 4, 1916.
80. Edgar B. Davis, Confidential Memorandum, 1949.
81. Wolf and Wolf, *Rubber, A Story of Glory and Greed*, p. 243.
82. Edgar B. Davis to David M. Figart, August 24, 1918.
83. *Ibid.*
84. David M. Figart, Notes made by D.M.F. from his diaries, 1933.
85. Lincoln K. Davis to Riley Froh, August 6, 1967.
86. David M. Figart to Riley Froh, July 22, 1967.
87. David M. Figart, Notes made by D.M.F. from his diaries, 1933.
88. David M. Figart to Riley Froh, June 23, 1967.
89. David M. Figart, Notes made by D.M.F. from his diaries, 1933.
90. *Ibid.*
91. *Ibid.*
92. David M. Figart to Riley Froh, June 23, 1967.
93. David M. Figart, Notes made by D.M.F. from his diaries, 1933.
94. "U.S. Rubber," *Fortune*, February, 1934, p. 60.
95. *Ibid.*, p. 58.
96. Lincoln K. Davis to Riley Froh, August 6, 1967.
97. "U.S. Rubber," *Fortune*, p. 60.
98. Wolf and Wolf, *Rubber, A Story of Glory and Greed*, pp. 209-210.
99. David M. Figart to Riley Froh, July 19, 1967.
100. David M. Figart to Lincoln K. Davis, August 17, 1967.
101. Wolf and Wolf, *Rubber, A Story of Glory and Greed*, p. 210.
102. "U.S. Rubber," *Fortune*, February, 1934, p. 128.
103. *Ibid.*
104. David M. Figart to Lincoln K. Davis, August 17, 1967.
105. *New York Times*, March 22, 1916, p. 14.
106. Edgar B. Davis to John Warren Bicknell, April 3, 1916.
107. Edgar B. Davis, Confidential Memorandum, 1949.
108. David M. Figart to Riley Froh, August 3, 1967.
109. Edgar B. Davis, Confidential Memorandum, 1949.
110. Edgar B. Davis to Colonel Samuel P. Colt, March 11, 1918.
111. *Ibid.*
112. David M. Figart to Lincoln K. Davis, July 20, 1967.

113. Edgar B. Davis to Colonel Samuel P. Colt, March 11, 1918.
114. Edgar B. Davis to Colonel Samuel P. Colt, March 11, 1918, Davis' Emphasis.
115. *Ibid.*
116. David M. Figart to Lincoln K. Davis, July 20, 1967.
117. Edgar B. Davis to David M. Figart, August 24, 1918.
118. David M. Figart, Notes made by D.M.F. from his diaries, 1933, November 16, 1918.
119. "U.S. Rubber," *Fortune*, February, 1934, p. 56.
120. Wolf and Wolf, *Rubber, A Story of Glory and Greed*, p. 242.
121. Edgar B. Davis, Confidential Memorandum, 1949.
122. "U.S. Rubber," *Fortune*, February, 1934, p. 55.
123. Wolf and Wolf, *Rubber, A Story of Glory and Greed*, pp. 462-463.
124. Edgar B. Davis, Confidential Memorandum, 1949.
125. Edgar B. Davis, Address given to the graduates of the Brockton Evening High School, March 27, 1928.
126. Barton, "Do You Believe in Luck? I Do," p. 160.
127. Edgar B. Davis, Confidential Memorandum, 1949.
128. Babcock, *History of U.S. Rubber*, p. 68.

Chapter IV

1. David M. Figart, Notes made by D.M.F. from his diaries, 1933.
2. Edgar B. Davis to John Warren Bicknell, April 3, 1916.
3. *Ibid.*
4. David M. Figart to Catherine Davis, July 18, 1953.
5. *Ibid.*
6. *Ibid.*
7. Edgar B. Davis to Howard E. Coffin, December 31, 1917; David M. Figart to Riley Froh, February 10, 1970; May 22, 1977.
8. David M. Figart to Riley Froh, May 22, 1977. The United States never got a plane to the Front, and American pilots flew British and French planes.
9. Edgar B. Davis to David M. Figart, November 11, 1917, David M. Figart Papers, Briarcliff Manor, New York; David M. Figart to Riley Froh, April 24, 1968; February 23, 1970.

10. David M. Figart to Riley Froh, June 23, 1967; July 15, 1967; David M. Figart, Notes made by D.M.F. from his diaries, 1933.
11. David M. Figart to Edgar B. Davis, June 1, 1918, David M. Figart Papers, Briarcliff Manor, New York.
12. David M. Figart to Riley Froh, June 24, 1980.
13. David M. Figart to Riley Froh, July 15, 1967.
14. Edgar B. Davis to Howard E. Coffin, December 31, 1917.
15. David M. Figart to Lincoln K. Davis, July 20, 1967.
16. David M. Figart, Notes made by D.M.F. from his diaries, 1933.
17. David M. Figart to Riley Froh, June 23, 1967; David M. Figart to Lincoln K. Davis, July 20, 1967.
18. Edgar B. Davis to David M. Figart (telegram), February 3, 1918.
19. Edgar Davis had agreed to U.S. Rubber demands that he leave his stateside war efforts and return to the Sumatra plantations only because he saw the limited possibility that he might go by way of Paris. He had thought that he might present his war plan to the Allies on his way to the plantations; however, when a passport through Europe could not be arranged, he felt obligated to go on to Sumatra via Japan.
20. Oscar C. Davis to Edgar B. Davis, May 22, 1918.
21. Edgar B. Davis to David M. Figart, August 24, 1918.
22. Pemberton, "Walking Under the Ladder," p. 83.
23. David M. Figart to Riley Froh, June 23, 1967.
24. Extract from the minutes of a meeting of the Executive Committee of the USRCO, held New York, January 9th, 1917.
25. Catherine Davis, Davis and the Plantations.
26. Edgar B. Davis, Confidential Memorandum, 1949.
27. Catherine Davis, Davis and the Plantations.
28. Wolf and Wolf, *Rubber, A Story of Glory and Greed*, pp. 444-447.
29. Edgar B. Davis to David M. Figart, July 2, 1925.
30. David M. Figart to Riley Froh, June 23, 1967.
31. *Ibid.*
32. Wolf and Wolf, *Rubber, A Story of Glory and Greed*, p. 245.
33. Edgar B. Davis, Confidential Memorandum, 1949.
34. Edgar B. Davis to Colonel Samuel P. Colt, April 3, 1919.
35. *Ibid.*

36. Edgar B. Davis, *The Dawn of a New Day: Containing Suggestions for the Introduction of a New Industrial Order*, privately printed, 1920.
37. *Ibid.*, p. 4.
38. *Ibid.*, p. 5.
39. *Ibid.*, pp. 5-6.
40. Oscar C. Davis to Edgar B. Davis, June 23, 1920.
41. Edgar B. Davis, *The Dawn of a New Day*, p. 6.
42. "Why Rubber Restriction Came About," Asia, June, 1935, p. 327.
43. Wolf and Wolf, *Rubber, A Story of Glory and Greed*, pp. 220.
44. *Ibid.*, pp. 224-225.
45. *Ibid.*, p. 223.
46. *Ibid.*
47. *Ibid.*, pp. 224-232
48. Whittlesey, *Governmental Control of Crude Rubber*, p. 25.
49. Edgar B. Davis, *A Proposal for the Organization of an Plantation Rubber Company*, privately printed, 1922.
50. *Ibid.*
51. Minutes of a meeting of the Rubber Growers' Association, September 22, 1922, London, England.
52. *Ibid.*
53. *Ibid.*
54. *Ibid.*
55. Wolf and Wolf, *Rubber, A Story of Glory and Greed*, pp. 222.
56. Minutes of Rubber Growers' Association, September 22, 1922.
57. *Ibid.*
58. *Ibid.*
59. *Ibid.*
60. *Ibid.*
61. *Ibid.*
62. Wolf and Wolf, *Rubber, A Story of Glory and Greed*, pp. 222-223.
63. Whittlesey, *Governmental Control of Crude Rubber*, p. 25.
64. David M. Figart to Riley Froh, July 9, 1967.
65. *Ibid.*
66. *Ibid.*
67. *Ibid.*
68. Wolf and Wolf, *Rubber, A Story of Glory and Greed*, pp. 222.

69. *Ibid.*
70. Edgar B. Davis to David M. Figart, February 23, 1923.
71. Edgar B. Davis to David M. Figart, May 5, 1923.
72. Godfrey E. Coombs to David M. Figart, May 23, 1968.

Chapter V

1. C. A. Warner, *Texas Oil and Gas Since 1543* (Houston, 1939), 132-133.
2. *Ibid.*, 1-2; Edgar Wesley Owen, *Trek of the Oil Finders: A History of Exploration for Petroleum* (Tulsa, 1975), 6, 8.
3. Carl Coke Rister, *Oil! Titan of the Southwest* (Norman, 1949), 4-6.
4. Warner, *Texas Oil and Gas*, 10-11.
5. Rister, *Oil!*, 109-111.
6. Warner, *Texas Oil and Gas*, 24-28.
7. Owen, *Trek of the Oil Finders*, 191, 196-198.
8. Warner, *Texas Oil and Gas*, 51-52.
9. Rister, *Oil!*, 109-111.
10. *Ibid.*, 115-117.
11. *Ibid.*, 145-150.
12. Mody C. Boatright, *Folklore of the Oil Industry* (Dallas, 1963), 4-5.
13. *The Tri-County News*, July 15, 1937.
14. *Ibid.*; Walter P. Webb and Eldon Stephen Brandon *et al* (eds.), *The Handbook of Texas* (3 vols.; Austin, 1976), II, 319.
15. *The Tri-County News*, July 15, 1937; The Luling *Signal*, Souvenir Edition, Luling Silver Anniversary Oil Jubilee, August 8, 1947; Berthold Z. Jackson, private interview, Gonzales, Texas, April 15, 1969.
16. John M. Talmadge, "A History of the Luling Oil Field," M.A. thesis, Southwest Texas State College, 1948), 22.
17. *The Tri-County News*, July 15, 1937; The Luling *Signal*, Souvenir Edition, August 8, 1947; Berthold Z. Jackson, private interview, Gonzales Texas, April 15, 1969.

18. The Luling *Signal*, Texas Centennial Edition, November 13, 1936; Hal Bridges, private interview, Luling, Texas, June 9, 1967; Edward L. Wilson, Biographical Sketch of Thomas Wilson (San Antonio, 1978), 2, 70; Dr. Francis W. Wilson, private interview, Luling, Texas, April 5, 1980.
19. Talmadge, "A History of the Luling Oil Field," 24.
20. *Ibid*, 26.
21. *Ibid*, 29-30; Morris O. Rayor to Riley Froh, July 24, 1967; August 2, 1967; William F. Peale testimony, *Commonwealth of Massachusetts vs. Edgar B. Davis*, Bexar County Court Transcript Copy, San Antonio, Texas, April 21, 1930, 6-8.
22. Talmadge, "A History of the Luling Oil Field," 29-30.
23. Morris O. Rayor to Riley Froh, July 24, 1967.
24. *Ibid.*
25. Talmadge, "A History of the Luling Oil Field," 30-31.
26. Riley Froh, "Edgar B. Davis and the U.S. Rubber Industry with Inclusive Dates," (unpublished M.A. thesis, Southwest Texas State College, 1968); a thorough discussion of the myth and reality of the self-made man is found in Irvin G. Wyllie, *The Self-Made Man in America: The Myth of Rags to Riches* (New Brunswick, 1954); Chapter 13 in Herman E. Kroos and Charles Gilbert, *American Business History* (Englewood Cliffs, 1972), discusses professional management in the early 20th century; Chapter 10 in Henry C. Dethloff, *Americans and Free Enterprise* (Englewood Cliffs, 1979), explains the role of the entrepreneur in business development.
27. Vern Woolsey, private interview, Luling, Texas, June 7, 1967.
28. Oscar C. Davis to Edgar B. Davis, July 17, 1919; September 18, 1919, Davis Papers, South Easton, Massachusetts.
29. Edgar B. Davis to Oscar C. Davis, December 2, 1919; December 5, 1919; Oscar C. Davis to Edgar B. Davis, December 4, 1919; December 6, 1919, Davis Papers, South Easton, Massachusetts. This arrangement also included the canceling of a $10,000 debt that Edgar owed Oscar.
30. Edgar B. Davis to Oscar C. Davis, December 8, 1919; December 10, 1919, Davis Papers, South Easton, Massachusetts.
31. William F. Peale to Edgar B. Davis, April 8, 1920, Davis Papers, Luling, Texas.
32. Talmadge, "A History of the Luling Oil Field," 46.

33. Notes of loans to Texas Southern Oil and Lease Syndicate, June 1919 to January 1921.
34. Edgar B. Davis to Oscar C. Davis, February 1, 1921, February 8, 1921; Oscar C. Davis to Edgar B. Davis, February 7, 1921, Davis Papers, South Easton, Massachusetts.
35. Edgar B. Davis to Oscar C. Davis, February 28, 1921, Papers, South Easton, Massachusetts.
36. Edgar B. Davis to Oscar C. Davis, March 15, 1921, Davis Papers, South Easton, Massachusetts.
37. William F. Peale testimony, *Commonwealth of Massachusetts vs. Edgar B. Davis*, Bexar County Court Transcript Copy, San Antonio, Texas, April 21, 1930, 8.
38. Edgar B. Davis to Oscar C. Davis, April 18, 1921, Davis Papers, South Easton, Massachusetts.
39. Kate Nugent, private interview, Luling, Texas, June 30, 1967.
40. Talmadge, "A History of the Luling Oil Field," 48-49.
41. Edgar B. Davis to Oscar C. Davis, August 23, 1921, Davis Papers, South Easton, Massachusetts.
42. Jess Stearn, *The Door to the Future* (New York, 1963), 60-61; David E. Kahn as told to Will Oursler, *My Life with Edgar Cayce* (New York, 1970), 70-80.
43. Maybelle Gurney to Edgar B. Davis, July (?), 1929; Edgar B. Davis to Maybelle Gurney, July 17, 1929; Hugh Lynn Cayce to Riley Froh, December 29, 1965; Gladys Davis Turner to Riley Froh, April 5, 1967.
44. Edgar B. Davis to Herbert Young and Joseph Machin, May 18, 1921.
45. Froh, "Edgar B. Davis and the U.S. Rubber Industry," p. 111.
46. David M. Figart, Notes made by DMF from his diaries, David M. Figart Papers, Briarcliff Manor, New York.
47. *Ibid.*; Edgar B. Davis, Confidential Memorandum, January 14, 1949.
48. Edgar B. Davis, Confidential Memorandum, January 14, 1949.
49. Kate Nugent, private interview, Luling, Texas, June 30, 1967.
50. Talmadge, "A History of the Luling Oil Field," 50.
51. Hal Bridges, private interview, Luling, Texas, June 9, 1967.
52. E. A. Haney to George H. Leach, July 25, 1922, Davis Papers, Luling, Texas. Haney is quoting a telegram to his Boston stock exchange from Peale.
53. Kate Nugent, private interview, Luling, Texas, June 30, 1967.

54. Hal Bridges, private interview, Luling, Texas, June 9, 1967.
55. Talmadge, "A History of the Luling Oil Field," 56-57.
56. Vern Woolsey, private interview, Luling, Texas, June 7, 1867.
57. Boatright, *Folklore of the Oil Industry*, 58, 78-79.
58. Morris O. Rayor to Riley Froh, July 24, 1967.
59. Owen, *Trek of the Oil Finders*, 647.
60. *Ibid.*, 848-849.
61. Edgar B. Davis, Confidential Memorandum, January 14, 1949.

Chapter VI

1. C. A. Warner, *Texas Oil and Gas Since 1543* (Houston, 1939), 66; C. C. Dauchy to Riley Froh, July 22, 1972; The Luling *Signal*, December 21, 1922.
2. K. C. Baker to Walter B. Mahoney, December 29, 1922; January 12, 1923.
3. Edgar B. Davis to Walter B. Mahony, April 16, 1923, Walter B. Mahony Papers, Pleasantville, New York.
4. Edgar B. Davis to Walter B. Mahony, June 25, 1923, Walter B. Mahony Papers, Pleasantville, New York.; Edgar B. Davis, Confidential Memorandum, January 14, 1949.
5. Edgar B. Davis to David M. Figart, May 5, 1923.
6. Edgar B. Davis to Walter B. Mahony, May 22, 1923, Walter B. Mahony Papers, Pleasantville, New York..
7. H. H. Halleck, Report to Magnolia Petroleum Company on Conditions of the Luling Field, August 11, 1923; Report to the Shareholders of the United North and South Oil Company Inc., June 29, 1923; Warner, *Texas Oil and Gas*, 422; Ernest W. Brucks, "Luling Oil Field, Caldwell and Guadalupe Counties, Texas," in Sidney Powers, ed., *Structure of Typical American Oil Fields* (Tulsa, 1929), I, 279; Edgar B. Davis to David M. Figart, May 5, 1923; Edgar B. Davis to Walter B. Mahony, June 28, 1923, Walter B. Mahony Papers, Pleasantville, New York.

8. Edgar B. Davis to Walter B. Mahony, July 25, 1923, Walter B. Mahony Papers, Pleasantville, New York; Davis was still extremely fascinated with oil strikes or news of discoveries occurring on birthdays of friends and relatives; he heard of the Lee Byrd No. 1 coming in at six thousand barrels a day on July 24, his brother Oscar's birthday.
9. Edgar B. Davis to Walter B. Mahony, August 1, 1923, Walter B. Mahony Papers, Pleasantville, New York; Edgar B. Davis, Confidential Memorandum, January 14, 1949.
10. Edgar B. Davis to Walter B. Mahony, August 8, 1923, Walter B. Mahony Papers, Pleasantville, New York.
11. Edgar Wesley Owen, *Trek of the Oil Finders: A History of Exploration for Petroleum* (Tulsa, 1975), 848.
12. James McIntyre, "Luling Field Could Produce 100,000 Barrels, *The Oil and Gas Journal*, XXIII, (May 15, 1924), 145; Edgar B. Davis Confidential Memorandum, January 14, 1949.
13. Walter Rundell, Jr., *Early Texas Oil: A Photographic History, 1866-1936* (College Station, 1977), 183.
14. Bruce Barton, "Do You Believe in Luck? I do," *The American Magazine*, CV (April 1923), 60.
15. Edgar B. Davis, Personal Note on Marines No. 1, April 14, 1932.
16. McIntyre, "Luling Field," 148.
17. *Ibid.*, 24, 145, Warner, *Texas Oil and Gas*, 68.
18. Owen, *Trek of the Oil Finders*, 848.
19. McIntyre, "Luling Field," 148.
20. Webb and Brands, eds., *Handbook of Texas*, II, 92, *Fifth Annual Report of the Agriculture Bureau of the Department of Agriculture, Insurance, statistics and History, 1891-1892* (Austin, 1893), 39-40.
21. Robert Carter, private interview, Luling, Texas, June 29, 1972; B. H. "Heavy" Chamness, private interview, Luling, Texas, June 27, 1972.
22. *Texas: A Guide to the Lone Star State*, compiled by the Workers of the Writers' Program of the Work Projects Administration in the State of Texas (New York, 1940), 601-602.
23. McIntyre, "Luling Field," p. 148; Robert Carter, interview, Luling, Texas, June 29, 1972.
24. *Ibid.*; Webb and Brands, eds., *Handbook of Texas*, I, 669.

25. John J. Jenkins and H. Gordon Frost, *"I'm Frank Hamer:" The Life of a Texas Peace officer* (Austin, 1968), 114, 121; B. H. "Heavy" Chamness, private interview, Luling, Texas, June 27, 1972.
26. Noble Griffin, private interview, Luling, Texas, June 28, 1967.
27. Inez Griffin, private interview, Luling, Texas, June 28, 1967.
28. Robert Carter, private interview, Luling, Texas, June 29, 1972.
29. Inez Griffin, private interview, Luling, Texas, June 28, 1967.
30. McIntyre, "Luling Field," 148.
31. Edgar B. Davis to David M. Figart, February 23, 1923; October 11, 1923.
32. Edgar B. Davis to Walter B. Mahony, May 29, 1924; undated clipping, Walter B. Mahory Papers, Pleasantville, New York.
33. David M. Figart to Riley Froh, July 15, 1967.
34. Edgar B. Davis to Walter B. Mahony, June 6, 1924, Walter B. Mahony Papers, Pleasantville, New York.
35. Edgar B. Davis to David M. Figart, April 20, 1925.
36. Edgar B. Davis to David M. Figart, October 20, 1923; July 3, 1924; September 6, 1924; Edgar B. Davis to Walter B. Mahony, June 6, 1924, Walter B. Mahony Papers, Pleasantville, New York.
37. Brucks, "Luling Oil Field," 268-272.
38. *Ibid.*, 261, 280; Edgar B. Davis to David M. Figart, December 26, 1924.
39. Edgar B. Davis to David M. Figart, January 1, 1925; January 29, 1925.
40. Edgar B. Davis to K. C. Baker, January 29, 1925.
41. Edgar B. Davis to David M. Figart, February 14, 1925.
42. J. Kenneth Blackmar, private interview, Luling, Texas. March 14, 1969.
43. Edgar B. Davis to David M. Figart, February 14, 1925.
44. Inez Griffin, private interview, Luling, Texas, June 7, 1967.
45. Edgar B. Davis to David M. Figart, March 18, 1925.
46. Report of E. W. Brucks to the United North and South Oil Company on the Subject of Deep Oil Tests, April (?), 1925/
47. *Ibid.*
48. Edgar B. Davis to David M. Figart, April 20, 1925.
49. Edgar B. Davis to David M. Figart, July 30, 1925.
50. Walter B. Mahony to W. J. Gallagher, September 22, 1925, Walter B. Mahony Papers, Pleasantville, New York.

51. David M. Figart, Notes made by DMF from his diaries, David M. Figart Papers, Briarcliff Manor, New York.
52. *Ibid.*
53. *Ibid.*
54. Edgar B. Davis to Herbert Hoover, December 19, 1925. Although Davis received a courteous reply, there was no follow-up of correspondence; Davis was thoroughly involved in his oil interests in the first six months of 1926; Herbert Hoover to Edgar B. Davis, January 23, 1926, Davis Papers, South Easton, Massachusetts.
55. Rister, *Oil!*, 219; Warner, *Texas Oil and Gas*, 422.
56. Warner, *Texas Oil and Gas*, 290; Owen, Trek of the Oil Finders, 849.
57. John R. Sandidge, "A Review of Edwards Limestone Production with Special Reference to South Central Texas," *University of Texas Bureau of Economic Geology*, Publication Number 5905, 1959.
58. Walter B. Mahony to F. Crosbie Roles, March 29, 1926, B. Mahony Papers, Pleasantville, New York.
59. Report of the Shareholders of the United North and South Development Company, April 27, 1948; Sandidge, "A Review of Edwards Limestone Production," 135; Owen, *Trek of the Oil Finders*, 848; Rister, *Oil!*, 175; Edgar B. Davis to David M. Figart, May 25, 1926.

Chapter VII

1. Edgar B. Davis to David M. Figart, May 25, 1926; *Ibid.*; Edgar B. Davis to Kate Nugent, July 31, 1935; Froh, "Edgar B. Davis and the U.S. Rubber Industry," 21-22.
2. The Luling *Signal*, June 3, 1926; June 10, 1926; Steve King, "He Gives Away His Millions," *The American Magazine* (August, 1951), 98-99. In the 1950s advertising agents used the Davis picnic as a take-off in full-page magazine advertisements to catch the reader's attention.
3. The Luling *Signal*, June 10, 1926.

4. Nobel Griffin, private interview, Luling, Texas, June 16, 1979; Willie J. Biggs, private interview, Luling, Texas, June 16, 1979; The Luling *Signal*, July 1, 1926; San Antonio *Express*, July 3, 1926; Houston *Chronicle*, July 3, 1926; Forth Worth *Star-Telegram*, July 3, 1926. The story appeared coast to coast and inthe London *Times*.
5. Willie J. Biggs, private interview, Luling, Texas, June 16, 1979. These prices were advertised in the Luling *Signal* during the summer of 1926.
6. Howard Wolf and Ralph Wolf, *Rubber: A Story of Glory and Greed* (New York, 1936), 244.
7. Vern Woolsey, private interview, Luling, Texas, June 7, 1967; C. C. Dauchy to Riley Froh, July 12, 1972.
8. David M. Figart to Sam Rabon, April 9, 1928. There is no reply from Kipling in Davis' extant papers.
9. The Luling *Signal*, April 21, 1927.
10. Hal Bridges, private interview, Luling, Texas, June 9, 1967.
11. Outline of transactions between Edgar B. Davis and members of the Management Committee.
12. *Ibid.*
13. J. M. Rabon, private interview, Luling, Texas, June 25, 1977.
14. The Luling *Signal*, January 6, 1927.
15. The black citizens made up roughly one fourth of the population of Luling, which might explain the smaller structure. This gesture to the Southern black became part of the Davis folklore in the incorrect story that he built a golf course for his servants when they were barred from the local white greens; see *Time*, October 22, 1951, 113.
16. Davis explained this philosophy in a speech he delivered in 1926 and 1927, "Farming in the Tropics--and Elsewhere"; see for instance, Brockton *Enterprise*, December 10, 1927.
17. The Luling *Signal*, February 24, 1926; "The Luling Foundation," typescript.
18. The Luling *Signal*, January 20, 1927; January 27, 1927; February 17, 1927.
19. The Luling *Signal* November 13, 1936; "The Luling Foundation," typescript; undated clipping.
20. Dawson Duncan, *The Luling Foundation* 1927-1948 (Luling: privately printed, 1948), 7.
21. *Ibid.*

22. Henry C. Dethloff, *A Centennial History of Texas A&M University* (2 vols., College Station, 1975) I, 298; II, 392, 505-506.
23. Charter of the Luling Foundation, 1927.
24. *Ibid.*
25. *Ibid.*
26. *Ibid.*
27. Duncan, *The Luling Foundation*, 36; Ed Kilman and Theon Wright, *Hugh Roy Cullen: A Story of American Opportunity* (New York, 1954), 221-223.
28. Brockton *Enterprise*, December 10, 1927.
29. *Ibid.*
30. The Luling *Signal*, November 13, 1936; Houston *Post*, December 13, 1936; "The Luling Foundation," typescript.
31. Duncan, *The Luling Foundation*, 33-34.
32. *Ibid.*, 28-29.
33. The *Luling Newsboy and Signal*, May 31, 1979; June 14, 1979. The Luling *Signal* and the Luling *Newsboy* combined as one newspaper in 1977.
34. The *Luling Newsboy and Signal*, June 7, 1979.
35. Statement to the papers, June 19, 1926, typescript, Davis Papers, South Easton, Massachusetts.
36. Boston Evening *Transcript*, February 9, 1927.
37. *Ibid.*
38. *Ibid.*
39. Brockton *Enterprise*, February 7, 1927.
40. *Ibid.*
41. Boston *American*, May 8, 1927, clipping.
42. Lincoln K. Davis, private interview, South Easton, Massachusetts, July 27, 1970.
43. The Boston *Herald*, July 23, 1926; The Brockton *Times*, June 2, 1926.
44. Brockton *Enterprise*, February 15, 1927.
45. Howard and Ralph Wolf, *Rubber*. 161.
46. Walter P. Webb, *The Great Frontier* (Austin, 1951), 20.
47. Howard and Ralph Wolf, *Rubber*, 156-160.
48. Quincy Tucker, *Pioneering in Rubber* (London, 1952), 11-12; Quincy Tucker to Riley Froh, March 17, 1970.
49. Edgar B. Davis to Walter C. Teagle, May 14, 1926.
50. David M. Figart to Edgar B. Davis, May 29, 1926.

51. *Ibid.*
52. David M. Figart to Edgar B. Davis, June 17, 1926.
53. Tucker, *Pioneering in Rubber*, 12; Quincy Tucker to Riley Froh, March 17, 1970; Howard and Ralph Wolf, *Rubber*, 161.
54. Henry Wickham to Edgar B. Davis, December 25, 1927.
55. Tommy Caylor, private interview, Port Aransas, Texas, August 21, 1960.

Chapter VIII

1. Webb and Brandon, eds., *The Handbook of Texas*, III, 230.
2. David M. Figart to Riley Froh, July 22, 1967; December 23, 1968; January 14, 1969.
3. J. Frank Davis, *The Ladder*, typescript. *The Ladder* was never published.
4. Quoted in *Familiar Quotations by John Bartlett*, Thirteenth and Centennial Edition, revised by the editorial staff of Little, Brown, and Company (Boston, 1955), 597.
5. Undated clipping.
6. *Ibid.*
7. Quoted in Stanley Walker, "Where Are They Now? Mr. Davis and His Millions," *The New Yorker*, XXV (November 26, 1949), 40-42.
8. *Ibid.*, 40.
9. *Ibid.*, 42-43; Murdock Pemberton, "Walking Under the Ladder," *Esquire*, XI (February, 1939), 83.
10. Pemberton, "Walking Under the Ladder," 82-83.
11. Undated clipping.
12. Walker, "Davis and His Millions," 43.
13. Alexander Woolcott, "Aladdin on Broadway," *Collier's* (February 18, 1929), 178; The New York *World*, April 28, 1927.
14. Walker, "Davis and His Millions," 44.
15. Pemberton, "Walking Under the Ladder," 157.
16. New York *News*, April 10, 1927.
17. Pemberton, "Walking Under the Ladder," 83; Tommy Caylor, private interview, Port Aransas, Texas, August 21, 1960.
18. Pemberton, "Walking Under the Ladder," 157.

19. David M. Figart to Riley Froh, July 22, 1967.
20. Walker, "Davis and His Millions," 44-45.
21. David M. Figart to Riley Froh, January 14, 1969; Pemberton, "Walking Under the Ladder," 82, 155.
22. Lincoln K. Davis, private interview, South Eason, Massachusetts, August 19, 1970.
23. David M. Figart to Riley Froh, January 14, 1969; Pemberton, "Walking Under the Ladder," 82, 155.
24. Los Angeles *Times*, September 10, 1935.
25. J. Frank Davis to Edgar B. Davis, June 23, 1929; July 9, 1929; November 25, 1929.
26. David M. Figart to Riley Froh, January 14, 1969.
27. Marie Seacord Lilly, "The Texas Wild Flower Painting Competitions," *The American Magazine of Art*, XX (June, 1929), 34.
28. J. Frank Dobie, *Tales of Old-Time Texas* (London, 1959), 141.
29. Helen Raley, "Texas Wild-Flower Art Exhibit," *Holland's Magazine* (July, 1927), 5, 49.
30. *Ibid.*
31. San Antonio *Express*, March 18, 1928.
32. Lilly, "Texas Wild Flower Competitions," 342, 345.
33. Houston *Post*, March 19, 1928; Dallas Morning *News*, March 19, 1928; *Christian Science Monitor*, April 3, 1928; New York Evening *Post*, March 28, 1928.
34. Chicago *News*, April 2, 1928.
35. *The New Yorker*, March 31, 1928; March 24, 1928.
36. San Antonio *Express*, January 30, 1929; February 1, 1929.
37. Lilly, "Texas Wild Flower Competitions," 346-347.
38. Larry McMurtry, *In a Narrow Grave* (Austin, 1968), 83, 121.
39. Lilly, "Texas Wild Flower Competitions," 346-347.
40. Pemberton, "Walking Under the Ladder," 155-156.
41. List of Artists and Hostesses at "A House in the Sand, Inc.," July 12, 1925 to July 10, 1926.
42. Fitzhugh W. Haensel to Edgar B. Davis, June 15, 1927; July 12, 1927.
43. San Antonio Evening *News*, April 7, 1928; San Antonio *Light*, April 7, 1929; The Brockton *Times*, April 7, 1928; The Brockton *Enterprise*, April 7, 1928.
44. Memorandum: Regarding Artists for Good Friday Concerts.
45. The Brockton *Enterprise*, April 7, 1928.

46. *Ibid.*
47. Riley Froh, "Edgar B. Davis and the United States Rubber Industry with Inclusive Dates," (unpublished master's thesis, Southwest Texas State College, 1968), 27-30; 111-118.
48. Frank Luther Mott, *A History of American Magazines* (4 vols.; Cambridge, 1938), II, 219-256.
49. *Ibid.*, 256-259.
50. Quoted in *Ibid.*, 258-259.
51. Walter B. Mahony to Edgar B. Davis, June 22, 1928; June 15, 1928.
52. Walter B. Mahony to Edgar B. Davis, June 22, 1928.
53. Edgar B. Davis to Walter B. Mahony, March 25, 1929.
54. David M. Figart to Riley Froh, August 3, 1967.
55. Walter B. Mahony to Colonel George Harvey, June 21, 1926.
56. Walter B. Mahony to Edgar B. Davis, June 15, 1928.
57. Mott, *History of Magazines*, II, 259-260.
58. Walter B. Mahony to Edgar B. Davis, June 15, 1928.
59. Walter B. Mahony to Edgar B. Davis, January 13, 1929.
60. Walter B. Mahony to Edgar B. Davis, March 14, 1929.
61. Walter B. Mahony to Edgar B. Davis, March 16, 1929.
62. Edgar B. Davis to Walter B. Mahony, March 15, 1929; Fred W. Murphy to David M. Figart, April 20, 1929; Walter B. Mahony to Edgar B. Davis, March 19, 1929.
63. Edgar B. Davis to Walter B. Mahony, March 25, 1929.
64. Walter B. Mahony to Edgar B. Davis, March 19, 1929.
65. Edgar B. Davis to Walter B. Mahony, April 1, 1932.
66. Mott, *History of Magazines*, II, 259-260.
67. Walter B. Mahony to Edgar B. Davis, March 22, 1933.
68. Edgar B. Davis to Walter B. Mahony, March 22, 1933. Davis had also mailed $1,000 the first of the month. Edgar B. Davis to Walter B. Mahony, March 2, 1933.
69. Edgar B. Davis to Walter B. Mahony, September 4, 1933.
70. Memorandum: Notes payable to Rumford Press, December 27, 1933.
71. David M. Figart to Riley Froh, August 3, 1967; Mott, *History of Magazines*, II, 260.
72. Mott, *History of Magazines*, II, 226, 260.

73. David M. Figart to Riley Froh, August 3, 1967; Theodore Peterson, *Magazines in the Twentieth Century* (Urbana, 1964), 229. Walter B. Mahony, Jr., who assisted his father at times on the *North American Review*, later became one of the top men with *The Reader's Digest* and now is directing the book publications of original manuscripts by that phenomenally successful magazine.
74. Peterson, *Magazines*, 146-148; *Time*, September 14, 1942, 46.
75. "About This Issue," *North American Review*, CCLXI (Summer, 1976), 2.
76. See particularly *Ibid.* for a graphic contrast between the reprinted articles and the contemporary offerings; also, see *North American Review*, CCLXII (Spring, 1977), an issue devoted to the short story which includes several examples of fiction lacking a refined sense of propriety.
77. Mott, *History of Magazines*, II, 261.

Chapter IX

1. The Luling *Signal*, July 1, 1926; San Antonio *Express*, June 26, 1926.
2. The Luling *Signal*, January 20, 1927.
3. Logs of Kelly No. 1 and Tiller No. 2.
4. The Luling *Signal*, January 20, 1927; Owen, *Trek of the Oil Finders*, 849-850; Warner, *Texas Oil and Gas*, 290.
5. Owen, *Trek of the Oil Finders*, 850; Warner, *Texas Oil and Gas*, 292; Outline of Transactions between Edgar B. Davis and Members of the Management Committee.
6. William F. Peale to Edgar B. Davis, July 9, 1929 (telegram).
7. Owen, *Trek of the Oil Finders*, 850; Noble R. Griffin, private interview, Luling, Texas, June 8, 1980.
8. Outline of Transactions between Edgar B. Davis and Members of the Management Committee.
9. The Luling *Signal*, January 3, 1930; January 10, 1930.
10. Sandidge, "A Review of Edwards Limestone Production," 136.
11. *Ibid.*
12. Warner, *Texas Oil and Gas*, 292-293.

13. Edgar B. Davis to Frank A. Seiberling, September 25, 1931; Sandidge, "A Review of Edwards Limestone Production," 136.
14. Edgar B. Davis to Frank A. Seiberling, September 25, 1931.
15. *Ibid.*
16. Edgar B. Davis to David M. Figart, August 14, 1931.
17. Kelts C. Baker, Personal Resume, 1931.
18. Vern Woolsey, private interview, Luling, Texas, June 7, 1967.
19. Outline of Transactions between Edgar B. Davis and the Management Committee.
20. Much of his personal correspondence throughout the depth of the Depression years from 1931 to 1932 will illustrate the high spirits Davis maintained. Particular references are Edgar B. Davis to David M. Figart, August 4, 1931; September 2, 1931.
21. Edgar B. Davis to David M. Figart, November 9, 1931.
22. David Figart worked out of the Davis New York office at Madison Avenue. From here he kept in touch with the New York offices of the major rubber concerns and read widely of overseas developments while keeping up a thorough correspondence with Davis on the latest news of the rubber industry.
23. David M. Figart to Riley Froh, June 23, 1967; Edgar B. Davis to Richard B. Ellis, May 9, 1928.
24. William McMasters to Richard B. Ellis, May 14, 1928; June 11, 1928; June 18, 1928.
25. Brockton *Enterprise*, January 24, 1928; February 1, 1928.
26. San Antonio *Evening News*, May 12, 1928; May 14, 1928; The Gonzales *Daily Inquirer*, May 8, 1928; Austin *American*, May 8, 1928; May 9, 1928; The Luling *Signal*, May 10, 1928.
27. Brockton *Enterprise*, June 27, 1928.
28. Ralph W. Steen, *Twentieth Century Texas* (Austin, 1942), 236.
29. Howard and Ralph Wolf, *Rubber*, 245.
30. Edgar B. Davis, "The Way Out - and On," *North American Review*, CCXXXIV (October, 1932), 290.
31. *Ibid.*
32. *Ibid.*, 291.
33. *Ibid.*
34. Brockton *Enterprise*, December 18, 1931; San Antonio *Express*, December 18, 1931.
35. Brockton *Enterprise*, December 19, 1931.
36. Edgar B. Davis to David M. Figart, December 17, 1931.

37. Report to the Stockholders of the United North and South Development Company, December 31, 1932.
38. Edgar B. Davis to David M. Figart, August 7, 1931; Report to the Stockholders of the United North and South Development Company, December 31, 1932.
39. Edgar B. Davis to David M. Figart, September 23, 1931.
40. David M. Figart, *History of Stoddard No. 1* (New York, 1932), 3-4.
41. Edgar B. Davis to Frank A. Seiberling, November 13, 1931.
42. Figart, *Stoddard No. 1*, 7.
43. *Ibid., The Oil Weekly*, September 19, 1932, 15.
44. Edgar B. Davis to David M. Figart, January 4, 1932.
45. Edgar B. Davis to David M. Figart, January 21, 1932.
46. Edgar B. Davis to David M. Figart, January 26, 1932.
47. Edgar B. Davis to David M. Figart, January 28, 1932.
48. Edgar B. Davis to Stuart Hotchkiss, February 12, 1932.
49. Edgar B. Davis to Fred Murphy, February 6, 1932, (telegram).
50. Edgar B. Davis to David M. Figart, February 29, 1932.
51. Edgar B. Davis to David M. Figart, January 28, 1932.
52. Edgar B. Davis to David M. Figart, February 23, 1932; February 26, 1932; David M. Figart to Edgar B. Davis, February 16, 1932; February 25, 1932.
53. Edgar B. Davis to David M. Figart, January 26, 1932.
54. Edgar B. Davis to David M. Figart, February 13, 1932.
55. Edgar B. Davis to David M. Figart, February 26, 1932.
56. Bertha M. Loheed to Edgar B. Davis, June 4, 1932; Figart, *Stoddard No. 1*, 9-11.
57. *The Oil Weekly*, September 19, 1932, 14.
58. *Ibid.*, 14, 16; Figart, *Stoddard No. 1*, 14-18.
59. Boatright, *Folklore of the Oil Industry*, 119.
60. Figart, *Stoddard No. 1*, 19.
61. *Ibid.*, 14.
62. Edgar B. Davis to David M. Figart, August (?), 1932.
63. Report to the Stockholders of the United North and South Development Company, December 31, 1932.
64. Sandidge, "A Review of Edwards Limestone Production," 136.
65. O. H. Holland to David M. Figart, April 29, 1970, David M. Figart Papers, Briarcliff Manor, New York. Holland was chief production geologist for Exxon's Houston Office.
66. Warner, *Texas Oil and Gas*, 219.

67. John W. Bicknell to Edgar B. Davis, September 1, 1932; November 10, 1932; John W. Bicknell to David M. Figart, February 25, 1937.
68. Lincoln K. Davis, private interview, Brockton, Massachusetts, June 19, 1970.
69. Edgar B. Davis to David M. Figart, July 10, 1933.
70. Edgar B. Davis to Mabel Lawrence, July 19, 1933.
71. Lorraine Crockett, private interview, Luling, Texas, July 3, 1980.
72. Edgar B. Davis to Mabel Lawrence, July 19, 1933.
73. David M. Figart to Riley Froh, August 19, 1967.
74. Edgar B. Davis to David M. Figart, August 11, 1933.
75. Edgar B. Davis, Personal Memorandum, September 11, 1933.
76. David M. Figart to Edgar B. Davis, November 23, 1933.
77. Edgar B. Davis to David M. Figart, December 4, 1933.
78. *The Tri-County News*, April 11, 1935.
79. Edgar B. Davis, Confidential Memorandum, January 14, 1949.
80. *The Tri-County News*, February 25, 1937.
81. *Ibid*, December 24, 1936; February 25, 1937.
82. Hazel Muenster, private interview, Luling, Texas, April 5, 1980.
83. *The Tri-County News*, April 8, 1937.
84. *Ibid.*, April 22, 1937.
85. *Ibid*, May 13, 1937.
86. *Ibid*, June 3, 1937; June 10, 1937; June 17, 1937.
87. *Ibid.*, June 4, 1937.
88. Warner, *Texas Oil and Gas*, 219.

Chapter X

1. James W. Bass, Collector of Internal Revenue, Austin, Texas to Edgar B. Davis, March 15, 1927.
2. Fred W. Murphy to Ralph W. Copeland, January 20, 1928, Davis Papers, South Easton, Massachusetts; David M. Figart, The Massachusetts Tax Case, Undated Memorandum, Davis Papers, South Easton, Massachusetts, 1-2.
3. The Luling *Signal*, December 30, 1926; Edgar B. Davis, Memorandum on Change of Residence, December 28, 1926, Davis Papers, South Easton, Massachusetts.

4. Edgar B. Davis, Memorandum on Change of Residence, December 28, 1926, Davis Papers, South Easton, Massachusetts.
5. David M. Figart, The Massachusetts Tax Case, Undated Memorandum, 3-4; Memorandum on Conference held July 16, 1928, at Campello, Massachusetts, in regard to Massachusetts Income Tax on Edgar B. Davis, Davis Papers, South Easton, Massachusetts.
6. David M. Figart, The Massachusetts Tax Case, Undated Memorandum, 3-4, Davis Papers, South Easton, Massachusetts.
7. Walker, "Davis and His Millions," 35.
8. David M. Figart, The Massachusetts Tax Case, Undated Memorandum, 4, Davis Papers, South Easton, Massachusetts.
9. *Ibid.*, 3-5; *Edgar B. Davis vs. Commonwealth of Massachusetts, Transcript of Record, Supreme Court of the United States, October Term, 1942* (Washington, DC, 1943), 77. The Supreme Court of the United States refused to hear the case.
10. *Ibid.*
11. Walker, "Davis and His Millions," 35.
12. Lincoln K. Davis to Riley Froh, July 1, 1971.
13. Edgar B. Davis, Confidential Memorandum, January 14, 1949.
14. Irving Perrine, Ph.D., Report of the Properties of the United North and South Development Company, March 13, 1933, Davis Papers, South Easton, Massachusetts.
15. Irving Perrine to Edgar B. Davis, September 29, 1933.
16. Edgar B. Davis, Confidential Memorandum, January 14, 1949.
17. Lincoln K. Davis to Riley Froh, July 1, 1971. One lower figure unofficially discussed was $25,000. Davis, as he said, would not pay a cent.
18. David M. Figart to Edgar B. Davis, October 13, 1937.
19. Edgar B. Davis to David M. Figart, November 16, 1937.
20. *Edgar B. Davis vs. Commonwealth of Massachusetts, Transcript of Record, Supreme Court of the United States, October Term, 1942*, 139-140.
21. David M. Figart to Riley Froh, November 12, 1968; Lincoln K. Davis to Riley Froh, July 1, 1971; Kate Nugent, private interview, Luling, Texas, June 30, 1967.
22. Wilber L. Matthews to Edgar B. Davis, August 15, 1951, Davis Papers, South Easton, Massachusetts.
23. Walker, "Davis and His Millions," 36.

24. Steve King, "He Gives Away His Millions," *The American Magazine* (August, 1951), 101.
25. Howard and Ralph Wolf, *Rubber*, 419-420.
26. Edgar B. Davis to Oscar C. Davis, July 16, 1916, Davis Papers, South Easton, Massachusetts.
27. David M. Figart, Memorandum on Seiberling Suits, October 16, 1939, 1-2. Walter B. Mahony Papers, Pleasantville, New York. The press often erroneously reported this friendly connection as stemming from a $57,000 loan from Seiberling to Davis in the wildcatting days before the Luling discovery. See, for instance, *Newsweek*, January 9, 1939, 47-48; *Time*, July 1, 1940, 64.
28. Howard and Ralph Wolf, *Rubber*, 448-450.
29. *Ibid.*, 450-451.
30. *Ibid.*
31. *Ibid.*, David M. Figart, Memorandum on Seiberling Suits, October 16, 1939, 2, Walter B. Mahony Papers, Pleasantville, New York.
32. Howard and Ralph Wolf, *Rubber*, 451; David M. Figart, Memorandum on Seiberling Suits, October 16, 1939, 2-3, Walter B. Mahony Papers, Pleasantville, New York; *Time*, July 1, 1940, 65.
33. Edgar B. Davis to E. J. Quintal, December 5, 1932, Walter B. Mahony Papers, Pleasantville, New York.
34. Edgar B. Davis, Memorandum to the Seiberling Rubber Company Debenture Holders, May 15, 1939, 2, Walter B. Mahony Papers, Pleasantville, New York; Howard and Ralph Wolf, *Rubber*, 457.
35. Howard and Ralph Wolf, *Rubber*, 451.
36. *Ibid.*, 478-480; Marcus Gleisser, *The World of Cyrus Eaton* (New York, 1965), 32-41.
37. Howard and Ralph Wolf, *Rubber*, 451.
38. Glenn D. Babcock, *History of the United States Rubber Company: A Case Study in Corporation Management* (Bloomington, 1966), 216-217.
39. David M. Figart, Memorandum on Seiberling Suits, October 16, 1939, 6, Mahony Papers, Pleasantville, New York; Gleisser, *Cyrus Eaton*, 40-41.
40. Cyrus Eaton to Walter B. Mahony, January 10, 1928, Walter B. Mahony Papers, Pleasantville, New York.

41. Edgar B. Davis, Memorandum to the Trustees of Seiberling Rubber Company, June 24, 1931, Mahony Papers, Pleasantville, New York.
42. David M. Figart to Riley Froh, August 19, 1967.
43. Notes on Luncheon Talks at the Savoy Hotel, London, England, October 3, 1929, Mahony Papers, Pleasantville, New York.
44. Gleisser, *Cyrus Eaton*, 49.
45. David M. Figart to Riley Froh, August 19, 1967.
46. Cyrus Eaton to Walter B. Mahony, February 18, 1930, Mahony Papers, Pleasantville, New York.
47. Howard and Ralph Wolf, *Rubber*, 478-479; Gleisser, *Cyrus Eaton*, 41-44.
48. Howard and Ralph Wolf, *Rubber*, 479-480; Gleisser, *Cyrus Eaton*, 60-69.
49. David M. Figart, Memorandum on Seiberling Suits, October 16, 1939, 8; Edgar B. Davis, Memorandum to the Trustees of Seiberling Rubber Company, June 24, 1931, Mahony Papers, Pleasantville, New York; David M. Figart to Riley Froh, August 19, 1967.
50. David M. Figart, Memorandum on Seiberling Suits, October 16, 1939, 8, Mahony Papers, Pleasantville, New York.
51. *Ibid.*
52. *Ibid.*
53. *Ibid.*, 10; Minutes of Meeting of Ohio Goodyear Securities Company, May 19, 1930, 9, Mahony Papers, Pleasantville, New York.
54. David M. Figart to Riley Froh, April 12, 1971.
55. David M. Figart, Memorandum on Seiberling Suits, October 16, 1939, 9, Mahony Papers, Pleasantville, New York.
56. Edgar B. Davis to Walter B. Mahony, September 24, 1936, Mahony Papers, Pleasantville, New York.
57. David M. Figart, Memorandum on Seiberling Suits, October 16, 1939, 9, Mahony Papers, Pleasantville, New York.
58. *Ibid.*, 9-10.
59. David M. Figart to Riley Froh, August 19, 1967.
60. *Time*, July 1, 1940, 64.
61. *Ibid.*, 66.
62. David M. Figart to Riley Froh, August 19, 1967.
63. *Ibid.* Frank Lausche became a United States Senator from Ohio in the 1960's.

64. *Ibid.*
65. Inez Griffin, private interview, Luling, Texas, June 7, 1967; Lorraine Crockett, private interview, Luling, Texas, June 28, 1967.

Chapter XI

1. David M. Figart to Walter B. Mahony, February 22, 1942; April 24, 1942; May 1, 1942; May 5, 1942, Walter B. Mahony Papers, Pleasantville, New York.
2. David M. Figart to Walter B. Mahony, October 10, 1942, Walter B. Mahony Papers, Pleasantville, New York.
3. David M. Figart to Walter Mahony, May 10, 1943, Walter B. Mahony Papers, Pleasantville, New York.
4. David M. Figart to Walter B. Mahony, June 26, 1944; July 30, 1944; August 11, 1944; August 30, 1944; September 14, 1944, Walter B. Mahony Papers, Pleasantville, New York.
5. David M. Figart to Riley Froh, June 24, 1980.
6. David M. Figart to Riley Froh, December 3, 1968; May 22, 1977.
7. David M. Figart to Riley Froh, June 17, 1977.
8. Raymond H. Fredette to David M. Figart, June 23, 1968; Hanson W. Baldwin to David M. Figart, January 21, 1965; David M. Figart Papers, Briarcliff Manor, New York.
9. Raymond H. Fredette, *The Sky on Fire: The First Battle of Britain* (New York, 1966).
10. Raymond H. Fredette to David M. Figart, September 2, 1968, David M. Figart Papers, Briarcliff Manor, New York.
11. David M. Figart to Riley Froh, May 22, 1977.
12. Edgar B. Davis, Memorandum, July 16, 1943, Walter B. Mahony Papers, Pleasantville, New York.
13. *Ibid.*
14. *Ibid.*
15. *Ibid.*
16. For the evolution of strategic bombing of transportation in the actual theatre of war, see Hanson Baldwin, *Battles Lost and Won* (New York, 1966), 51, 404; and Lord Tedder, *With Prejudice* (Boston, 1967), 488-489, 502-503.

17. George Ball, *et al., Strategic Bombing Survey* (Washington, DC, 1945), 59-61.
18. David M. Figart, "A Statistical Analysis of Aerial Bombardments," October, 1918, 27, David M. Figart Papers, Briarcliff Manor, New York.
19. Ball, *Strategic Bombing Survey*, 63. In a reverse procedure, David Figart continued by letter to attempt to influence the government's bombing operations during the Viet Nam War. This time Figart, who opposed the war in principle, argued against the massive bombing raids. He pointed out that this fruitless warfare rarely cut any transportation or command lines because supplies always moved over jungle trails. The bombing, Figart argued, rarely accomplished any military objective, often killed more civilians than soldiers, and strengthened the people's will to resist.
20. Inez Griffin, private interview, Luling, Texas, June 7, 1967; Lorraine Crockett, private interview, Luling, Texas, June 28, 1967.
21. The Luling *Signal*, Souvenir Edition, Luling Silver Oil Jubilee, August 8, 1947.
22. King, "He Gives Away Millions," 24-25.
23. Walker, "Davis and His Millions," 45.
24. Edgar B. Davis to George H. Leach, March 20, 1945; November 21, 1945.
25. Edgar B. Davis to L. D. Tompkins, January 4, 1947.
26. Quoted in Edgar B. Davis, Memorandum for Whoever Writes My Biography, If Done At All. It Will Not Be Done By Me, undated memorandum, Davis Papers, South Easton, Massachusetts.
27. Noble R. Griffin, private interview, Luling, Texas, June 8, 1980.
28. Lorraine Crockett, private interview, Luling, Texas, June 28, 1967.
29. *Ibid.*
30. Report to the Stockholders of United North and South Development Company, February 5, 1945.
31. Sandidge, "A Review of Edwards Limestone Productions," 136-137.
32. Report to the Stockholders of United North and South Development Company, April 19, 1947.

33. Report to the Stockholders of United North and South Development Company, April 27, 1947.
34. Inez Griffin, private interview, Luling, Texas, June 7, 1967.
35. Report to the Stockholders of United North and South Development Company, April 30, 1951; Tommy Caylor to David M. Figart, October 20, 1950; November 20, 1950, David M. Figart Papers, Briarcliff Manor, New York.
36. Edgar B. Davis to Walter B. Mahony, December 1, 1949, Walter B. Mahony Papers, Pleasantville, New York.
37. San Antonio *Light*, October 18, 1951.
38. William A. Schan to Lincoln K. Davis, September 24, 1954, Davis Papers, South Easton, Massachusetts.
39. Lincoln K. Davis to Riley Froh, July 1, 1971.
40. *Ibid.*
41. Kenneth Foree, Jr., *Citizen Of Luling* (Magnolia Petroleum Company, 1947); James A. Clark, "How Davis Found Luling," *Big Orange* (Spring, 1965), 22-27; Frank X. X. Tolbert, "Wild Flower Wildcatter," *Texas Star* (July 18, 1971), 10-11; Thomas Ricks, "The Incredible Life of Edgar B. Davis," *Texas Parade* (August 1972), 32-35; Jo Hoskinson and Vera Holding, "Unforgettable Edgar B. Davis," *Drilling* (February, 1976), 66-70; Frank X. Tolbert, "The Wild Flower Wildcatter," *Vision* (October, 1979), 8-10. The second Tolbert article is slightly different from the earlier version he did. All of these accounts borrow liberally from the Kenneth Foree booklet listed first in this footnote.
42. Branda (ed.), *Handbook of Texas*, III, 229-230.
43. James Presley, *A Saga of Wealth: The Rise of the Texas Oilmen* (New York, 1978), 340-345. For the basis of Presley's sketch see Stanley Walker, "Where Are They Now? Mr. Davis and His Millions," *New Yorker* (November 26, 1949), 35-44.
44. Edgar B. Davis to Walter B. Mahony, December 6, 1934, Walter B. Mahony Papers, Pleasantville, New York.
45. *Ibid.*
46. Lincoln K. Davis to Riley Froh, May 31, 1967.
47. C. C. Dauchy to Riley Froh, July 12, 1972.

BIBLIOGRAPHY

PRIMARY SOURCES

Private Collections of Papers

The Edgar B. Davis Papers, Texas A&M University, College Station, Texas. This collection includes the files from the offices of the United North and South Development Company at the Time of Davis' death in 1951.

The Edgar B. Davis Papers, South Easton, Massachusetts. These files, collected by Edgar Davis' nephew Lincoln K. Davis, are from the New York and Massachusetts business offices which Davis maintained. In this repository are numerous personal and family letters. There are also the papers on the personal life and business career of Lincoln Davis' father Oscar Davis.

The David M. Figart Papers, Briarcliff Manor, New York. As employee, friend, and confidant, David Figart was closely associated with Edgar B. Davis for forty-five years. Papers in Figart's files related to all aspects of Davis' career.

The Walter B. Mahony Papers, Pleasantville, New York. As a close friend and associate for nearly half a century, Walter B. Mahony and Edgar B. Davis corresponded regularly. These papers, though relating primarily to Mahony's business career and personal life, contain much information of a biographical nature on Davis.

Newspapers

Austin *American*, 1928.
Brockton *Enterprise*, 1927, 1928, 1931.
Dallas *Morning News*, 1928.
Fort Worth *Star-Telegram*, 1926.
Houston *Chronicle*, 1926.

Houston *Post*, 1928, 1936.
San Antonio *Evening News*, 1928.
San Antonio *Express*, 1926, 1928, 1929, 1931.
San Antonio *Light*, 1928, 1951.
The Gonzales *Daily Inquirer*, 1928.
The Luling *Newsboy and Signal*, 1979.
The Luling *Signal*, 1926, 1927, 1930, 1936, 1947.
The Tri-County News, 1935, 1937.

Interviews

Biggs, Willie J., June 16, 1979, Luling, Texas.
Blackmar, J. Kenneth, March 14, 1969, Luling, Texas.
Bridges, Hal, June 9, 1967, Lulling, Texas.
Carter, Robert, June 29, 1972, Luling, Texas.
Caylor, Tommy, August 21, 1960, Port Aransas, Texas.
Chamness B. H. "Heavy," June 27, 1972, Luling, Texas.
Crockett, Lorraine, June 28, 1967, Luling, Texas.
Davis, Lincoln K., June 19, 1970, Brockton, Massachusetts.
Griffin, Inez, June 7, 1967; June 28, 1967, Luling, Texas.
Griffin, Noble, June 28, 1967; June 16, 1967; June 8, 1980, Luling, Texas.
Jackson, Berthold Z., April 15, 1969, Gonzales, Texas.
Muenster, Hazel, April 5, 1980, Luling, Texas.
Nugent, Kate, June 30, 1967, Luling, Texas
Rabon, J. M., June 25, 1977, Luling, Texas.
Wilson, Dr. Francis W., April 5, 1980, Luling, Texas.
Woolsey, Vern, June 7, 1967, Luling, Texas.

SECONDARY SOURCES

Books and Monographs

Babcock, Glenn D., *History of the United States Rubber Company: A Case Study in Corporation Management*. Bloomington: Indiana University Press, 1966.
Baldwin, Hanson, *Battles Lost and Won*. New York: Harper & Row, 1966.

Ball, George, et al. *Strategic Bombing Survey.* Washington, DC: Government Printing Office, 1945.

Boatright, Mody C. *Folklore of the Oil Industry.* Dallas: Southern Methodist University Press, 1963.

Dethloff, Henry C. *A Centennial History of Texas A&M University.* 2 vols. College Station: Texas A&M Press, 1975.

Dobie, J. Frank. *Tales of Old-Time Texas.* London: Hammond, Hammond and Company, 1959.

Duncan, Dawson, *The Luling Foundation* 1927-1948. Luling: privately printed, 1948.

Fifth Annual Report of the Agricultural Bureau of the Department of Agriculture, Insurance, Statistics, and History, 1891-1892. Austin: Ben C. Jones and Company, State Printers, 1893.

Figart, David M. *History of Stoddard No. 1 Well.* New York: privately printed, 1932.

Foree, Kenneth, Jr. *Citizen of Luling.* Magnolia Petroleum Company: privately printed, 1947.

Fredette, Raymond H. *The Sky on Fire: The First Battle of Britain.* New York: Holt, Rinehart, and Winston, 1966.

Gleisser, Marcus. *The World of Cyrus Eaton.* New York: A. S. Barnes and Co., Inc., 1965.

Hart, Moss. *Act One: An Autobiography.* New York: Ballantine Books, 1970.

Jenkins, John H., and Frost, H. Gordon. *"I'm Frank Hamer": The Life of a Texas Peace Officer.* Austin: The Pemberton Press, 1968.

Kahn, David E., as told to Will Oursler. *My Life with Edgar Cayce.* New York: Doubleday and Company, 1970.

Kilman, Ed, and Wright, Theon. *Hugh Roy Cullen: A Story of American Opportunity.* New York: Prentice-Hall, 1954.

Kipling, Rudyard. *Rudyard Kipling's Verse.* Definitive Edition. Garden City: Doubleday and Company, Inc., 1940.

Kroose, Herman E., and Gilbert, Charles. *American Business History.* Englewood Cliffs: Prentice-Hall, Inc., 1972.

McMurtry, Larry. *In a Narrow Grave.* Austin: The Encino Press, 1968.

Mott, Frank Luther. *A History of American Magazines.* 4 vols. Cambridge: Harvard University Press, 1938.

Owen, Edgar Wesley. *Trek of the Oil Finders: A History of Exploration for Petroleum.* Tulsa: The American Association of Petroleum Geologists, 1975.

Owens, Williams A. *Fever in the Earth.* New York: G. P. Putnam's Sons, 1958.

Peterson, Theodore. *Magazines in the Twentieth Century.* Urbana: University of Illinois Press, 1964.

Presley, James. *A Saga of Wealth: The Rise of the Texas Oilmen.* New York: G. P. Putnam's Sons, 1978.

Rister, Carl Coke. *Oil! Titan of the Southwest.* Norman: University of Oklahoma Press, 1949.

Rundell, Walter, Jr. *Early Texas Oil: A Photographic History, 1866-1936.* College Station: Texas A&M Press, 1977.

Stearn, Jess. *The Door to the Future.* New York: Doubleday and Company, 1963.

Steen, Ralph W. *Twentieth Century Texas.* Austin: The Steck Company, 1942.

Tedder, Lord. *With Prejudice.* Boston: Little, Brown and Company, 1967.

Texas: A Guide to the Lone Star State. Compiled by the Workers of the Writer's Program of the Work Projects Administration in the State of Texas. New York: Hastings House Publishers, 1940.

Tucker, Quincy. *Pioneering in Rubber.* London: E. J. Parsone, Ltd., 1952.

Warner, C. A. *Texas Oil and Gas Since 1543.* Houston: Gulf Coast Publishing Company, 1939.

Webb, Walter P., and Brandon, Eldon Stephen (eds.). *The Handbook of Texas* 3 vols. Austin: The Texas State Historical Association, 1952, 1976.

Webb, Walter P. *The Great Frontier.* Austin: University of Texas Press, 1951.

Wilson, Edward. *Biographical Sketch of Thomas Wilson.* San Antonio: privately printed, 1978.

Wolf, Howard, and Wolf, Ralph. *Rubber: A Story of Glory and Greed.* New York: Covici-Friede Publishers, 1936.

Magazine Articles and Published Bulletins

"About This Issue." Editorial. *North American Review,* summer, 1976, 2.

Barton, Bruce. "Do You Believe in Luck? I Do." *The American Magazine,* April, 1928, 60, 158-160.

Brucks, Ernest W. "Luling Oil Field, Caldwell and Guadalupe Counties, Texas," in Sidney Powers (ed.) *Structure of Typical American Oil Fields.* Tulsa: American Association of Petroleum Geologists, 1929, 632-651.

Clark, James A. "How Davis Found Luling." *Big Orange*, spring, 1965, 22-27.

Davis, Edgar B. "The Way Out--and On." *North American Review*, October, 1932, 289-291.

Hoskinson, Jo, and Holding, Vera. "Unforgettable Edgar B. Davis." *Drilling*, February, 1976, 66-70.

King, Steve. "He Gives Away His Millions." *The American Magazine*, August, 1951, 24-25, 96-101.

Lilly, Marie Seacord. "The Texas Wild Flower Painting Competitions." *The American Magazine of Art*, June, 1929, 342-347.

McIntyre, James. "Luling Field Could Produce 100,000 Barrels." *The Oil and Gas Journal*, May 15, 1924, 24, 145, 148.

Pemberton, Murdock. "Walking Under the Ladder." *Esquire*, February, 1939, 82-83, 155-157.

Raley, Helen. "Texas Wild-Flower Art Exhibit." *Holland's Magazine*, July, 1927, 5, 49.

Ricks, Thomas. "The Incredible Life of Edgar B. Davis." *Texas Parade*, August, 1972, 32-35.

Sandidge, John R. "A Review of Edwards Limestone Production with Special Reference to South-Central Texas," in *University of Texas Bureau of Economic Geology, Publication Number 5905*, 1959, 132-140.

Tolbert, Frank X. "The Wild Flower Wildcatter." *Vision*, October, 1979, 8-10.

_____. "Wild Flower Wildcatter." *Texas Star*, July 18, 1971, 10-11.

Transcript of Record, Supreme Court of the United States, October Term, 1942. Washington, DC: Judd & Detweiler, Inc., Printers, 1943.

Walker, Stanley. "Where Are They Now? Mr. Davis and His Millions." *New Yorker*, November 26, 1949, 35-44.

Woolcott, Alexander. "Aladdin on Broadway." *Collier's*, February 18, 1928, 17, 32, 35.

Newsweekly Magazines

Newsweek, January 9, 1939, 47-48.
The Oil Weekly, September 19, 1932, 15.
Time, July 1, 1940, 64-65; September 14, 1942, 46; October 22, 1951, 113.

Theses

Froh, Riley. "Edgar B. Davis and the U.S. Rubber Industry with Inclusive Dates," unpublished M.A. thesis, Southwest Texas State College, 1968.
Talmadge, John M. "A History of the Luling Oil Field," unpublished M.A. thesis, Southwest Texas State College, 1948.

INDEX